THE DIGITAL DEPARTED

The Digital Departed

How We Face Death, Commemorate Life,
and Chase Virtual Immortality

Timothy Recuber

NEW YORK UNIVERSITY PRESS
New York

NEW YORK UNIVERSITY PRESS
New York
www.nyupress.org

References to Internet websites (URLs) were accurate at the time of writing. Neither the author nor New York University Press is responsible for URLs that may have expired or changed since the manuscript was prepared.

Library of Congress Cataloging-in-Publication Data

Names: Recuber, Timothy, 1978– author.
Title: The digital departed : how we face death, commemorate life,
    and chase virtual immortality / Timothy Recuber.
Description: New York : New York University Press, [2023] |
    Includes bibliographical references and index.
Identifiers: LCCN 2022059271 | ISBN 9781479814947 (hardback) |
    ISBN 9781479814961 (paperback) | ISBN 9781479814978 (ebook) |
    ISBN 9781479814985 (ebook other)
Subjects: LCSH: Death—Social aspects. | Internet—Social aspects. |
    Immortality—Social aspects.
Classification: LCC HQ1073 .R43 2023 | DDC 306.9—dc23/eng/20230123
LC record available at https://lccn.loc.gov/2022059271

New York University Press books are printed on acid-free paper, and their binding materials are chosen for strength and durability. We strive to use environmentally responsible suppliers and materials to the greatest extent possible in publishing our books.

Manufactured in the United States of America

10 9 8 7 6 5 4 3 2 1

Also available as an ebook

CONTENTS

Introduction

From Digital Self to Digital Soul

"I am dead." So began a November 18, 2006, post on the personal blog of an author who went by the handle AkumaPRIME. The twenty-five-year-old blogger continued: "Ok so, I'm not dead yet, not really. Obviously, I'm writing this post. But by the time You read this, I WILL be dead." This blog post, it turned out, was a digital suicide note—a fairly novel development in and of itself in the year 2006. Yet it held a further surprise. "I thought it would be interesting to post my suicide note out over the course of time. So even though I'm dead, new material will still pop up here now and again. Freaky huh? Yeah well, I thought I'd do sth creative." AkumaPRIME had indeed scheduled twenty different posts to gradually appear on the blog over the course of the next six months, with the final one emerging on what would have been his twenty-sixth birthday. It read simply, "Happy BIRTHDAY!!! Yay I'd be 26."

As he explained in the initial post of his suicide note, "the goals of these posts are simple: Explain my suicide as best as possible, say things I've wanted to say, and entertain weirdos that like to read suicide notes (which, btw, is most of us. We all have a macabre voyeuristic side. This is your chance to get a glimpse of the mind at war with itself . . . anonymously . . . I hope you enjoy)." And indeed, the posts did just that, discussing the author's many interests, his relationships with friends, his struggles with his mental health, his apologies for things he had done wrong in his life—including killing himself—and a variety of other topics. In these ways, this extended, pre-scheduled suicide note served as a kind of legacy for its author, a testament to his beliefs, his personality, and his creativity—one that remained online almost fifteen years after his death.

Yet almost immediately, his blog began to serve other social functions as well. A handful of friends and family commented on his posts as they emerged. Some of these comments contained simple sentiments like "AkumAPrime was one of my best friends. I love you . . . I will never forget you." Others made their own attempts to define his legacy, as did one comment from a friend that explained,

> He spent the last night of his life here with the people that he loved and cared about, buying them drinks and spending time with them. He looked in everyone's eyes and poured his love into them. He saw them from a deep and pure place of love and non-judgment. That is what he would want to leave them with. Everyone should try to remember the way he looked at them the last time each of you saw him. He wasn't sad at all. He just couldn't do it anymore . . . He's just moved away, but he is NOT dead. He lives on to make another life and more choices and move closer to that which created him.

Others mused about the medium of this suicide note itself, as in one comment that read, "If this blog doesn't count as getting the last word in, than I don't know what does . . . You must of Cared enough to leave so many messages, which are greatly appreciated, by the way." Another early comment read in part, "You wanted to be a time traveler. Keep in touch. I will be waiting for your posts."

Among all of these comments, those written by AkumaPRIME's mother were the most poignant, revealing over time her passage through various stages of grief and mourning. Her first post, written a day after the initial suicide note, read, "my darling . . . i have watched you struggle for a long time. your brillant mind was awesome, admired by people around the world. i am so grateful for your last 5 years, so exciting, so full. and now, finally, that you are at rest. peace and love, your mom." Six months later, on a different post, she commented, "it's been 6 months—seems like both forever ago, and just yesterday. i miss you so much . . . i had such a rotten mothers' day . . . i can't remember why you had to go, i just want you back. Mom." Years later she left the last comment on the site, which was written in response to his final birthday post. It read, "it's been 6 years without you, my son. still i miss you every day . . . so many people cared for you—i'm so sorry you had to leave us. peace out, my boy. love, mom."

Five years after AkumaPRIME's suicide, and a year before this final comment was posted, someone on Reddit, a news site and discussion forum that bills itself as "the front page of the Internet," discovered the blog. In a 2011 post called "TIL a redditor posted his suicide note posthumously on his blog over a period of six months," hundreds of Redditors debated AkumaPRIME's choice. One wrote, "Wow, what a way to string out a painful event over a long period of time. I hope his parents weren't following his blog, that would have been Hell to endure." But another countered with "His mom is going to grieve either way. This way at least she can still kind of do it 'with' him. The comments she has on the blog (where she goes through the process of grief) would have been internal feelings regardless. Who's to say letting it out this way doesn't make it easier?"

Other Redditors pondered the larger meaning of these kinds of scheduled posthumous posts. One wrote, "This is both incredibly sad and unbelievably clever. He had pretty much all of his final thoughts in waiting posts. It's a bit scary knowing they were published after his death (by him), but I'm unsure if I've ever seen a better use of the function. Indeed, I will have to remember this as an option for if I ever get something terminal." Another asked, "Doesn't the posthumous publishing of material hint towards his desire to live? By carrying out the actions of the living whilst dead, it's almost like he's displaying some unconscious desire to be alive." A Redditor responded to that question by positing that "Humans have the inherent desire to be creative, to add something new to the world, that might help the future generations. Some folks are driven to do this genetically, others memetically. Even suicidal folks have these desires."

Though Reddit arrived at no consensus on the meaning or morality of AkumaPRIME's suicide note, those debates remain relevant today, as do the various comments of his friends and family members, and his posthumous posts themselves. After all, in 2006 his suicide note via scheduled blog post may have struck most observers as very unusual, but a decade and a half later these kinds of phenomena are more commonplace. Family, friends, and loved ones routinely use social networking profiles as spaces to mourn and commemorate the dead, or even to continue a kind of one-way conversation with them. The dying themselves now often use blogs or other digital platforms to explain themselves to a larger audience of friends and sometimes strangers as they face down a terminal illness. Digital suicide notes are more common now as well, across a host of digital spaces.[1] Postmortem messaging services will even store your written or recorded messages until after you die, and send them to specially selected loved ones for years or even decades to come. Indeed, social networking platforms and digital technologies enable a whole host of new or novel ways of thinking and communicating about death, many of which were contained proleptically in AkumaPRIME's early experiment with postmortem digital communication.

Of course, it has always been possible to leave posthumous messages behind for loved ones, either intentionally or incidentally. Letters, time capsules, diaries, old photo albums, and any number of other artifacts have served as a testament to the inner lives of the dying and dead for hundreds of years. Sometimes these messages have provided comfort and closure, and at other times—though perhaps less frequently—they have revealed potentially painful secrets and challenged existing understandings of the identities of the deceased. But digital technologies open up a host of new possibilities for such postmortem self-presentation. As we detail the minutiae of our daily lives on Facebook or rant about the political system on Twitter or share vacation photos on Instagram or examine our personal lives with the help of Blogger or Medium, we leave behind more than just traces of who we are: in many ways these are the elements of which selfhood is constituted in the digital era. What becomes of this digital self when we die?

This question has been the subject of a significant amount of scholarly research and a whole host of news stories. Much of that work has focused narrowly on the ways that our social networking profiles become spaces for grief, mourning, and commemoration after we die—similar to how AkumaPRIME's suicide note was used by his own family and friends.[2] And just as in the Reddit discussion about that suicide note, many scholars have commented on the continuities between digital, networked forms of grieving and more traditional funerary processes. Others have stressed the novel elements of digital grieving, with either laudatory effects[3] or darker implications.[4]

But what is at stake when people *purposefully* use digital platforms and online technologies to craft messages that will outlast their physical bodies? What does the ability to digitally continue a relationship six months or six years after one's death say about the nature of the self? What happens to the processes of grieving and mourning when we can reinsert ourselves into the lives of our loved ones for years after our bodies have grown cold? What is the nature of one's responsibility to one's families and friends in an age when such posthumous social interaction is relatively easy to achieve? Is it really possible to maintain agency over one's own legacy after one's death? How does the memory of a departed loved one change when new interactions are potentially just around the corner? What sorts of inequalities or biases are liable to emerge in a future where digital technology promises to extend our interactions beyond this mortal coil, and what role do the various platforms and technologies themselves play in encouraging or discouraging postmortem forms of sociality?

While digital mourning and commemoration practices associated with Facebook pages of the dead have been heavily researched, there has been very little academic attention thus far on the technologies and platforms that allow the dead themselves to have agency in these processes. One small exception is a paper based on interviews with fourteen social networking site users, which asked respondents to predict their reactions to receiving digital messages from recently deceased loved ones.[5] The paper described the ways that such messages might enhance conventional forms of mourning and coping, and also the ways that these might be challenged by changing our definitions of mortality and our expectations surrounding the possibilities for connecting with the deceased. Important though this work may be, it is still focused on the living, and how they might perceive communications from the dead. The dead and dying themselves do not figure into the research design— for obvious reasons. Yet postmortem messaging services that offer this kind of communication from beyond the grave proliferated during the previous decade. Companies with names like Afternote, Safe Beyond, Postumo, and Wishes Keeper have all offered similar experiences, but remain largely understudied.[6]

Of course, postmortem messaging services are not the only ways that people are taking advantage of online tools to extend themselves beyond their living years. Other digital suicides besides AkumaPRIME have also made use of the unique affordances of online platforms to do things that were not possible with paper suicide notes. For instance, former sportswriter Martin Manley killed himself on his sixtieth birthday and arranged for a meticulously crafted website called MartinManley.com to go live that same day. The site contained thousands of words and hundreds of pictures describing his family, his career, and his reasons for ending his life.[7] It quickly garnered extensive news coverage and generated heated public debate.

The terminally ill use digital spaces to confront death and make meaning out of their suffering as well. Charlotte Kitley was a thirty-six-year-old mother of two who blogged about her experiences with terminal bowel cancer for two years. Her final post, uploaded by her husband on the day of her death, urged her readers to "enjoy life" and "Take it by both hands, grab it, shake it and believe in every second of it." It was viewed more than two million times.[8] Similarly, Peter Short was a fifty-seven-year-old Australian man who blogged about his own terminal esophageal cancer as a way to advocate for physician-assisted death legislation. His blogging attracted significant political attention to this issue before he succumbed in 2014.[9]

Such uses of digital technology are not without their critics. In January 2014 *Guardian* columnist Emma Gilbey Keller profiled blogger Lisa Bonchek Adams. At the time, Adams was busy detailing her experiences with terminal breast cancer in her blog and on various social media accounts. Keller questioned the propriety of this, wondering whether "her tweets [were] a grim equivalent of deathbed selfies, one step further than funeral selfies?" She also interrogated her own fascination with Adams's blogs and tweets, declaring her embarrassment at her own "voyeurism."[10] Days later, Keller's husband, Bill, wrote a similar column about Adams in the *New York Times* as a means of advocating for increased palliative care, rather than the "battlefield strategies" he accused Adams of promoting.[11] Both columns were the subject of a fierce public backlash, in which readers took to Twitter and to the comments sections of the two articles to defend Adams's right to record and represent her experiences in any way she saw fit.[12] Adams passed away in May 2015, but controversies like these suggest that norms concerning end-of-life communication remain in flux.

Not everyone gets to exercise that much control over their digital legacies, however. Sandra Bland was a twenty-eight-year-old African

American woman who was stopped by police in her car and taken into custody in Waller County, Texas. She was later found dead in her jail cell of an apparent suicide. The events surrounding her arrest were captured on police dashboard camera footage and her own cell phone video, both of which were viewed millions of times on YouTube. The suspicious events surrounding her particular death, and its broader similarities to other high-profile deaths at the hands of police suffered by people like Mike Brown and Eric Garner, inspired hashtags on Twitter like #SayHerName, which aimed to ensure that Bland would not be erased or forgotten. They also inspired the hashtag #IfIDieInPoliceCustody, in which people of color told their friends, family, loved ones—and really the world—what they should know if, like Bland, they were taken by police and never came back alive. In cases like this, we can certainly speak of a digital afterlife for Bland, but it is one enacted more by the structures of racism and inequality, and the mass resistance to those structures, than by Bland herself.

Yet even when a deceased person is in total control of their digital afterlife, criticisms abound. Postmortem messaging applications have drawn a particularly large amount of critical venom. One UK tabloid noted "a HUGE rise in the popularity of morbid social media apps which allow users to tweet 'after they die.'" It labelled such apps "sickening and twisted," "disconcerting and troubling," and quoted the founder of a bereavement charity as worrying that such companies were simply "cashing in on death."[13] Using an episode of the dystopian science fiction television show *Black Mirror* as a jumping-off point, another critic weighed in on the ethics of postmortem communication: "Some may argue that pretending to conduct conversations with the dearly departed is merely a coping mechanism, but to me it's like Norman Bates keeping his mother in the fruit cellar. Sometimes it's good not to talk."[14]

Such discussions often conflate conventional forms of posthumous digital mourning on social networking sites with a much more cutting-edge, science fiction–inspired ideal of using new technologies to literally live forever. Mark O'Connell has written about the ways that "transhumanist" philosophy has inspired Silicon Valley entrepreneurs to try to make such death-defying technologies a reality. O'Connell classifies transhumanism as "a liberation movement advocating nothing less than a total emancipation from biology itself."[15] Major figures like Peter Thiel, of Facebook and PayPal fame, and Google's Eric Schmidt have bank-rolled efforts at "radical life extension" through biotechnology. More than that, new tech companies and think tanks are aiming to create "mind uploading" technologies that will eventually be able to recreate an entire human personality based on brain scans loaded into a sophisticated computer.[16] But as Abou Farman has pointed out, "The question 'Why should life be extended?' is impossible to detach from the social and political question 'Whose life is being extended?'"[17] Given the costs associated with the kinds of technology that mind uploading would require, it makes sense to wonder whether such efforts would exacerbate current inequalities, or even create a new class divide between wealthy digital immortals and the poor and working-class, forced to die as usual.

It is worth pointing out that mind uploading and other radical life extension technologies may not ever reach the heights prophesied by their most radical proponents. But more mundane digital technologies have already been put to use, by everyday people, to extend the boundaries of the self beyond the realm of the living. These technologies—blogs, social networking sites, hashtags, postmortem messaging services, and artificial intelligence (AI) chatbots, to name a few—are in use right now, not in some utopian or dystopian future. They are conquering death, in their own pragmatic and populist ways, and allowing our loved ones to speak with us when they are gone, or to cement a reputation in death that they could not quite achieve in life, or to make a political statement, or to share the lessons they have learned, or to simply remind the world that they were here, that they refuse to be forgotten.

How can we understand these posthumous social actions and actors? Some of the earliest social scientists to write about the World Wide Web commented on its liberatory possibilities for personal identity. In the earliest days of the Internet, our self-presentations consisted of text with no images or sounds attached, leading some early digital theorists to believe that people online would be able to break free of the bonds of gender, sexuality, race, and nationality, and engage in interactions more accurately befitting their core selves.[18] Some early researchers also rightly called these assumptions into question,[19] but in any case the appeal of digital self-presentation has only grown more powerful with the rise to prominence of social networking sites. In the absence of physical presence, tactile engagement, and face-to-face interaction, human sociality can still thrive. For some critics, these new networked forms of digital interaction were inherently inferior to face-to-face conversations.[20] But despite the steady stream of op-eds in major newspapers decrying this or that form of online interaction, researchers have found that Internet connectivity can enhance community and even result in increased levels of face-to-face interaction as well.[21]

Still, the migration of huge amounts of human sociality into digital realms makes the dead members of our social networks very potent figures today. The dead no longer possess physical bodies, but in digital spaces none of us do. Like the living, the digital dead lay claim to profiles, text messages, videos, and photos that circulate among us, that help to create the same sort of connections and the same sense of identity or personhood that we are all crafting each time we tweet or blog or post or share. The affordances of many digital platforms encourage or at least enable this kind of intermingling.

So how do we distinguish between the living and the dead online? Debra Bassett uses the term "digital zombies" to describe the dead who move among us in digital spaces, but this is, strictly speaking, inaccurate.[22] A zombie retains the corporeal presence of the deceased person while losing all traces of personality, all attachments to community, all affect. A zombie is a body without a self. The digital dead are almost precisely the opposite—selves without bodies. Unlike zombies, they are still embedded in networks and communities, still engaged in limited forms of contact and conversation, still exchanging affect with other members of digital society.

Other scholars prefer to label these actors "ghosts." Candi Cann uses the term "Internet ghosts" to describe the "program-generated prompts" on social networking sites that have ended up suggesting that users "like" or "friend" the profiles of dead people, especially before sites like Facebook adopted a memorialization process for the profiles of deceased users. This "created the notion of a virtual ghost that lingered around the Internet, acting on behalf of the deceased."[23] The transhumanist Eric Steinhart has speculated that eventually we will all be able to create ghostly versions of ourselves that could digitally converse with our friends and loved ones convincingly enough to pass as us when we die. In his context, a "digital ghost" is "composed of a diary and an animator. Your diary is all the information recorded about your life. Your animator is an artificially intelligent program that tries to reconstruct your internal first-person perspective from your diary. Your animator tries to replicate your psychology (your character, personality, preferences, etc.)."[24] Tech entrepreneurs like Marius Ursache and his Eternime project have already attempted to use artificial intelligence to do this sort of ghostly work, though with very mixed results.

Unlike ghosts from horror films, however, these sorts of digital ghosts are often seen as comforting figures. The need to be able to continue to "speak" to the recently deceased is a key factor here, one that bridges the gap between the digital and the spiritual.[25] In a thoughtful philosophical exploration of such "ghosts in the machine," Patrick Stokes has pointed out that our "desire to hold onto the dead" and our "familiarity with the experience of electronically mediated communication" have psychologically prepared us to extend the moral identity of the dead beyond their mortal lives.[26] Stokes has explained that social networking sites allow one's mediated presence

> to be reconstructed across time, even when the origin of the "signal," so to speak, has ceased to exist, like the light from a distant star that appears normal to us but has long since gone supernova. Continued online presence helps preserve the individual particularity of the deceased self from the corrosive effects of time and the decay of memory.[27]

Stokes ultimately argues that "persons" live on after death, via social networking sites like Facebook, though "selves" do not, because selves are dependent on a first-person experience of the present.[28] But this view of the self is somewhat at odds with many social scientific conceptions of the term. For instance, in George Herbert Mead's canonical work of social psychology, *Mind, Self, and Society*, the concept of the self emerges out of a physical body but is analytically separate from it. For Mead, the self is created by our perceptions of the attitudes of others and our attempts to communicate a sense of who we are within our social environments. Mead explains, "Such a self is not, I would say, primarily the physiological organism. The physiological organism is essential to it, but we are at least able to think of a self without it. Persons who believe in immortality, or believe in ghosts, or in the possibility of the self leaving the body, assume a self which is quite distinguishable from the body."[29] Similarly, for Charles Horton Cooley—also a foundational figure in the discipline of sociology—the faculty of imagination figured prominently in the formation of selfhood. In large, complex societies with many members, most people are real for us only to the extent that we can imagine them. As such, Cooley considered "persons who have no corporeal reality, as for instance the dead," real people, full-fledged "members of society." "What indeed, would society be," he asked, "if we associated only with corporeal persons and insisted that no one should enter our company who could not show his power to tip the scales and cast a shadow?"[30] The communication theorist John Peters provocatively summed up the implications of Cooley's position: "The imagined, the mediated, and the dead may be as socially alive as those whose flesh presses on the furniture."[31] What, then, to make of the digital self, in life as well as in death?

This book argues that the digital self is *reenchanted*. Over the past two decades or more, we have moved our social interactions and self-presentations online in myriad ways. This has brought a sense of magic and mystery back to the modern project of selfhood. Yes, the self has always been a social construct,[32] it has always been something we perform in order to manage the perceptions of others,[33] it has always been a narrative that we tell ourselves to make meaning of our lives.[34] But by rendering those constructed, narrative, performative elements of selfhood into legible textual and audiovisual information, and by publicly circulating that information to others in ways determined by opaque algorithms, and of course by allowing that narrative information to persist and continue to circulate after someone dies, our digitally networked society has brought a sense of wonder—and sometimes dread—back to the process of creating and maintaining a self.

The significance of this digital reenchantment of the self will be discussed in more detail later in the book, but for now it suffices to say that one of the fundamental concepts of classical sociology has been Max Weber's theory of *disenchantment*. Put simply, Weber argued that the ascendance of modern, rational, scientific means of understanding the world had gradually robbed social life of the kind of spirituality and mysticism that dominated premodern worldviews. From time immemorial, people had sought "recourse to magical means in order to master or implore the spirits," but in a modern, scientifically oriented age, "technical means and calculations" have replaced such mysterious powers.[35] For Weber, this was not an entirely salutary development, as modern notions of progress and means-ends rationality had, he asserted, engendered a kind of meaninglessness for modern humans. After all, scientific rationality helps us gain control of the natural world, but it cannot tell us "what shall we do, and how shall we arrange our lives?"[36]

Today, by contrast, the affordances of online, digital, networked technologies reenchant the modern self. Becoming "friends" with hundreds or thousands of people from hundreds or thousands of miles away; having those people "like" or otherwise encourage the particular ways in which you have curated a sense of self on a particular digital platform; going viral and suddenly becoming the topic of discussion, and maybe abuse, from hundreds of thousands of distant strangers; interacting with other people who might not be people at all but are actually bots created to mimic online personas—these are just a few of the ways that the digital era has not only reorganized our times and our lives, but added irrationality, mystery, and enchantment back into our understanding of what it means to have a self or to be a member of society.

At the same time, the various reenchanting elements of the Internet depend upon a vast network of highly rational technological infrastructures run by massive, private corporations and government bureaucracies.[37] The Internet would not be around to dazzle us without the geological minerals that are harvested and turned into semiconductors and cables and smartphones, in locations throughout the developing world, often under grueling, exploitative labor conditions.[38] The digital self would not be reenchanted today without the sophisticated data-harvesting and surveillance technologies that render us all legible to advertisers and governments.[39] These are all highly disenchanting facts—the relative openness and amateurism of the early Internet have been captured and reconfigured today in an example of what Weber called the "iron cage of rationality."[40] It makes sense, then, to think of the Internet's various magical or spiritual affordances as part of a dialectic of disenchantment and reenchantment that has long been a feature of modern life.[41]

I use the term *affordances* to signal a commitment to a specific school of thought around the social uses and meanings of technology. Social scientific scholarship about technology can often fall into a kind of technologically determinist perspective in which technology itself is seen as monolithically causing major social changes, with no consideration for the local variations in those changes or how human perception and decision making play roles in such processes. At the same time, there is a countervailing tendency among other scholars to downplay the features of technologies that are genuinely new and different from older forms, and to minimize the social effects of those new features. Affordance theory exists between these extremes. It has grown in popularity in studies of science, technology, and the Internet precisely because it offers a way around the "unpalatable choice between undersocialized and oversocialized conceptions of technology."[42] As the sociologist Jenny Davis put it, "Technologies don't *make* people do things but instead push, pull, enable, and constrain. Affordances are how objects shape social action for socially situated subjects."[43] This perspective will animate the book's analysis of the digital death-related platforms and technologies described throughout.

As previously mentioned, the book concentrates on the way users of technologies exercise *agency* in their engagements with death and dying online. Though some argue that this concept "has become a source of increasing strain and confusion in social thought,"[44] the term "agency" generally refers to the ability of an individual to purposefully navigate social structures in pursuit of their own goals. Some social theorists use "agency" simply to mean the capacity for any individual to act, whereas for others it involves acting independently of social structures altogether,[45] though the idea of action that is completely outside social structures seems hard to fathom. Still, the concept of the self, on which this book is focused, presents a good example of the use of agency. People create a sense of self over time not because they are socially programmed automatons, but by thinking reflexively about themselves and exerting influence over their environments in the service of immediate, routine, and long-range goals.[46] Their ability to achieve these goals is mediated by the affordances of their environments, including the technologies through which they perceive and communicate with the world around them.

How, then, to study the affordances of digital technologies and online platforms as they intermingle with death and dying? To date, researchers have focused mainly on the experiences of the living as they navigate mortality online, by studying the posts of living persons on Facebook walls of their dead friends and loved ones, or by interviewing the living about those practices. This book relies primarily on another category of data that scholars have yet to fully explore: texts generated by the dying and dead themselves. Blogs written by the terminally ill provide one example of such texts. Chapter 3 examines 927 blog posts by 20 different terminally ill authors who eventually passed away, and reviews 1,566 comments on those blog posts. Suicide notes offer another example. Chapter 4 analyzes 51 digital suicide notes taken from personal websites, Facebook pages, and other social networking platforms, and compares them with 112 paper suicide notes from three different time periods. Even hashtags can tell us something about the new ways that digital spaces encourage contemplation of one's own death. Chapter 5 in fact focuses on 990 tweets from two hashtags grappling with the deaths of Black people at the hands of police, as well as 23 digital videos of these killings. These data show people making sense of their own lives, legacies, and mortality in their own words, and help us see the ways in which earthly inequalities and prejudices factor into all of this.

The book also uses more traditional forms of data. Chapter 1 examines 228 news articles about digital death and dying, in order to better understand the range of digital death-related practices being discussed in the news and the nature of public discourse about them. Chapter 2 reviews historical and archaeological research in order to chart the relationship between death and communication technologies from prehistory to the present day, showing how media technologies as old as writing created the phenomenon of *absent presence* that is at the heart of our digital communications with the dead. And because chapter 6 focuses on cutting-edge technologies like mind uploading that have for the most part yet to be realized, it also must rely on measuring present-day public opinion about these technologies, in this case through interviews with a handful of tech entrepreneurs and an analysis of 977 posts to the ten most popular Reddit threads dedicated to these topics.

The book also reports the results of an original survey, undertaken on October 7 and 8, 2021, in which 574 people shared their opinions about the various ways of engaging with digital death and dying covered in this book. I used the SurveyMonkey Audience service to recruit respondents. The service enlists its survey takers, called "panelists," from among the millions of people who take surveys using its service each day. Panelists are given fifty cents to donate to charity for each survey they complete.[47] As will become clear in the coming chapters, I used this survey data as a kind of check on the things I was finding in my discourse analysis, a way to further understand public opinion about digital death and dying as it was emerging in my work. Although these data are not the result of a random sample, and so must be taken with the proverbial grain of salt, a variety of research has shown that the reliability and accuracy of SurveyMonkey data are comparable to similar services like Amazon's Mechanical Turk and to other, larger, and more extensive kinds of market research surveys.[48] Furthermore, online surveys with participants recruited from platforms like Mechanical Turk and SurveyMonkey may generate more attentive respondents and a more demographically and politically diverse set of respondents than the large surveys of undergraduates that are typical in many academic fields.[49]

The substantive results of these surveys will be revealed in subsequent chapters, but I will report the demographic data now. Although the non-random nature of this sample means that we cannot know whether SurveyMonkey panelists are significantly different in some way from the general population, the respondents to this survey were fairly diverse: 13 percent of my respondents were between eighteen and twenty-four years of age, 29 percent were between twenty-five and forty, 29 percent were between forty-one and fifty-six, 14 percent were between fifty-seven and sixty-six, and 14 percent were sixty-seven or older. In terms of gender identity, 52 percent of my respondents identified as female, 46 percent as male, and 2 percent identified with one of the trans, nonbinary, or "prefer not to answer" categories I provided. In terms of racial or ethnic identity, 11 percent of my respondents identified as Asian, Indian, or Pacific Islander; 6 percent identified as Black or African American; 8 percent chose Hispanic, Latino, or Latin/x; 2 percent chose Native American or Alaskan Native; 67 percent identified as White or Caucasian; 3 percent identified as Multiracial or biracial; and 3 percent chose "Prefer not to answer" or "A race/ethnicity not listed here." I chose to send my survey only to panelists in the United States, and as it turned out these demographic proportions are fairly similar to the demographics reported by the US census.[50]

In any case, the survey data in this book were designed as a way to double check the much more extensive textual data drawn from a variety of online platforms and spaces. To understand these data—the digital texts produced by the dead and dying—the book primarily employs the method of *digital discourse analysis*. This approach entails "systematically collecting, reading, and analyzing what gets left behind in the small, sometimes forgotten sites of online discourse that are scattered throughout the World Wide Web."[51] That means coding the themes and counting the frequencies of those themes in the texts I have collected, but always keeping my analytic schemes close to the meanings that the authors of the texts themselves have explicitly created. Susan C. Herring was one of the earliest researchers to formalize methods for this sort of work, which she labelled "computer-mediated discourse analysis." My approach, like hers, "takes into account the technological affordances" of digital spaces and systems, and makes sure that its "analyses are socially, culturally and historically situated in the larger Internet context." Where my approach may differ from hers, and others like it, is that I do not aim to identify "patterns in language structure and use that may have been produced unconsciously."[52] Instead, I focus on the largely explicit meanings of each digital text being analyzed. I am still able to develop understandings of the issues at play that move beyond what individual texts' authors express by comparing the frequencies with which certain meanings appear in the data, and by noting the surprising or counterintuitive findings that emerge from these comparisons. In this way I am able to tease out the broader social significance of a set of digital data without suggesting that there are any subconscious or unconscious processes at work.

Of course there are a variety of other approaches to studying the creation of meaning in digital spaces. In *Coming of Age in Second Life*, Tom Boellstorff successfully adapted the method of ethnographic participant observation to his study of the online game Second Life. He created a digital anthropologist avatar and explained to all the other avatars he met in the game that he was engaged in a research project, without ever attempting to study them outside the game space. Boellstorff argued that "since people find virtual worlds meaningful sites for social action . . . our task as ethnographers is to study them."[53] But other researchers have sought to better integrate the on- and offline lives of those they study. Some notable examples include sociologist Jeffrey Lane's *The Digital Street* and communication scholar danah boyd's *It's Complicated*.[54] Both of these works combine the more traditional ethnographic study of places like urban neighborhoods or schools with an investigation of the digital lives and interactions of the people within those spaces.

However, when one's research subjects have already died, neither traditional ethnographic methods nor hybrid on- and offline ethnographic approaches seem as well suited as a discourse analytic approach. Like many other researchers on death and dying, I employ qualitative methods as a way to "search for how individuals construct meaning in the face of death."[55] In my data, much of this meaning-making was made explicit. Questions that I might have wanted to ask my research subjects when they were alive were often answered—unprompted, of course—in the hundreds of their blogs, tweets, posts, and other digital media that I have collected and analyzed in this book. Indeed, a certain amount of introspection, analysis, and social commentary were baked into the genres of the texts I collected—blogs of the terminally ill, suicide notes, and hashtags decrying racism and police brutality tend not to be written in a naïve state but instead are published with fairly explicit goals and meanings. As much as possible, then, I preferred to let these digital texts speak for themselves. Of course, what people say is no guarantee of what they do, and this often poses problems for interview-based research.[56] But this problem is minimized when one is less interested in behaviors anyway. I am more concerned with how people understand themselves in relation to the norms and technologies animating their social worlds. In aggregate, and all on their own, these digital texts provided a robust description of contemporary meanings and values regarding death, dying, and digital technology. I simply played the role of their post hoc collector and interpreter.

Digital discourse analysis also avoids an epistemological problem common to all participant observation and interview methodology— the extent to which researchers themselves influence the results. Ethnographers tend to take a position like Mitch Duneier's that social structures are typically rigid enough to ensure that "a certain set of situations will arise over time" in the field, regardless of the researcher's presence.[57] Nonetheless, one can never fully be sure that the things one observes during participant observation, and the reports of one's interviewees, are not to some unknown degree altered by the researcher's presence. Ethnographers' accounts often obscure this uncertainty.[58] Of course, contemporary ethnographers have found many valid ways to address these criticisms and produce thoughtful, reflexive work that takes such critiques into account, but in any case digital discourse analysis retains the advantage of relying on data gathered after the fact, from spaces and sites where the author was never a participant and thus exerted no influence at all.

Like many other subjects that qualitative researchers investigate, death and dying are highly personal and often very private matters. The ethics of studying death and dying in online spaces are therefore quite important. However, the issue of privacy is somewhat muted in this case, because the texts I examine in this book all came from publicly available online spaces and platforms. The major ethical standards governing research on human subjects typically treat such publicly available texts as exempt from ethical review.[59] Moreover, the dead are not considered human subjects at all within this ethical framework. Still, this does not mean that they are not deserving of ethical treatment. It is certainly true that many people who have posted text and images online, while aware that the Internet is public, might not have realized that their posts could turn up in an academic research paper or book.[60] In light of this, some have argued that academic researchers ought to take care to subject their qualitative data to the process of "un-Googling"—that is, beyond the standard anonymity granted to many qualitative research subjects, one might also remove all "contextual details of the environments where ethnographic encounters happened and the country or collaboration context where the research was conducted."[61] For this reason, some digital researchers have even advocated "cloaking" direct quotes—altering them so as to make them untraceable by search engines.[62]

Cloaking presents significant problems for digital discourse analysis, however. As in all discourse analysis, it is important to use the text as it originally appeared. Moreover, search engines can often still identify even reworded quotes.[63] On top of that, the practice of cloaking quotes, much like the more widespread practice of anonymizing the names of one's research subjects, can be harmful to the reliability of sociological work.[64] Although the practice is rare, sociological research still ought to be able to be fact-checked if need be, and too much anonymizing makes this impossible.[65] There are of course many instances where the well-being of one's research subjects still requires such measures, but I do not believe that to be the case for most of the data here. For one thing, the authors of the most intimate digital texts analyzed in this book—the blogs by terminally ill authors and the digital suicide notes—were highly aware of the public nature of what they were writing. Indeed, the suicide note authors often mentioned this explicitly, and some of the terminally ill bloggers received significant media attention as they developed larger audiences. In fact, I was able to easily confirm the identities of all of these authors, so as to make sure that the blog posts and suicide notes were genuinely written by people who had died. This suggests that their words were already firmly entrenched in the public domain. These texts were not posted naïvely or with an assumption of anonymity—indeed, these authors wanted to share their thoughts, experiences, and life stories with others.

Given all of this, the direct quotes in this book—and there are many—have not been cloaked or altered in any other way. Any typos or spelling errors have been left intact. I have also not used any pseudonyms or changed any identifying information. At the same time, out of an abundance of caution for what loved ones of the decedents might feel, on the slim chance that they were to read this book, I have used only the names or Internet handles of authors whose deaths and death-related communications have already received a substantial amount of news coverage and those whose web pages have remained online for many years after they died. Otherwise I have simply not provided the names of the people I quote. I have also not directly quoted the few authors of these texts who were under the age of eighteen, though their writing was used to determine the frequencies of various themes in the larger collections of data. The one exception to this rule was a transgender teen whose suicide note in support of trans rights was very widely covered in the press. When I directly interviewed living people, however, I did quote them by name, and I did edit their quotes slightly to remove words such as "um" or "like." In all, I am confident that these decisions balance the potentially sensitive nature of this topic with the need for research transparency and, more importantly, with a desire to honor the research subjects themselves, who in most cases had already made the decision to share their words with the world well before I came upon them.

As in all qualitative social research, the data examined here are inherently limited. There is no way to garner a statistically representative, random sample of digital suicide notes or blogs of the terminally ill. Indeed, there may be reasons why the blog posts and suicide notes that I was able to find are significantly different from others that might have been deleted by family members or whose authors simply didn't make plans to have them hosted for long after they died. This is an unavoidable obstacle to data collection around the dead and dying, and it has meant that there have been some forms of online death-related content that I could not collect enough of to make any kind of systematic analysis.

But rather than aim for the kind of generalizability that comes with quantitative measures of statistical significance, my work—and discourse analytic work in general—aims for a sense of *transferability*. This term implies that the data here have been presented with enough contextual information that readers can apply my theories and analyses to other similar contexts and other kinds of data.[66] To ensure the transferability of my data, I have drawn from a variety of different sources—the aforementioned blogs and suicide notes, as well as tweets, news articles, Reddit threads, interviews, surveys, and a historical review. The aim of this sort of triangulation was simply to gather as robust an archive as I could, with as diverse an array of data as I was able to collect, in keeping with the ideal of the qualitative researcher as *bricoleur*.[67] Internet platforms and technologies change quickly, as do the norms surrounding their use, but I am confident that the arguments put forth here about the social meanings imputed to digital media and death will be valuable for future researchers working in a variety of similar contexts, and to readers of all sorts simply hoping to understand these topics in the years to come.

The Digital Departed will show how the dead and dying can now make use of digital platforms and social networking sites to create a new sense of self, or to enshrine a legacy for posterity, or to think about race and identity under threat of police violence, or to communicate with friends and loved ones from beyond the grave, or even to attempt to achieve immortality. For most, this is a kind of "symbolic immortality" that allows a person "to live without overwhelming anxiety in the face of the certainty of death."[68] Indeed, the digital dead and dying discussed here combined two separate kinds of symbolic immortality—the "creative mode" in which one feels that one's art work or inventions will live on after one's death, and the more standard "theological mode" in which one's soul is seen as transcending death.[69] Though scholars have debated the extent to which modern societies experience terror or anxiety around death,[70] this book suggests that the ad hoc forms of transcendence available in our online age have the benefit of salving fears around mortality in otherwise secular populations.

The book argues, then, that rather than zombies or ghosts, our posthumous digital traces and interactions are best understood as evidence of a *digital soul*. I use *digital* here as a rhetorical commonplace for online communication technologies of all sorts. And I use *soul* as an umbrella term for a variety of related beliefs about the ways that humans may individually or collectively transcend death—from being kept alive in others' memories to living on in an actual afterlife. But crucially, this is a sociological argument, not a metaphysical one. Whether or not the soul exists as a spiritual reality, the concept of the soul is as old as humanity itself, and it provides us with a way to talk about the portion of the self that is felt by many to live on when we die. Sociologists are interested in understanding the meanings behind social practices, and a wide variety of social customs and traditions have been motivated by the notion that some ineffable part of us lives on after death. "Immortality is ultimately a social relation," as the sociologist Zygmunt Bauman once put it.[71] In fact, archaeological and historical research allows us to track a variety of changes in the ways humans have envisioned the nature of the immortal soul over time, as well as the aesthetic and technological means with which we have attempted to care for it, cultivate it, and communicate with it.

Today, almost as a by-product of its reenchanting properties, the digital self may be transubstantiated into a kind of digital soul, at least among those who believe. There have been a small number of scholarly discussions of the term "digital soul." Patrick Stokes's recent book, *Digital Souls: A Philosophy of Online Death*, explores some of the same phenomena as those discussed here.[72] But it doesn't really use the term "digital soul" anywhere except in the title, and its argument concerns the moral obligation of the living to preserve the digital remains of the dead. A much earlier book, Thomas Georges's *Digital Soul: Intelligent Machines and Human Values*, deals with the social, ethical, and religious issues raised by the prospect of super-intelligent, self-aware artificial intelligences, not with human decisions about how to generate their own sense of transcendence or digital immortality.[73] So although there are some overlaps and resonances with these other works, this book is uniquely situated to show how online, digital technologies enable the dying and dead themselves to control the narratives about themselves and their lives from beyond the grave.

Many of the online spaces and platforms in this book have thereby provided a kind of agency for the dying and dead, what sociologist Robert Zussman once called "narrative freedom"[74] and which I have repurposed as *mnemonic freedom*. This is the freedom to purposefully construct a digital soul that will outlive one's corporeal body, at least to some extent, and to engage in the kinds of memory work around one's own life story that was previously available only to the very powerful or famous. In this way the digital soul represents a kind of populist, democratizing phenomenon—a repurposing of our enchanted digital spaces to extend the self beyond its corporeal form.

On the other hand, as the book will also show, this kind of freedom or agency is refused to many based on class, race, and gender, among other factors. In fact, for a growing number of transhumanists, the apotheosis of digital immortality is mind uploading, a technology that promises literal immortality once our brains can be successfully mapped and emulated in computers. Yet despite the protestations of its biggest boosters, if mind uploading is ever possible it will almost certainly be tremendously expensive, and the demographics of those who are willing and able to pay for it might end up looking a lot like the largely white, male, and wealthy demographics of the contemporary Silicon Valley tech industry.[75] Thus while digital souls may be associated with new kinds of spirituality, they are also deeply entwined with the kinds of modern, rational systems that generate many everyday inequalities.

In the end, however, all of these efforts to extend the self, to redefine the boundaries between life and death, or between the digital and the spiritual, ultimately reinforce the profoundly social nature of mortality. The father who can't fathom not being there as his children grow up, the mother blogging her struggles to stay alive in the face of incredible odds, the suicide making sure that his life story is recorded for posterity, or the young Black woman speculating about what her own legacy would be if she were victimized by racist police—they all exhibit a dedication to life, not any kind of macabre fascination with death. There are, of course, different power dynamics behind all of these cases. But they all demonstrate that life is powerful, and that being a living, thinking, feeling person in the world, connected to other living, thinking, feeling persons, is so meaningful that it is hard to imagine just letting it go. Not while all these new media technologies present so many possibilities for self-extension and symbolic immortality, and while new ones seem to be invented every day. The digital data in this book are sad, to be sure, and they have often brought me to tears as I collected and analyzed them. Yet ultimately this book about terminal illness, suicide, police violence, mind uploading, and digital selves and souls of all sorts is not just about how we die in the digital age, but how we live as well.

1

News Coverage of Digital Death and the Birth of the Digital Soul

"To my dearest Gert, my love for you will never fade. It will continue to grow for all my days. I'll keep you safe in my heart until we are together again." This Facebook status update, by then thirty-two-year-old Belle Petersen, addressed to her recently deceased husband, appeared in a 2014 newspaper article about Facebook and bereavement. In an accompanying interview, Petersen explained, "I often type statuses to Gert . . . I tell him how much I miss him and how I wish he was here to watch our little girl grow up. It's probably silly, but I like to think that he reads the messages. It makes me feel less alone."[1]

Petersen is not alone in using social media to interact with deceased loved ones. Indeed, 61 percent of the respondents to my survey—described in the book's introduction—reported in the last year having viewed a social networking page of someone who had died. And since the mid-2000s, these types of interactions have drawn the attention of the mainstream press, which has not only reported on the increasingly wide variety of such postmortem digital interactions, but has also interrogated the ethics of digital death. The digital era has presented us with a fundamentally new set of social questions: What to do with what is left behind online when we die? Is it healthy to maintain social connections through those digital traces of the dead? Is it authentic to grieve in public, online, and for those we may have known only in digital spaces? What does it mean that so much of who we are gets left behind online when we die, and what sorts of social obligations are attached to this digital detritus?

A 2014 opinion piece in the *New York Times* entitled "Retweet If You're Grieving" pondered whether the Internet was perhaps pulling Americans and others in the Western world into a more collective, public way of grieving. Today, "the question of how we should actually behave when mourning online" involves everyone from parents and close friends to minor acquaintances and complete strangers.[2] The potential audiences for one's digital traces are almost limitless, a fact that makes many critics uncomfortable. Coupled with the increasing online prominence of dead celebrities, whose deaths frequently elicit a torrent of tweets and Facebook posts from fans across the globe, it seems to some that the "tone of social media—true loss mixed in with memes—can feel off."[3] "Retweet If You're Grieving" then asked readers to consider whether it was a good thing that Facebook and Twitter had become the public squares in which communal grieving takes place, or whether there was still something more tasteful or noble in keeping one's grief private.

Although much of the press coverage of digital death has focused on the popular social media platforms, more creative or boundary-pushing digital death-related experiences have also received scrutiny. Reporting on India's first digital memory portal, one news article quoted a user who had just created an extensive page for his deceased father-in-law. "Instead of paying a fortune on print media for the announcement," the son-in-law noted, "this online profile will be up for 30-odd years. And by uploading all the pictures and videos, my wife and I are making sure that he will be 'alive' for our 12-year-old son in the future."[4] But later in the article, the reporters noted that there is a "flipside" to such practices: "In the real world there is a period of mourning, people come to offer condolences and then, it is time to move on. Cyberspace may not allow this clean transition from grief and mourning to a semblance of routine. The thing about having such a digital memoriam is that grieving does not really end." Indeed, the authors quoted a clinical psychologist who recommended that memorial pages should remain online for no more than fifteen days, because "grief has to stop and loved one's routines have to continue."[5] The vast difference, in this story, between the thirty years of digital posterity imagined by the son-in-law and the fifteen days recommended by the psychologist, deserves further investigation.

This degree of divergence suggests that ideas about what is appropriate in the realm of digital death are still heavily contested. Grief itself is a social construction, after all, not a hard-and-fast biological or psychological process.[6] What's more, the notion that uploading copious amounts of videos and images of a dead loved one is a way to keep that person "alive" implies that our understandings not just of grief and mourning, but of what it means to live in the digital age are shifting. In an era where so much of who we are is carefully curated and presented online to family, friends, co-workers, and relative strangers, are our online legacies qualitatively different than the photographs, letters, or diaries that were left behind when we died in the days before the Internet? When even very intimate, deeply personal aspects of our selves are dispersed across multiple public, online networks, how do we account for the interactions that they continue to generate with their postmortem circulation? How should we understand the popular practice of maintaining lines of communication with dead social networking profiles?

This chapter uses news coverage of digital death and online mourning to begin to answer these questions. The news articles analyzed here revealed two things: the variety of practices surrounding digital death and dying that have been discussed in the popular press, and the framing of these practices—the way they were subjected to normative, moral, or ethical debates. Discourse analytic work is a good way to uncover such social norms and moral frameworks,[7] and given this book's concern with the self and its various digital reenchantments, my analysis of these articles pays particular attention to the connections between norms about dying or mourning online and larger understandings of the nature of the self and the soul in digital spaces. As such, the first half of this chapter reports the results of my analysis of these news articles, while the second half of the chapter uses that analysis as a springboard to engage with literature from sociology, psychology, media studies, and history in order to make sense of the ideas about selfhood and digital transcendence revealed there.

This sample of news stories yielded several important findings, which I will briefly summarize. To begin with, public discourse was divided in its views of digital death practices. Many journalists and their interview subjects pointed to the continuities between older, time-honored ways of grieving and today's digital practices, but just as many others emphasized the new and radical elements of digital death. There was a similar divide on the ethics of digital death and mourning practices, with many commentators alleging that the new digital ways of dealing with death were unhealthy, while just as many suggested that they were therapeutic—possibly more so than the older traditions. Taken together, these articles questioned what it meant to mourn authentically in online spaces. They asked us to consider what constituted a healthy digital existence, and whether digitally mediated interactions and emotions were fully human, or in some way diminished.

The intersection, in these articles, of issues surrounding personal self-presentation and underlying spiritual health also pointed to a redefinition of selfhood in the digital age. Indeed, the most interesting set of findings from this sample concerned the ontological framing of our digital dead. I examined the news stories in this sample in order to understand how they described the existence of our postmortem digital data: what sort of things are our digital traces, exactly, according to mainstream news accounts? It turns out that a surprisingly large percentage of these articles portrayed digital remains as not just, or not only, heirlooms or memorials, but in fact as a component of a kind of digital soul—a part of us that lives on online. This, the chapter argues, points to an intertwining of self and soul in digital spaces. As we use the Internet to construct, refine, and perform a distinct sense of self, and as that self connects with overlapping networks of other selves, those selves become, in a sense, *reenchanted*. Part of that reenchantment appears to be the ability to transcend death, at least in some limited form. However, I argue that this constitutes a highly *rationalized* sense of what transcendence means. It turns the metaphysical ambiguities of the afterlife, which have haunted human beings for the whole of our existence, into technological certainties dependent only on ones and zeros. In this way, we see modernity's dialectical, back-and-forth fluctuations between disenchantment and reenchantment at work.

Digital Death and Mourning in the News

This chapter is based on a discourse analysis of 228 mainstream news articles from 2006–2018 that had to do with digital death and dying.[8] To code these 228 articles, I began with an initial, unsystematic read-through in order to understand the major topics covered in these pieces and their most prominent themes. From that unsystematic read-through I created a coding scheme with four major categories of discourse, and then broke the responses to each of those categories down into several types. Articles were placed into multiple categories if they contained more than one theme, which many did.

The first of these major categories concerned the newness of digital death practices. Some articles emphasized the unique or novel elements of digital dying or grieving, while others pointed to continuities with older, pre-digital death practices. The second major category concerned the overall evaluation of digital death and mourning practices—is it healthy or unhealthy to grieve online, or to continue one's relationship with the dead by tweeting or posting about them? Is it authentic or phony to publicly share one's grief on social media? The third category had to do with power and control. These were stories that discussed who benefitted from digital death and mourning and who was able to make decisions about the postmortem use of digital texts and spaces: giant social networking platforms, smaller entrepreneurs, or families and friends themselves? Finally, the last major category dealt with what I am calling the ontological quality of the digital dead. These articles framed the status of digital traces in a few different ways—as memorials and monuments, as heirlooms and artifacts, or in a third possibility, as evidence of a digital soul.

Table 1.1 details the frequency of these themes in all 228 news articles in the sample. Well over half of the articles made evaluations about whether digital death-related practices were good or bad, which usually meant whether they were healthy and authentic or unhealthy and inauthentic. Over half of the articles also made ontological claims about the nature of the digital dead. Almost half discussed digital death, grief, and mourning as either radical changes or continuous with more traditional ways of dealing with death, while a smaller percentage discussed the power, profit, and control of digital death-related content.

TABLE 1.1. Most prominent themes in the news coverage of death and dying online

Themes	Frequency of news stories in sample featuring this theme (%)
Evaluation: Good/ healthy/authentic?	64
Ontological qualities	55
Traditional or new?	49
Power/control	43

Having established that these were prominent themes in the news coverage, we can dig deeper and understand the nature of the discussion in each category by breaking them down into eleven distinct types of responses within the total sample, as in table 1.2.

Table 1.2 reveals quite a bit about the prevailing norms surrounding digital death and mourning, and about the ways that these issues are conceptualized in the mainstream press. The main idea to emerge here is the sense that norms are in flux, or still unresolved, or that a consensus has yet to emerge on many aspects of our engagement with death online. This was apparent when I coded the articles to see whether the authors thought that the way we grieve online represents some sort of major change in social practices around death or whether they described digital mourning in terms of its continuities with traditional forms of grieving. The articles ended up being fairly evenly split in this regard, with 25 percent describing continuities and 32 percent describing shifts or changes to mourning traditions. "My parents' generation grieved in graveyards. People my age mourn online," wrote one author emphasizing such continuities.[9] Another article quoted a psychology professor in order to emphasize these similarities by comparing digital death-related practices to ancient means of communication: "The Phoenicians had to

TABLE 1.2. Distinctions within thematic categories

Themes	Distinctions within themes	Frequency of news stories in sample that feature these distinctions (%)
Evaluation	Healthy/authentic	51
	Unhealthy/inauthentic	46
Ontological qualities	Obituary/grave/memorial	42
	Ghost/self/soul	36
	Estate/heirloom/artifact	18
Traditional or new?	New/changes	32
	Traditional/continuities	25
Power/control	Platform control/rules	31
	Family and friends control	10
	Platform clicks & money	9
	Entrepreneur clicks & money	9

chip it into tablets," said professor Bennett Leventhal, and digital mourning "is just a different form of communication. I don't think it changes
the subject or intent. . . . It's just another form of public grieving."[10] But
other articles framed social media as "redefining the way people grieve"
such that "death and mourning are no longer a private matter,"[11] or lamented that there is "no protocol" yet for offering condolences in the age
of social media, texting, and online memorial pages.[12]

The ramifications of this debate about change or continuity are significant. Public acceptance of digital death practices might be tied to
the sense that they are simply extensions of existing traditions, whereas
newness can be seen as a reason for rejection, or at least skepticism toward the seemingly radical changes that digital death and mourning
might bring with them. On the other hand, novelty itself can be seen
as a positive too, a way to overcome faults in conventional grieving and
mourning practices. Of course, the fact that this sample of newspaper
articles reveals a split on many of these questions probably has something to do with the conventions of modern journalism, where reporters
typically seek out perspectives on either side of an issue, regardless of
how representative each of those sides is. Nonetheless, these 228 articles
produce a strong sense that public discourse frames digital death and
dying as alternately traditional or radical, without a clear consensus one
way or the other.

The public is clearly split on whether our ways of dealing with death
and grief on the Internet are ultimately socially or ethically appropriate as well. Writing about the ultimate goodness or badness of digital death and mourning came in a form that mixed notions of health
with other notions of what might be called authenticity. In other
words, when digital death practices were criticized it was either on
the grounds that they were inauthentic and phony or mentally unhealthy, whereas when they were lauded it was on the grounds that
they elicited genuine or authentic emotion, or that they were therapeutic. Of the articles I studied, 51 percent said that digital engagements
with death were healthy or authentic, while 46 percent said that they
were unhealthy or inauthentic. One psychologist specializing in grief
worried that "sometimes, people will only grieve in private, plugging
themselves into the computer at night and not grieving with their family or with people directly in their community" and stated that "the

Internet shouldn't be a substitute for human contact."[13] Another critic wrote, "There's a difference between remembering someone who's died and who you miss, and creating an inauthentic version of them online that has little to do with who they were and everything to do with how you want to remember them."[14] Other commentators worried about the potential hurtfulness of online trolls and the incompatibility of the Internet's ironic stance with the respectful tones usually required at mourning rituals: "Online, where pseudonymous message boards flourish, the response to death is more like a free-for-all than the respectful hush of yore."[15]

On the other hand, many commentators pointed to the therapeutic benefits of online grieving. One columnist in the *Washington Post* wrote that "commenting on a deceased friend's MySpace profile is a lot like group therapy. Friends of the deceased can find some sort of comfort in reading thoughtful messages from others who are equally upset."[16] Similarly, an essay reported on a bereaved mother's use of Facebook after the death of her daughter and noted that "after a major loss, many find comfort in having a constant outlet for their feelings. While individual and group therapy can help, therapists, counselors and pastors aren't always available during a person's loneliest and most trying hours. That's where social media fits in."[17] Another journalist described the process of deciding what to do with the social media accounts of her recently deceased mother:

> Sure, my family could take it upon ourselves to shut down her e-mail, Facebook and LinkedIn accounts; but in some way, allowing her online ghost to continue to exist also allows my mother's memory to take up real space in a culture that typically denies death, dying and grief outright. To scrub the internet clean of any trace of my mom's life feels a bit like denying she ever existed. . . . The e-mails she sent, the posts she made on Facebook and even her network on LinkedIn all provide insight into who she was, how she thought and the experiences she had. These dormant accounts are proof that she existed in the 21st century and participated in its online culture.[18]

One thing that was rarely questioned was the platforms'—especially Facebook's—control over these processes. Beginning in late 2009 with

Facebook's "memorialize" feature, there was a good deal of coverage of Facebook's policies and their effects. Yet there was very little critical discussion of whether or not these are the ways we ought to be doing things, even though the authors did not mind editorializing on other related subjects. This was reflected in my own survey data as well. When asked what they would like to happen to the social networking pages of someone close to them who was still living when that person died, 52 percent said they would like those pages to be memorialized. By contrast, only 20 percent said they would like those pages to remain online in their normal state, while 15 percent would like to see those pages taken offline immediately, and 13 percent would like those pages to be taken offline but only after the respondent had been sent all the raw files and data. These results thus confirm the sense in the news coverage that norms about this topic remain in flux, but that memorializing social networking pages of the dead has become the most conventional way of treating one's digital remains.

Overall, in my sample of news coverage, 31 percent of the articles discussed some aspect of the platforms' official control over digital death practices, whereas only 10 percent discussed the informal ways that families and friends decided to make rules to limit or encourage engagement with the digital dead. There was almost no discussion of what we ought to ask or demand of the platforms—social media companies made the rules and at best people followed them or occasionally made ad hoc adaptations in a small number of cases, at least according to this news coverage. In fact, only 9 percent of the articles discussed the idea that social media platforms make money off of our data, even potentially when we're dead, while 9 percent also discussed smaller-scale digital death entrepreneurs and their efforts to monetize other aspects of mortality online.

One of the 31 percent of articles that discussed Facebook's control noted that "while a person might stop sharing data with a service, the company still owns it" and asked, critically, "What happens to all this data social networks are controlling once [the users] disappear?"[19] The answer to that question is often a serious point of contention for family and friends of the dead. One article in the sample told the story of Ann Grant, a woman whose son had died and whose page had been "memorialized" at someone else's request. Grant wanted access to the page, in order to be able to send messages and correspond with her son's friends. But memorialized pages did not allow for such features, and at the time could only be seen by those who were "friends" with the user when they were alive, which Grant was not. Grant tried many times to get Facebook to change this policy, and even took the desperate step of emailing Facebook founder Mark Zuckerberg directly, pleading that "if you returned my son's Facebook page to what it was, you would bring a small bit of joy to a grieving mother's heart. . . . I still have the rest of my life to remember my son. Just to see his photos, his status and his comments before he died, and the memories friends and family continue to post, means more than anything to me."[20] Zuckerberg did not respond, but Facebook eventually relented after much pressure from Grant and help from others.

When articles did describe everyday people asserting control, it often had to do with their ability to work around the social media platforms' own policies. One article described the experiences of a bereaved mother named Wendy Rebman Lefever, who used social networking sites to maintain ties to her deceased son Zach. It noted that

> although Zach's personal Facebook page is private and only allows those who are "friends" with him to post messages, Lefever created the "In Memory of Zach Lefever" page on Facebook as a daily journal, of sorts, to memorialize her son. The page is filled with messages not only from his mother, but other relatives and friends who post sentimental, and sometimes funny, thoughts to whomever wishes to read the posts.[21]

Another article emphasized the rise of online obituaries as a new tool for family members to share the legacy of the deceased with larger potential audiences. The dying themselves are even increasingly writing their own obituaries, as was the case with a man named Val Patterson, whose 2012 self-composed obituary on Legacy.com was quoted in another article: "Now that I have gone to my reward," Val wrote, "I have confessions and things I should now say. As it turns out, I AM the guy who stole the safe from the Motor View Drive Inn back in June, 1971."[22]

So despite their ubiquity, Facebook and the other major social media platforms do not wholly dictate public views of death and dying online, at least not yet. One last category of responses illustrates this point.

Articles concerning the ontological quality of the digital dead revealed some views of the fundamental nature of our digital remains that contrasted with Facebook's own policy preferences in interesting ways. As previously mentioned, when a person has died, Facebook provides two options—either deleting their profile or memorializing it. When an account is memorialized, it no longer appears in ads, birthday reminders, or suggestions of people you may know. The memorialized account includes the word "Remembering" across the top, and although the person's previous "friends" can post messages to the timeline, new content can't be added.[23] This policy was presumably put into place at least partly in response to the uncanny and often unsettling ways in which recently deceased people would pop up in all sorts of algorithmically generated Facebook notifications, a problem that several of the articles in the sample mentioned. Memorialized pages do not circulate in that way. In any case, given that "memorialization" is really Facebook's only option besides complete deletion, and given that Facebook was by far the most prominent and powerful social networking platform for most of the time period covered by my sample, one would expect that the overwhelming majority of ontological framing concerning our digital traces in this sample would describe them as memorials, or use other similar metaphors such as gravesites or monuments. But that wasn't exactly the case. This category was the most prominent theme, at 42 percent, but not by much.

Of course, even before Facebook's dominance over the social media landscape, the memorial was a common framework for understanding the social media pages of the dead. One 2007 article noted that "MySpace avoids deleting the deceased's profiles unless asked by family members, which means the profiles-turned-memorials can stay active for years. Other social-networking and blogging sites, such as Xanga and LiveJournal, also host memorials tied to deceased users' pages."[24] Another early article explicitly compared social media pages to physical remembrances while reporting on the social media practices of the friends of a young soldier who had been killed in Iraq. "For them, the MySpace profile has become the virtual equivalent of the boots, rifle and helmet of a military memorial ceremony, their words the electronic form of a small memento left at a gravesite. It's an electronic monument for a war that doesn't yet have a tangible one."[25]

The idea that sites left behind by the digital dead are akin to physical spaces of remembrance like memorials, monuments, or gravesites predates Facebook, then, although Facebook has enthusiastically adopted it, and it showed up prominently in the sample. But another way of thinking about the digital data that we leave behind when we die is as an artifact, heirloom, or part of an estate—something to be passed down to future generations.[26] Even Facebook now allows you to nominate a "legacy contact" to make decisions about your account when you die,[27] and a host of private companies offer digital estate protection services for your postmortem data. As such, one might expect the heirloom/estate/artifact framing to be prominent in the sample as well, but this was the smallest theme of the three ontological categories, appearing in only 18 percent. The author of one such article wondered, "What of all those photos, tweets, comments, updates we post daily? For many of us they add up to an important and detailed picture of our lives. They matter to us. One day these digital files will be the equivalent of the old photo album or grandparents' love-letters."[28] Some other articles adopting this framing did so because they were explicitly covering new digital services designed to help store and pass on one's digital ephemera. One such article noted that "when people die, they leave behind more than physical objects. They also have digital assets such as email accounts, automatic bills, banking accounts and photos. If they do not leave instructions and passwords, loved ones may not be able to access those things."[29] That article went on to provide advice about how to manage such "digital assets" in the event of a death, but even in the context of such practical advice, the piece closed with an anecdote about a woman who continued to send Facebook messages to her deceased brother, and commented that "in a digital world, websites can become conduits to a spiritual world."[30]

This brings us to the third ontological category in the sample, which was the idea that online death has the potential to create a kind of digital ghost, or virtual immortality, or simply the idea that a dead person's profile contained some essence or some remaining form of selfhood—I have labelled this the *digital soul*. Despite the fact that "memorializing" is the only official Facebook response to dead profiles, and despite the fact that a host of other entrepreneurs now encourage us to think of our digital data as part of an estate to be passed down when we die, this third way of thinking about digital death—as means to a kind of extended selfhood or digital soul—was very prominent in the sample, appearing in 36 percent of the articles. For example, a professor studying grief and mourning was quoted as saying that interacting with a dead person's social media page means that "the person you cared about is still virtually living in some way."[31] Another article exclaimed simply, "We'll all live on as digital ghosts. In a nitty-gritty sense it sounds awful, but in the long term, I think that it sounds a bit wonderful: What seems like nothing now will be the something that lives on."[32] Some of these "digital ghosts" have been created quite purposefully. One article quoted a man who was using the website DeadSocial to create postmortem messages: "As I was looking at the camera, I thought, gosh, I'm not only talking to my kids, I'm talking to my grandkids, and all my generations for years to come. It's always going to be out there, in the cloud. There's something comforting about that. . . . Through DeadSocial, you can make sure the essence of who you are remains on the internet. It cheats death."[33] Or as another piece put it, "Logically, we know the departed can't read comments on their memorial sites, but we keep leaving them months, even years, after they've passed. Social networking connects us to people across the earth—and to people who have left the Earth, too."[34]

The Reenchantment of the Self and Rationalization of the Soul

This digitally enhanced connection to the dead would have certainly been seen as pathological for the better part of the twentieth century. Freudian psychologists viewed grief as a process of cutting away attachments to the deceased. Only in the late 1990s did the field of psychology begin to accept the importance of what became known as "continuing bonds," in which mourners seek to ease their pain by maintaining connections to those who have passed away. As the authors of the first book on the subject explained, in their research they found that "remaining connected seemed to facilitate both adults' and children's ability to cope with the loss and the accompanying changes in their lives. These 'connections' provided solace, comfort and support, and eased the transition from the past to the future."[35]

Though the healthfulness of such an approach to grief and mourning may seem obvious today, it appears to have emerged at least partly in response to the "denial of death" that many associate with modern life.[36] In the latter part of the previous decade, scholars began to argue that death under modernity was "routinely hidden from view," and often treated as "a technical matter, its assessment removed into the hands of the medical profession."[37] By contrast, death in the Middle Ages often took the form of a "ritual organized by the dying person himself. . . . It was also a public ceremony. The dying man's bedchamber became a public place to be entered freely."[38] As the historian Philippe Ariès has noted, "Death has always been a social and public fact," but "after the second half of the nineteenth century, an essential change occurred." Death became increasingly concealed, such that the dying person and her friends and family were encouraged to act as if "life goes on" and "nothing has changed."[39] Simple, public protocols led by the dying in their own homes fell out of favor—even the summoning of a priest was seen as something to only do at the last possible minute, or once the dying person was unconscious or actually dead, lest the impending death be acknowledged too early. In this way, time-honored strategies for making meaning out of mortality were lost. According to Ariès, these developments were connected to changing views of self-hood beginning in the late Middle Ages, at least among the wealthy and powerful, for whom "the sense of one's own identity prevailed over submission to the collective destiny," and thus "the traditional relationship between self and other was first overthrown."[40]

Many scholars have made the case that some form of death denial is a fairly fundamental part of modern life, due to a variety of factors such as the decline of organized religion, the rise of individualism, the declining death rates associated with modern medicine, and the cordoning off of death and the dead in hospitals and cemeteries.[41] Such arguments are not without their critics, however. Some contend that modern, Western societies like the United States are both death-denying and death-accepting, depending on the circumstances.[42] Others like British sociologist Tony Walter have offered a variety of modifications and limitations to the death-denial thesis, suggesting instead that we may simply lack a coherent language for discussing death, or that death denial may be limited to only a few influential occupational classes, or that there was previously a taboo on discussing death that had begun to fade by the later part of the twentieth century.[43] It is certainly also true that modern, multicultural societies like the United States have a variety of different cultures around death and mourning, many of which may not engage in anything resembling denial.[44] Though these critiques certainly have merit, they don't refute the basic point that death is likely a fundamental source of unease for self-aware human beings,[45] and that modern, medicalized death in highly secular cultures may create new forms of death-related anxiety. In the coming pages and chapters, we will learn more about how this unease affects the modern self.

But what is the self? As Irving Howe once reminded us, "No one has ever seen the self. It has no visible shape, nor does it occupy measurable space. It is an abstraction, like other abstractions equally elusive: the individual, the mind, society."[46] For academics across a variety of fields, from philosophy to psychology to anthropology to sociology, "the self" can be a tricky concept to define. Some argue that the self is a fundamental part of embodied human cognition, some argue that the self is a cultural construct but one that has real consequences, and some argue that the self is merely a linguistic trick with no greater reality behind it.[47] Despite this dissensus, and without taking a position on the objective reality of the self, we may summarize the key features of the modern self that social scientists have identified. As Giddens put it, "The idea that each person has a unique character and special potentialities that may or may not be fulfilled is alien to pre-modern culture."[48] He went on to list the features of this unique character as modern societies have conceived it: it is a "reflexive project, for which the individual is responsible," and it "forms a trajectory of development from the past to the anticipated future."[49] In other words, the self is not simply an essence with which we are imbued at birth, but a sense of who we are that we as modern individuals are tasked with more or less continuously thinking about and working on. It is a kind of narrative we tell ourselves about where we've been and where we are headed, and how this passage of time marks us as authentic individuals.[50]

Death, as the mysterious end to the self, has serious consequences for modern individuals. After all, the modern self is "a project to be worked on, something open to new designs, new methods of construction."[51] However, "since this reflexivity is 'chronic' its completion is never envisaged. This means that when individuals inevitably die their self-projects will be incomplete, their fragile attempts at personal meaning left shattered by the brute fact of death."[52] Death presents itself as a fear of the self's ultimate incompleteness, and thus becomes a powerful motivating factor behind the experimentation with postmortem digital communication described in this chapter and the rest of this book. The desire to continue bonds with the dead may pull mourners to send messages to Facebook profiles of deceased friends and family, as was featured so prominently in the news stories analyzed here. But by the same token, the desire to "complete" a self-project, or to provide narrative closure or cohesion to one's life, may push dying persons, or those contemplating dying, to experiment with new digital death technologies as a way to capture a lasting sense of self, and to broadcast that to the rest of the world—as we will see in the coming chapters as well.

Indeed, this was an explicit goal of early postmortem messaging services like DeadSocial or If I Die, which were themselves the subject of many news articles in the sample. As one journalist explained,

> Sites like DeadSocial can let people control how friends and family perceive them after death. For instance, by sending out personalized messages after death, they can help people remember them as who they were in life. Sure, they can also exaggerate how much of a good person they are, but on the other hand, users can make fun of themselves at the same time. They can find humor in life and in death.[53]

That author concluded that in addition to helping loved ones grieve, such postmortem messaging services are really just "another way to ensure that while you may be gone when you die, you won't be forgotten."[54]

Some critics in the sample found such digitally aided life extension ethically dubious. One writer, reporting on the postmortem digital messaging service Safe Beyond and a postmortem avatar project called Eternime, wrote that "the desire to live forever—and it does seem that in the future that will be a technological outcome rather than a medical one—is the ultimate act of narcissism." For such critics, postmortem self-extension technologies are examples of "our compulsion to be online, even when we're not alive any more."[55] In some ways these criticisms echo those made four decades ago about America's "culture of narcissism."[56] Yet this remains an area of exploration and boundary pushing for many. One *New York Times* article detailed the work of Gordon Bell, whose project called MyLifeBits archived all his email as well as "digital records of Web pages visited, scanned versions of paper notes, recordings of routine conversations and tens of thousands of snapshots taken every 30 seconds by a digital camera that dangles from his neck." Bell was quoted in the piece as explaining that the point of digital technology is in fact "to capture one's entire life" and to "leave a personal legacy."[57]

Many would quibble with this vision of what digital technologies are supposed to do, but in any case at this point it is clear that digital engagements with death have the capacity to fundamentally challenge our notions of selfhood. Information communication technologies are certainly "technologies of the construction of the self," which "affect who we are, who we might become, and who we think we might become."[58] Digital information and communication technologies have, at least since their popularization beginning in the late 1990s, brought with them renewed attention among scholars and laypeople to what exactly it means to be social, to have "friends," to make connections, and to present oneself to others beyond one's physical environment. Some scholars, most notably Sherry Turkle, have been opposed to the sort of fracturing of selfhood that she viewed as emerging from the rapid growth of online, digital personas. Beginning with her 1990s studies of interactions in online "multiuser domains" or "multiuser dungeons" known as "MUDs," Turkle argued that such interactions made possible "the construction of an identity that is so fluid and multiple that it strains the very limits of the notion."[59] She saw these early online communities, where people created elaborate alter egos bearing little or no resemblance to their physical bodies or social statuses, as a way of fragmenting selfhood beyond repair. "What is the self," she asked, "when it divides its labors among its constituent 'alters'?"[60]

But what Turkle and other critics may have really been responding to was the digital reenchantment of the self, in which relatively commonplace features of selfhood were given a sheen of novelty, mystery, or even danger. Through the bright lights of an IBM or Macintosh screen, the self may have looked fragmented beyond repair. In actuality, the self had always been performed differently for different audiences and in different situations—this was Goffman's key insight in the middle part of the last century.[61] Online spaces in the late 1990s simply recorded these performances in new ways, and allowed them to take riskier and more extreme turns. In fact, other early Internet scholars found in this state of affairs a vast emancipatory potential. In "A Declaration of the Independence of Cyberspace," John Perry Barlow famously described the Internet as a space where people could cast off the shackles of race or class and connect on a purer level.[62] This was an early, highly influential, and highly enchanted vision of the Internet as a venue for the kind of transcendence that analog media and physical bodies could not provide.

Of course, time has generally not been kind to the idea that cyberspace can allow us to escape embodiment.[63] Moreover, the development of social networking sites and the rise of a more image-based Internet have rendered some early scholarship on the fragmentation of digital identity somewhat outdated. MUDs and their users are no longer representative of the Internet, and haven't been for a long time.[64] And although it remains possible to play with alternate or secret identities in digital spaces, most of us are engaged in a fairly stable and coherent set of self-presentations online.[65] Partly this is due to the influence of social networking sites like Facebook, whose founder, Mark Zuckerberg, famously quipped that "you have one identity. . . . The days of you having a different image for your work friends or co-workers and for the other people you know are probably coming to an end pretty quickly."[66] This is an overstatement, of course, but it is likely true that the in-depth metadata collection and targeted advertising sales on which social media platforms now rely are more effective when people maintain a single, coherent online identity.[67]

What all this means, in any case, is that the Internet has not changed the nature of the self, it has simply made fundamental elements of selfhood more explicit, made them more overtly and visibly a part of our social behavior, and connected them to one another in novel ways, thereby rendering them new, exciting, enigmatic, or even magical. We have always performed an at least slightly different version of ourselves for our co-workers than for our drinking buddies or our grandparents, but moving our social interactions online makes the performance of self and the consideration of audiences necessarily a more deliberate and potentially riskier endeavor. Face-to-face self-presentation often comes with built-in physical barriers between the front and back stage, "since performers behave out of character there."[68] Online, with the strong possibility that previously separate audiences will intermingle,[69] and the somewhat more remote possibility of the viral circulation of one's self-presentations to huge audiences of strangers, people—especially young people—are often urged to be on their best behavior.[70] But that does not stop the creative forms of self-construction that digital platforms provide, such that "interaction in cyberspace perpetuates the same self-ing that exists in the offline world."[71]

In fact, foundational figures in sociology, social psychology, and philosophy, including pragmatists like George Herbert Mead, Charles Sanders Peirce, William James, and Charles Cooley, have described the process of modern self-construction in ways that continue to resonate today. Norbert Wiley synthesized the works of these thinkers to argue that the self was a form of "inner speech," a way of talking to oneself about one's self.[72] At the same time, that inner conversation was embedded in cultural norms and social relations—we have always been "networked" even before the term became fashionable—so when we talk to ourselves about ourselves we are also imagining what others may think about us based on the clues we get in everyday life and our sense of the degree to which we are living up to norms and expectations. We achieve a state of selfhood by crafting a coherent narrative for ourselves, but always embedded within a host of social and cultural influences. Thus, despite the chaos of actual human events and the thousands of unknown and unknowable structural factors contributing to our personal lives, "we make our existence into a whole by understanding it as an expression of a single unfolding and developing story."[73] This was true in the twentieth century and it remains true in the twenty-first as well.

This modern form of selfhood has sometimes been described as disenchanted. In Max Weber's terms, when Calvinism turned away from clergy as the mediator between the sacred and the profane, and established each individual as the arbiter of their own destiny, the result was a sense of inner loneliness and the disenchantment of the self.[74] More recently, William Whyte's critical 1956 book *The Organization Man* identified the ways that bureaucracies had shaped our modern personalities to eschew individual creativity in favor of corporate conformity.[75] In a way, the counterculture of the 1960s and the lifestyle consumption of the 1970s were attempts to reenchant the self in response to this critique.[76] Painting in broad strokes, by the 1990s American selfhood was once again viewed in disenchanted and alienated terms, if popular trends like "grunge" music are to be taken as indicators.[77] One might argue that this alienation helped set the stage for the widespread excitement around digital technologies at the turn of the twenty-first century—an excitement that resulted in the dot com bubble that burst in 2000, but that nonetheless helped set the world on a course of ever-increasing digitalization.[78] No doubt this sort of grand narrative about enchantment and disenchantment in American life leading up to the advent of the Internet is too monolithic, and misses tremendous amounts of variation and nuance. But the larger point is simply to illustrate that, as Richard Jenkins once put it, "the historical record suggests that disenchantment—no less than power and discipline—provokes resistance in the shape of enchantment and (re)enchantment."[79]

Given this sort of dialectical ebbing and flowing of disenchantment and reenchantment, it makes sense that the digital revolution of the 2000s can also be seen as renewing the sense of possibility and magic around the self. Indeed, magic works by playing on distinctions between the visible and the invisible to create a false sense of causality, and the Internet does this too. By giving users an exaggerated sense of control of their digital devices while hiding the more disenchanting elements around these products—like the labor conditions used to create them, their vacuuming up and selling of user data, or the hidden algorithms secretly dictating what we see and hear while using them—media and tech companies reenchant the spaces and artifacts we use to create a sense of who we are.[80] And this sense of reenchantment persists when the dead appear to be resurrected with new digital media.[81] The Internet imbues the self-presentation of both the living and the dead with a new kind of promise and possibility.

It makes sense, then, that philosopher Patrick Stokes has argued that our digital remains come with an ethical requirement not to delete, and that postmortem deletion of our social networking profiles constitutes a kind of "second death."[82] Such profiles have a right not to be deleted because, "insofar as SNS profiles are materially implicated in the action of remembrance that allows SNS users to persist as practical identities, . . . cessation of memorialisation (in a broad sense) is the destruction of the person."[83] Though Stokes uses the term "person" rather than "self" to describe the status of our postmortem social networking profiles, it is worth noting that the "self" concept frequently came up in the news coverage reviewed in this chapter. For example, a counseling psychologist wrote in one of the sampled news stories,

> Although these persistent digital "selves" have not existed for long, many people now expect them to be there and rely on them in working through their grief. Bereaved individuals interviewed for my research had one overriding fear: profile removal. "If we lost it," said one, "it would be like losing him all over again."[84]

This sentiment was echoed in coverage of the legal battle between Facebook and the partner of a jazz musician whose profile was mysteriously deleted two years after his death. The partner claimed that "the disappearance of the Facebook pages was like he had 'died a second time.'"[85] It appears that Stokes's "deletion as second death" philosophical framework accurately matches many laypersons' and journalists' ontological framing of our digital traces.

The Rationalization of the Soul

The "life" with which digital profiles are imbued in these descriptions, their ability to transcend the death of the physical organism, thus reveals a linkage between the self and what might be thought of as the soul. Indeed, the concepts of self and soul have always been deeply intertwined. In ancient Greece, Socrates and Plato had argued for the existence of an immortal soul, and in the Roman era, philosophers like Cicero urged people to develop a sense of their authentic selves.[86] But early notions of the soul were not the same as the very self-concerned visions that developed into the modern era. The "tame death" of the early Middle Ages, where simple rituals in the dying person's bedchamber were attended by community members, was meant to express "the conviction that the life of a man is not an individual destiny but a link in an unbroken chain, the biological continuation of a family or a line that begins with Adam and includes the whole human race."[87] That view of death and the soul changed throughout the Middle Ages and into the Enlightenment, resulting in a much more individualistic view. This new, "fully conscious soul . . . expressed the individual's desire to assert his creative identity in this world and the next, his refusal to let it dissolve into some biological or social anonymity."[88]

Over time, then, a more scientifically oriented, secularizing society eventually began to require a new vision of human individuality. "The notion of a unified self was introduced into scientific theory in the seventeenth century, particularly in the theories of Descartes and Locke, as a replacement for the notion of soul, which had fallen on hard times."[89] As Norbert Wiley put it, "The self, based on reflexivity rather than immortality, became the center of the human being."[90] Raymond Martin and John Barresi have spoken of a "naturalization of the soul" that began when "new natural philosophers of human nature turned away from dogmatic assertions about the essence of the soul in favor of investigating the mind's activities as found experience."[91] Whereas personal identity had been rooted in an immaterial and immortal soul, it came to be seen as a product of the mind—a biological fact, not a metaphysical article of faith, but without the accompanying possibility of an afterlife. "As a consequence, the debate over how to understand ourselves, over what it is essentially that each of us is, provoked not only intellectual controversy but existential horror."[92] This is, essentially, the same existential horror that pushes us to deny or sequester or create taboos around death, according to many of the death-denial theorists mentioned earlier.

It is certainly true that one's own death still occupies a space just beyond any person's ability to fully prepare for or comprehend. No technologies can tell us how it feels to be dead, or let the dead tell us this, but the digital technologies and online spaces described in these news articles do seem to be salving many of the other consequences of death for one's self and one's loved ones. As we have seen, the Internet allows the living to maintain their bonds with a variety of technologically achieved selves circulating online. It affords the possibility of sending messages to loved ones after we die, either intentionally or serendipitously. It allows for a kind of co-construction of memorials between the dead and their mourners, made up of the raw stuff of one's own digital life. Photos, posts, statuses, and networks of friends in social media sites become a testament to one's self, extended beyond the bounds of mortality. As the news coverage studied here has shown, these ideas about the continuity of the postmortem self figure quite prominently in mainstream discourse; there is a socially constructed sense of the immortality of digital souls at work in these data.

However, in order for our digital selves to become immortal, somewhat paradoxically, we need to also rationalize the very concept of a soul. Weber used the term "rationalization" to describe the process whereby Western, capitalist societies gradually replaced decision making based on tradition or emotions with a kind of means-ends rationality, based on modern values like efficiency, predictability, calculability, and technological control.[93] Indeed, the process of rationalization has often been viewed as the catalyst for the widespread disenchantment of modern life.[94] But clearly new digital technologies and online platforms blur these distinctions. Magic and enchantment are critical to capitalist economies,[95] and in many cases "science and new technology now provide the fuel for a re-enchantment of society."[96] The term *rationalization of the soul* describes the comparatively predictable, controllable ways that this digital transcendence of death plays out in everyday life. When you die, your digital self clearly remains right where it was, in the exact same state, doing the same sorts of things that it used to do before your corporeal existence had ended. By contrast, many traditional, religious conceptions of a soul or afterlife rely on rituals, uncertainty, and heavy doses of hope and faith—with far less in the way of visual or virtual proof to back them up.

In this sense, then, the rationalization of the soul stems from the reenchanting capabilities of online, digital media. But it also redefines what counts as a soul by treating human immortality as a technical achievement rather than a metaphysical abstraction. It treats the conquest of death as a digital certainty rather than a matter of spiritual faith or belief. This is not the transcendence offered by religion, it is a diminished version but a more tangible and immediate way to think about individual human persistence after death. We know for certain that our digital self-extensions will outlast our physical bodies, and since these digital parts of our selves were so firmly ingrained in our senses of who we were while we were alive, so deeply embedded in online networks of other selves, our digital remains can be seen as containing such a soul.

This view came up again and again in my sample of newspaper articles. In one such article, a grieving young person explained that her group of friends still interacted with a deceased friend's social media profile because "we don't want her spirit to go away. . . . We want the world to know that this was an amazing person and that her spirit should be alive forever. . . . Her grave is just a resting spot, her memorial is where she passed away, but they're just places. MySpace is actually a piece of her."[97]

At the same time, this vision of the soul is not really devoid of emotion or values in the same way that the term "rationalization" is treated in classical sociology. In fact, one way to conceive of this notion of the digital soul is as a means to combat the existential dread of death in a modern, secular age. With no other guarantee of the self's transcendence upon death, and yet having invested so heavily in the lifelong project of building a self—both on- and offline—we see our digital avatars and social media profiles as something more than simply datalogical corpses. As another article in the sample put it, "With Facebook, a profile becomes the online embodiment of the soul. . . . It's as close as we can get to a living spirit."[98] An essay in the *Huffington Post* similarly intoned, on the question of life after death, "In the age of Facebook, we keep on living. We live on through memories. We live on through videos. We live on through stories. We live on through pictures. We live on, through Facebook."[99] This is a simultaneously banal and profound and, for some, horrifying thought. But regardless of one's ethical or aesthetic reaction to the idea of Facebook as a kind of afterlife, we see the cultural work that the rationalization of the soul is doing in mainstream discourse. It consoles us with the fact that, at the very least, the selves that we so carefully crafted in our profiles and selfies and blogs will not simply vanish when we are gone. It may be a diminished version of immortality, as compared to many traditional notions of the afterlife, but there is something undeniable about it. It requires no faith, no religion, just an Internet connection.

Conclusion

In a 2018 *Financial Times* article, a woman named Emma Jacobs explained how she had grieved her deceased father by sending him text messages many months after he passed away. She went on to make the connection between her personal, seemingly idiosyncratic form of grieving and the variety of digital death-related practices available now.

"Today," she wrote, "there are digital services . . . which will send your prewritten messages to loved ones after your death. Facebook accounts can be memorialised. There are virtual graves where families can pay their respects and chatbots that converse with the living, based on texts and social media posts left by the dead. The virtual cloud is an afterlife of sorts, hosting the dead's photographs, documents and memories."[100]

The image of cloud servers as a kind of afterlife is a fitting one for this chapter and its argument about the rationalization of the soul. After all, the language of "the cloud" may lend itself to notions of angels floating blissfully above the earth, but in reality cloud data centers are "low-rise, endlessly bland warehouses. . . . There is nothing ethereal about these buildings."[101] The transcendence of our digital souls depends heavily on servers that "burn up millions of dollars of electricity every month and produce an enormous amount of heat that requires cooling."[102] It is worth remembering, then, that this kind of immortality depends on a vast infrastructure rooted firmly in the material world.

The philosopher Hans Ruin wrote that "there is no social space outside the shared space with the dead. To learn to live is to learn to inhabit this space in a responsible way."[103] But it remains unclear what exactly are the responsible ways to live with the digital dead, if the news articles reviewed in this chapter are to be believed. These articles took a wide variety of stances on digitally mediated grief over, mourning for, and interactions with the dead. However, if we pull back far enough, we can see one central theme emerge. This is the simple fact that all of these articles took the digital dead seriously as social actors. They recognized an obligation between the living and the digital dead, even in those articles that espoused an obligation to give the dead their privacy, to leave them alone, to forget. They saw our digital souls as worthy of moral consideration. Granted, they also occasionally worried about the traumatic or otherwise unhealthful possibilities for such digitally mediated interactions with the dead, but this tended to come out of a sense that the appropriate way to treat the dead was to let them rest. By contrast, the ethic of those who embrace the digital afterlife tends to be one of circulation and continuing presence.

The precise ontological nature of that presence was also often at issue, and these articles showcased varying ways of conceptualizing the digital traces we leave behind when we die. But it may be the case that these seemingly competing conceptions were not really so different. An artifact or heirloom, a gravestone or memorial, a spirit or soul—all three of these are means of keeping the dead present, honoring them, remembering them, and interacting with them. These three interrelated frameworks remind us of the sociological importance of death and dying. Studying who dies, how, in what patterns, and with what meanings attached can tell us about the broader norms, morals, and relations of inequality animating the societies in which we live.[104] In short, the dead have always remained among us, with much to say about the societies in which they lived and died, no matter how we envision them. The digital rationalization of the soul simply enables us to see them more easily, to watch them circulate among the living in new and uncanny ways, and to hear what the dead have to say with more clarity than ever before.

2

Absent Presence, Death, and the History of Communication Technologies

A middle-aged woman, clad in a long pale skirt and a thin purple sweater, stands in front of a large green screen. A virtual reality headset covers most of her face and black gloves cover her hands, as a camera operator circles briefly into frame. In the next moment, we see the woman immersed in a computer-generated park, with tall grass and wooden benches. A little girl runs around a corner and calls out, "Mom!" This is how Jang Ji-Sung, a South Korean mother of three, is reunited with her seven-year-old daughter Nayeon, who had died of blood cancer three years prior. Nayeon wears a light purple dress with a pink purse, and smiles as she chats with her mom in this pristine virtual space. Jang Ji-Sung speaks softly to her daughter while gently weeping. She crouches down to stroke the girl's hair and squeeze her shoulders, but Ji-Sung's hands pass through her daughter's body without actually making contact.

These images come from a nine-minute clip of a South Korean television documentary called *Meeting You*, which details the efforts of six virtual reality studios to create this digital resurrection. Moments later in the clip, which has been viewed over twenty million times on YouTube, the pair float upwards, away from the park and into a new land with a purple sky, a small bed, and a smattering of Nayeon's favorite foods laid out on a white table—a kind of digitally imagined child's afterlife. At the end of the clip, we see how their time together comes to a close: Nayeon lies sideways on her bed, and tells her mother she is no longer in pain. As she gently falls asleep she says, "I love you, Mom." Then the purple afterlife scene fades away, and Jang Ji-Sung is back in the virtual park, alone.[1]

As journalist Violet Kim noted, "Jang may not have been the first mother to lose a child, but she is perhaps the first who got to meet her deceased daughter as a VR simulacrum."[2] But beyond the novelty of the technology itself being put to this purpose, it is worth pondering the larger significance of this virtual reality experiment. To what extent does *Meeting You* speak to new ways of understanding death and dying, and to what extent does it represent timeless elements of humans' engagement with mortality? Are digital technologies fundamentally changing the ways that we communicate about death and dying and the types of things that can be communicated? Or do new media simply allow us to draw deeper from the same well of human emotion into which death and dying have always fed? Is this another in an ancient line of attempts to access the afterlife through technological or aesthetic means? Or are we entering an era in which high-tech computing can create new kinds of afterlives altogether? Answering such questions requires a deeper dive into the social and historical context for our digital communication with the dead.

It is likely true that humans have always had an understanding of death that sets us apart from the rest of the natural world. "Because we humans are aware that we exist, we also know that someday we will no longer exist."[3] To the progenitors of the psychological school of thought known as *terror management theory*, "this awareness of death is the downside of human intellect."[4] Although animals can certainly recognize death in other animals, and some species have shown quite complex levels of death awareness and expressions of grief, "the mortal challenge" for humans consists of "the anticipation of death's arrival and reflection on its possible meanings, or even more, entertaining the possibility that death might have meanings at all."[5] At the same time, this knowledge of one's own mortality has not necessarily had the same meaning or implications throughout human history.

The current archaeological consensus is that humans began to view death in this self-conscious manner as early as 120,000 years ago.[6] They began to believe that death was not the end of one's existence, that there was some kind of soul that lives on after we die and an afterlife where that soul resides. These sorts of beliefs are often considered definitive features of Homo sapiens as a species, although the extent to which they were also present in our late Neanderthal antecedents remains a matter of significant debate.[7] All that we really know for sure is that eventually in this period, our human ancestors started to communicate about death in ways that left physical evidence suggestive of these beliefs, and that some of this evidence remains today. This is a key point. Beliefs, values, traditions, and affect around death and dying can be known only through communication, and what gets communicated is influenced by the technologies available in a given time and place. These technologies render ideas legible, and in the case of ancient peoples, some tiny fraction of what was once rendered legible has remained for modern archaeologists to uncover and study. It is essentially impossible to disentangle the ideas themselves from the cultural and technological conditions that made them expressible.

Such a perspective on communication technologies falls under the rubric of what is often labelled "affordance theory." Initially, James J. Gibson defined an affordance as "a specific combination of the properties" that an environment "offers animals, what it provides or furnishes, for good or ill."[8] Don Norman later applied the term to the design and manufacture of man-made things, such that it referred to "those fundamental properties that determine just how the thing could possibly be used."[9] The affordances framework helps explain how technologies may push or pull users toward certain behavior, or merely make such behavior possible in a more neutral sense, but always "through variations in perception, dexterity, and cultural and institutional legitimacy."[10]

Adopting the affordance framework is a way of acknowledging that no technologies are neutral, but at the same time, that humans can exercise creativity and agency in the ways they put technologies to use. With that guiding principle in mind, Jenny Davis has identified six mechanisms for how technologies afford things. Objects or technologies may be said to *request* or *demand* things of users when they bid users to do certain things. On the other hand, when users make bids of technologies or objects, objects or technologies may *encourage*, *discourage*, or *refuse* such bids. The final mechanism, *allow*, refers to situations where users may take a line of action with a technology or artifact but there is no pressure from the artifact to do so.[11] Using this terminology enables us to move beyond a binary where media technologies either do or do not afford something, and instead understand the intensities with which technologies and media shape human interaction, and the relative ease or difficulty with which humans may exert their own agency on such technologies. Though it is not always easy to distinguish between an affordance and a simple outcome or feature of a technology,[12] the larger point is that technologies present a range of possibilities for actions, but these exist in a dialectical relationship with the specific social, cultural, and perceptual frameworks of users.

With this perspective in mind, this chapter describes the relationship between death and communication technology throughout history. It focuses on the ways that a handful of important technologies have afforded new ideas about death, the afterlife, and the soul. And it shows how those technological affordances shaped and were shaped by their social-historical milieu. Though a historical chapter of this length cannot possibly allow for a comprehensive account of these themes, it nonetheless enables us to see the central function that a handful of very important communication technologies have played in the ways that we talk and feel about mortality today, and to distinguish between the new and the eternal features of digitally mediated death and dying moving forward.

The following brief historical overview will cover five key time periods that speak to the role played by media technologies in this changing relationship between the living and the dead. Though the amount of time covered here is vast, and thus requires painting with very broad strokes, these examples touch on some of the most important developments in human communication surrounding mortality. The ascendance of Homo sapiens, with their use of red ochre in burial sites and cave art, shows us how fundamental death-related communication has been to our species as a whole. The creation of alphabetic writing cemented the problem of absent presence, and made it possible for one's own words to outlive one's corporeal presence. The Victorian era intensified the problem of absent presence with a host of mechanical and electronic technologies that cleaved distance from time, most distinctively photography and telegraphy. Then, beginning in the period after World War I, we see a gradual movement away from Victorian mores and toward a shunning of death. In this era, death was fully medicalized, death and dying were removed from public view, and mourning became stigmatized. Finally, the digital era has arrived in conjunction with a backlash against this denial of death, as technologically adept members of modern societies have begun to use new technologies to continue their bonds with the deceased and to try to preserve those relationships with the souls of the departed. These may not be new desires for humans, but digital technologies do offer more ways to address them, and to potentially shift our sense of the social obligations between living humans and those who no longer draw breath.

This chapter thus argues that absent presence links these death-related communication technologies together across history. The uncanny ability to stand in for people who are distant or even dead is a fundamental affordance of almost all communication media. However, issues of power and privilege have always mediated the extent to which average people could make use of such affordances. In some cases, modern media technologies add a democratizing, populist element to the ways that individuals are able to relate to death and the dead, and in some cases they appear to offer more agency for the dead and dying themselves. Yet ultimately, the kind of posterity associated with physical media around death and remembrance is merely simulated by digital media, and largely imagined by users—no communication medium is guaranteed to stand the test of time.

Death and Communication in Prehistory

The Paleolithic period—from roughly 2.5 million years ago until about 11,500 BCE—bore witness to tremendous developments in human biology, technology, culture, and communication. Of course, these changes proceeded extremely slowly. "At least 99 percent of human evolution passed before significant changes in human behavior occurred, changes that are attributable more to cultural evolution than biological evolution."[13] Advances in communication are one product of this cultural evolution. Speech itself is a trait likely common to both Neanderthals and our species, Homo sapiens, who succeeded them, but the creation of stone tools probably predates even speech.[14] The earliest human communication technologies, then, were stone tools used for carving and engraving. But as Paleolithic art—a term that encompasses engravings, carved bone, statuettes, drawings, and cave paintings[15]—advanced around 40,000 years ago in the period called the Upper Paleolithic, the pigment known as ochre played an increasingly important role. As one scholar put it, "Prehistory has produced evidence for two meaningful regularities in human evolution: tool making and the collection and use of ochre."[16] Perhaps because this period is popularly known as "the Stone Age," however, the significance of ochre has been somewhat overlooked.

Ochre is defined as any iron-rich rock that can be used as a pigment, but it is most frequently associated with the mineral known as hematite, which makes red ochre.[17] Though many researchers speak of a universal human color triad of black, white, and red,[18] archaeological research attests to the fact that red ochre was by far the most commonly used of these pigments in prehistoric times.[19] Neanderthals may have utilized it as early as 300,000 years ago, and it has been found in early Homo sapiens burial sites from Africa to Europe to the Pacific, where it has typically been deployed around the heads and pelvises of buried corpses. The Blombos Cave in South Africa, a site dated to around 100,000 years ago, appears to have been a prehistoric red ochre factory.[20] A slightly later site, the 92,000-year-old Qafzeh Cave in Israel, shows some of the earliest evidence of the purposive use of red ochre in burials specifically. But the ritual use of red ochre in mortuary practices grew more common throughout the late Middle Paleolithic and into the Upper Paleolithic period.

It makes sense, then, to think of red ochre as a technology with certain affordances for the communication of concepts related to death and dying. For one, ochre has a versatility in that it adheres to skin, dirt, and cave walls, and lasts for great periods of time when need be. In that sense, there may have been very practical reasons for marking grave sites with red ochre, namely, making sure that bodies were not inadvertently dug up later on.[21] But the increasingly complex social life that accompanied the ascendance of anatomically modern humans may have begun to necessitate the use of ochre as a status signifier too. Indeed, one can think of ochre as both responding to and enabling the growing complexity in Homo sapien forms of social organization. Ochre may have been used to "stimulate the formation of social and economic relationships, reinforce group solidarity and ensure cooperation. Or it would discern different statuses, achievements or affiliations amongst group members."[22]

Those things would have been true in death as well as life, thereby determining the kinds of mortuary practices that accompanied one's demise. Although the archaeological record is necessarily incomplete, the practice of decorating gravesites with red ochre tells us that for as long as there have been anatomically modern humans, death has held a deeper meaning than simply the end of one's corporeal existence. Despite the lack of consensus on exactly why red ochre was the preferred pigment of our Paleolithic ancestors, most scholars take this practice as evidence of newly evolved symbolic and meaning-making powers.[23] This pigment afforded early humans opportunities to meaningfully engage with their mortality. Red ochre, and the symbolism it evoked, was an important mechanism for bonding together prehistoric communities through collective rituals in both life and death.[24]

Most researchers consider the use of complex symbolic systems to be the defining feature of Homo sapiens, and the use of red color symbolism at so many burial sites suggests that some of the earliest symbolic, abstract thinking was occurring around the topic of death and through the medium of red ochre.[25] It is important to note that our human ancestors were also often buried with material goods. When we consider these grave goods alongside other mortuary practices, we see early humans creating elaborate forms of symbolic communication to aid the dead in the transition to other states of being. Of course, death was not the only subject of prehistoric art and communication—fertility, female goddess imagery, and hunting also figured prominently in Paleolithic art.[26] But in terms of what went inside prehistoric graves, archaeologist David Lewis-Williams has explained that "people used meaningful items . . . to construct their identities in life and to construct a special, perhaps enhanced, identity for specific dead."[27] As societies became more complex, so too did individual identities become more variable and more differentiated within evolving hierarchies, so some individuals became more worthy of more elaborate forms of ritual and commemoration.[28]

Indeed, death required these kinds of mortuary practices because it posed problems not only for the survival of the rest of the group, but for the meaning of their own existence. As one paleoanthropologist succinctly put it, with the realization that one's own life will end someday, "there arose the need for a belief in the afterlife in which the identity would be preserved at least to some extent."[29] Archaeologists and other researchers who point to the Upper Paleolithic period as the moment when human beings gained a fully symbolic sense of self do so because of the confluence of burials, personal adornment, and representational art that flourished between 60,000 and 30,000 years ago.[30] This time period has been described as the "creative explosion," in human development due to the rapid emergence of deep cave art alongside mortuary practices involving red ochre pigmentation, grave goods, and other signs of symbolic and ritualistic ways of engaging with death.[31] As science journalist John Pfeiffer put it, "Excavated grave goods and other traces of ritual state collectively, and as clearly as if it had been spelled out in plain English that 'the dead are still among us,' invisible but not far away, requiring attention and sustenance and commemoration."[32] Though the idea of a short and dramatic creative explosion may be more a product of the vagaries of where archaeological digs actually occur,[33] it is nonetheless true that our early Homo sapien ancestors have bequeathed this sentiment to most of the major world religions today.

As such, we can think of red ochre as affording particular perceptions of time and mortality that transcend individual lives. The red markings around a gravesite may have requested that our ancestors think about those deceased members of a tribe or clan who had lived long ago, while, dialectically, the things like handprints on the cave wall may have been encouraged by these ancient peoples' desires to leave something of themselves behind when they were gone, or to represent their own transformation into other postmortem states of being. Of course, interpreting the meaning of prehistoric art is contentious and difficult work.[34] Nonetheless, it seems clear that red ochre's permanence called forth a sense of absent presence—people and times and moments from the past could remain a visible, symbolic presence in the present, and conceivably into the future. This symbolic element of red ochre likely worked in tandem with prevailing belief systems in which "the principal value of the soul's immortality [was] its life-giving transformation into another being, into an ancestor, ghost, animal, or another human."[35] Absent presence has thus been a key feature of death-related communication technologies for as long as such communication technologies have existed. It helped the dead to remain vital social members of premodern hunter-gatherer societies, and it continues to do so into the present day.

In his 1907 study of collective representations of death, the sociologist Robert Hertz examined death rituals of hunter-gatherer tribes, especially the practice of providing multiple burials for a single corpse. Hertz found that death was seen by hunter-gatherers in a variety of regions as a transition between one state and another, not an ending. "In the same way as the body is not taken at once to its 'last resting place,' so the soul does not reach its final destination immediately after death."[36] Instead, Hertz claimed that peoples like the Olo Ngaju of Indonesia believed that the soul undergoes a kind of probation after death, wandering around the places it inhabited while alive, and only entering the land of the dead for good at the time of the second funeral and second burial. The goods found in many Upper Paleolithic burial sites suggest that some form of this belief—that the soul in the afterlife requires help from the still-living, at least for some period of time after death—was extremely common for our early ancestors. "In burial," the philosopher Hans Ruin noted, "there is always a question not just of handling a body but of responding to a relation to an other that does not end with death."[37] Grave goods and red ochre afforded prehistoric peoples the ability to express their care for the dead, through mortuary rituals that left traces on the bodies themselves and at other places around the burial sites of deceased members of their communities.

Hertz's mentor Emile Durkheim, one of the foundational figures in sociology, also studied the prehistoric roots of modern views of death and spirituality. He surveyed the anthropological literature about Australian hunter-gatherer societies in order to make some fundamental claims about the sociological nature of religion and society. He focused partly on the idea of the soul, because he thought that some version of this concept was a part of all religious systems. For Durkheim, the concept of the soul spanned the gap between the individual and the collective, "at once a discrete being and an ethereal substance," as the sociologist Karen Fields explained.[38] "Belief in the immortality of souls," Durkheim wrote, "is the only way man is able to comprehend a fact that cannot fail to attract his attention: the perpetuity of the group's life. The individual dies, but the clan survives, so the forces that constitute his life must have the same perpetuity."[39] In this way, society itself is the source of religion's power. Religion makes society's norms intelligible; it puts them into action and binds people to a cause greater than themselves. As the archaeologist Clive Gamble summed up, "Religious life is not a special, separate activity. . . . Instead religious behavior, in all its varied ethnographic forms, lies firmly rooted in the practices of social life."[40]

In sum, social organization, self-concept, and communication technologies surrounding death and the afterlife have been deeply intertwined since the dawn of humanity. Scholars differ on the exact time period when these concepts fully took root in hominins, perhaps more so than this brief summary has made apparent. But without a doubt human brain size increased alongside the growth of human social networks and the complexity of early human societies, and the notion of a soul and an afterlife has likely been with us for as long as our ancestors were able to "think outside the box, go beyond the immediate world where interaction is mediated by the senses."[41] And to reiterate an earlier point, our species' unique imaginative capacities appear to have been turned toward death as soon as those capacities came into existence. The problems posed by death—the loss of the individual and the potential destruction of the whole community that depended on that individual—were resolved by early humans with the aid of their newly evolved symbolic powers, which evolved dialectically with their capacity to utilize technologies like red ochre.

Death and the Written Word

If the afterlife and the soul were made possible by the growth of human imagination and religious-moral socialization, and if they solved the problems to group cohesion posed by the death of the individual, they also crystalized the philosophical problem of absent presence. Social life for our hominin ancestors was limited to small bands of family and kin, but as the Neanderthals gave way to Homo sapiens, human social networks expanded far beyond one's immediate physical or geographical proximity. The souls and ancestors who populated the afterlife were one class of absent presence, but people in neighboring clans and tribes and trading partners from the outskirts of one's territory were also absent presences of a different sort. With the emergence of agrarian societies, and then the eventual ascendance of urban life in ancient city-states, the problem of imagining and managing the outer limits of one's territory became more than existing oral and aesthetic practices could accommodate. Though critics like David Graeber and David Wengrow caution against a simplistic historical narrative in which societies inevitably evolve from small, egalitarian bands of hunter-gatherers to advanced agrarian empires,[42] it is nonetheless true that when ancient political empires did emerge, writing and scripts eventually became essential.

Writing was a crucial means of increasing what Anthony Giddens called the "storage capacity" of societies.[43] Power can be extended over increasingly larger spaces and collective memory can be controlled more effectively if ruling classes have the ability to hold ever larger amounts of information, which writing provided. But alphabetic writing increased the problem of absent presence in a variety of ways as well, and these ways have had tremendous impacts on contemporary communication around death and dying.

"More than any other single invention, writing has transformed human consciousness."[44] This is a fundamental point for the school of thought known as media ecology, identified with thinkers like Walter Ong, Marshall McLuhan, and Neil Postman. "Writing is a visual enclosure of non-visual spaces and senses," as McLuhan put it. "It is, therefore, an abstraction of the visual from the ordinary sense interplay."[45] This form of abstraction allows one's words, thoughts, and ideas to take on a life of their own. They can travel to places one has not been, they can be shared with people who are not nearby, and they can be read in times when their authors are no longer living. Writing essentially severed the connection between physical presence and information transmission. With each new development in communication technologies the precise contours of this rift have shifted, but it would never be repaired. Thus, even though functional literacy did not become widespread for many centuries after it was invented, writing's repercussions for the ways we communicate about and with the dead reverberate throughout history.

Consider, for instance, the last will and testament. In the early medieval period, according to Philippe Ariès, "the written will seems merely to have formalized and rendered obligatory the instructions and prayers that [had been previously understood as] spontaneous impulses on the part of the dying."[46] Over time, though, the will became "an act of foresight and caution that [was] performed in expectation of death, but of death as a distant possibility rather than an impending reality."[47] Wills also became a part of a vision of the "good death" in prosperous, bourgeois societies: "To make a good death was viewed as a significant financial and legal management challenge."[48] Writing was itself fundamental to the last will and testament. In 1677 the English Statute of Frauds insisted that any disposition of land at death had to be in writing.[49] This was the end result of several centuries—from 1066 to 1307—in which medieval states cultivated early forms of literacy by requiring written forms in matters of business and law.[50] And it occurred well before Gutenberg's 1440 invention of typography, which is often thought to have spurred mass literacy.[51] Typography's importance cannot be overstated, of course, but even before people were reading pamphlets, newspapers, and novels produced by the printing press, many of them were engaging with the written word as a kind of conduit between the living and the dead. In this sense, writing created a new level of agency for the dying and the dead, who could now influence the actions of the living from a postmortem state. But it also generated a new set of social obligations between them.

Agency is, of course, a tricky concept to apply to the dead. The traditional sociological view of agency refers to the ability of human beings to act with intention, or to navigate social structures in pursuit of a given end. In this way of thinking, the dead cannot have agency. But some contemporary social philosophers have challenged this view, especially those informed by Bruno Latour's "actor-network theory." In that perspective, nonhumans—animals, microbes, and machines, for example—have agency inasmuch as they cause things to happen or produce perceptible reactions.[52] Mikkel Bille suggests that when we think of the agency of the dead, it makes sense to move from the concept of intentionality to that of potentiality—if one believes that the soul of a dead loved one may potentially still interact with the living, or may influence events in the world, then these dead souls retain a kind of agency.[53] Of course, this brings us back to a fairly straightforward social constructionist view—if the dead are *felt* by people to be a real kind of social presence, then they are "real in their consequences," to borrow from the famous sociological maxim of W. I. Thomas.[54] Suffice it to say at this point in our discussion that writing affords possibilities in both directions—for the dead to influence the living and for the living to interact with the dead—and that these possibilities are often deeply meaningful.

After all, the written word also provided a means for family members, friends, and even journalists to commemorate the life of the deceased in genres like the obituary. Early seventeenth-century obituaries consisted of a biography of the deceased—usually a nobleman or other notable public figure—and sometimes a moral or religious lesson drawn from their lives. By the mid-seventeenth century this practice began to be expanded, as "newspaper and magazine obituaries made public a narrative that would otherwise be confined to family and community."[55] This practice was of course as much about providing a salve for the grief of survivors as it was about the dead themselves. But in this way, alphabetic writing and its mass production in books, newspapers, and the like greatly democratized the sense of what sorts of people deserved to be remembered. One finds biographical inscriptions about the dead in artifacts as old as the walls of ancient Egyptian tombs, but these belonged exclusively to kings and other nobility.[56] The notion that less powerful or historically noteworthy people also deserved a similar kind of biographical preservation was in many ways quite radical.

The posthumous publication of diaries and letters also demonstrates another major affordance of the written word—its ability to circulate after one is dead, and in many cases to disseminate one's intimate, personal, and seemingly private thoughts and feelings to a wider audience. Though critics often claim that the Internet has degraded the boundaries between public and private communications, the letter had also blurred these boundaries many centuries before. Despite the fact that, dating back to the ancient Greeks, letters had been seen as a form of conversation between absent friends, and even as a "mirror of the soul," they were frequently circulated beyond their addressees and leaked to the public, or published as parts of newsletters and other collections.[57] Suicide notes are another prominent form of death-related writing, though due to the stigma associated with suicide these have, with some historical exceptions, been kept private.[58] Like wills, but unlike obituaries, they afford the dead themselves some control over how their descendants will remember them, and often give directions for the dispersal of property and resources. The notion that one can reach out from beyond the grave to reveal the reasons behind one's decision to end one's life, or to reestablish a relationship, or to apologize for wrongdoing, and thus to have a better chance at having one's final wishes heeded—these are hallmarks of the suicide note[59] and a testament to the haunting nature of the written word itself.

It is true, of course, that the myriad forms of ancestor worship categorized by anthropologists have typically been part of a system of beliefs in which the dead may influence the affairs of the living. But even for anthropologists who view ancestor worship as a universal feature of human culture, and who have studied the veneration of the dead in hunter-gatherer societies, the ancestors' influence on the living is typically seen as a means of strengthening kin ties and enforcing social traditions.[60] The dead communicate their expectations of the living "in social norms that reinforce social solidarity, consensus, and conformity as living religious leaders communicate with the deceased ancestors and convey their expectations to their descendants."[61] This sort of communication from the dead is, then, a far cry from the often uncanny ways that a written will or a suicide note can convey a particular—often idiosyncratic or highly personal—message from a specific individual who has died.

As a matter of fact, ancient peoples who bore witness to the transition from orality to literacy immediately made a connection between writing and death, and envisioned writing as something otherworldly and unnatural. Plato quoted Socrates at length on the subject in the *Phaedrus*. Socrates argued that writing produced "forgetfulness in the souls of those who have learned it . . . as through reliance on writing they are reminded from outside by alien marks, not from within."[62] As opposed to the time-honored medium of face-to-face speech, writing was for Socrates an invisible consciousness exerting a potentially malignant influence on the reader. Walter Ong was fascinated by the paradox at the root of Socrates's critiques: "The deadness of the text, its removal from the living human lifeworld . . . assures its endurance and potential for being resurrected into limitless living contexts by a potentially infinite number of living readers."[63] This point is illustrated by Socrates's own life and legacy. The great philosopher did not write down any of his thoughts; we know of them only because his student Plato was much more comfortable with the emergent literate culture of the time, and so recorded his mentor's arguments in writing—though we have no way of knowing how faithfully or fancifully.

In his own lengthy commentary on the *Phaedrus*, the communication theorist John Peters elaborated on the importance of that ancient text to contemporary media scholars: "The deprivation of presence, in one way or another, has always been the starting point of reflection about communication."[64] Peters recognized, more than anyone else, the ethereal qualities of all communication media. In his magisterial *Speaking into the Air*, he noted that "writing allows all manner of strange couplings:

the distant influence the near, the dead speak to the living, and the many read what was intended for the few."[65] But this quality is not unique to writing—as he put it, "every new medium is a machine for the production of ghosts."[66] Indeed, "the two key existential facts about modern media are these: the ease with which the living may mingle with the communicable traces of the dead, and the difficulty of distinguishing communication at a distance from communication with the dead."[67]

As such, the philosophical problem of absent presence really began to haunt every media technology from writing onward, allowing for otherworldly traces of communication to escape the fates of their authors and instead circulate across a diversity of contexts. Though there are obviously a wide variety of materials and technologies and genres in which writing takes place, it seems clear that as a technology itself it requests a different way of thinking about language and posterity from users, such that over time conventions about written versus oral speech greatly diverge. Moreover, it demands a different way of thinking about what communication is—language and information are no longer momentary events, lost as soon as they are created. They have a physical presence, they remain instead of instantly evaporating, and they can be held, copied, and transported. If media ecology theorists are to be believed, these qualities have transformed social and intellectual life more than those of any other communication technology.

Digital media are often treated by contemporary critics as engendering new or more intense versions of absent presence, however. For example, in arguing that mobile phones and other information and communication technologies were going to eradicate the social importance of physical space, the social psychologist Kenneth Gergen wrote,

> In terms of absent presence the Internet promises to be much more profound in its consequences than the development of print. Here we have a technology that enables instantaneous connections to be made among persons throughout the world. Alien voices from any locale and around the clock may instantaneously insert themselves into one's consciousness.[68]

Note the way he echoed Socrates's critiques of writing's "alien marks." It is this uncanny quality of mediated communication, again and again, that makes it feel as if each new communication technology offers new means of speaking to the dead. Yet that very feeling is at least as old as writing itself. On the other hand, certain technologies in certain time periods certainly do seem to have very pronounced effects on the sorts of things we think we can say to the dead—and on what we think they might say back to us.

Death and Communication Technology in the Victorian Era

The people of the mid-nineteenth century lived and died in a time of exploding technological possibilities with wide-ranging social implications. While the photograph enabled the masses to hold on to an image of the deceased, the telegraph created new forms of absent presence, opening and enflaming the possibilities of spiritual communication for nineteenth-century publics. Before the electric telegraph, human communication was tethered to the speed of transportation—the fastest message could only go as fast as a horse or steamship could carry it. But as the telegraph began to wire the world together, it created what David Harvey has called "time-space compression," in which social life gets sped up and distance has less bearing on the speed of communication.[69] Taken together, "in the 1830s and 1840s, the photograph overcame time and the telegraph overcame space."[70]

Photography offers a powerful testament to the way communication technologies have enabled new forms of grieving and commemoration. Grief, as we know, appears to be as old as humanity, but the possibility of using a likeness of a particular deceased individual as an aid in memory or grieving is much more recent. A relative handful of very wealthy people throughout history may have been able to experience this phenomenon via painted portraits, but for most people portraiture was far too costly. Photography democratized portraiture. Beginning in 1839 the daguerreotype, together with other methods of photographic image production, began to supplant painted portraiture. Within a few decades, the middle classes in Europe and the United States could afford to own likenesses of themselves and their loved ones. This meant that one could hang on one's wall or hold in one's hand a very accurate image of a family member, friend, or loved one that would of course remain once that person was no longer living.

But the uncanny nature of photographic imagery struck many observers at the time as well. Daguerreotypes especially contained a sort of ghostly quality, almost like a hologram on a novelty trading card today, as there appeared to be a kind of depth to the image, which also seemed to move or disappear as the light hit it from different angles.[71] And in 1861 a photographer named William Mumler discovered "spirit photography" when he took a picture of himself alone that, once developed, revealed an image of another figure beside him—purported to be his dead cousin.[72] Spirit photography became a way to help mourners cope with loss, "by purporting to expose the ghosts of dead friends and relatives to their survivors."[73]

Although he later used the term differently in his famous essay "Art in the Age of Mechanical Reproduction," Walter Benjamin wrote about the *aura* surrounding photographic images of living people who had since died. He spoke of "the tiny spark of contingency, of the here and now," with which such images had been imbued.[74] Matthew Brady's haunting photographs of Civil War dead were another powerful example of early death photography. Although these battlefield photos of soldiers' corpses violated a taboo, Brady and others justified them by citing both the need to preserve history and the desire to expose the horrors of war.[75] In both cases—domestic photographs of the dead and battlefield photos—there was a sense that this new technology provided greater detail, greater intimacy, and overall a greater access to the reality of death than we may otherwise have comprehended.

Victorian photographers leveraged that sense of intimacy and realism to provide access to the dead in other ways as well. From the 1840s to the 1880s, in both the United States and Europe, postmortem photography was fairly commonplace. This practice typically involved taking photographs of the recently deceased either lying in a casket or in a bed, as if asleep.[76] Sometimes it even meant "photographing your dead as though they were alive" and "photographing the living with the dead," thus "blur[ring] the line between life and death itself."[77] "The practice was common across all classes and allowed families to maintain a concrete visual link to the deceased and to memorialise persons at the final stage of life."[78] Indeed, the practice of postmortem or memento mori photography is a sign of a changing orientation toward individualism and selfhood.[79] Roland Barthes, inspired by a photograph of his deceased mother as a child, once described such images as containing a kind of "punctum"—a sting, cut, or accidental prick that captures the attention or affect of the spectator.[80] Like other reliquary commodity forms, the photograph of the deceased attests to the fact that "what has been lost . . . was an utterly unique, singular being, a whole that can never be replaced, duplicated, encompassed (even in memory)."[81]

In addition to outlining six mechanisms that explain *how* technologies afford things, Davis's work also asks us to consider the question "for whom and under what circumstances?"[82] The possibilities of an artifact will never be realized if potential users cannot perceive them, lack the dexterity to make use of them, or encounter them in a setting in which those affordances do not have "cultural or institutional legitimacy."[83] These questions draw out the kind of democratizing, populist appeal of photography relative to painted portraiture or other ways of producing a likeness by hand. Once photographic technology was commonplace, visual likenesses of the deceased joined the written word as important symbolic legacies of tragedies and loss for people across a wider socioeconomic spectrum.

Tragedy and loss are at the root of another of the nineteenth century's most important inventions in communication technology, the electric telegraph. Before he invented telegraphy, Samuel Morse had been a very sought-after portrait painter. On an assignment in Washington, DC, in 1825, he received a letter that his wife was gravely ill at their home in Connecticut. Although he dropped everything and travelled as fast as he could back home, by the time he arrived she was already dead.[84] Historians like Tom Standage have theorized that this was a primary motivating factor in Morse's subsequent experiments to improve the speed of communication; indeed, Morse's son Edward once suggested that his father hoped that the telegraph might be able to "bring a husband to the bedside of a dying wife,"[85] among its many other potential benefits.

The growing sense of the unacceptability of personal loss was also an increasingly common feature of life in the nineteenth century. Modern societies tend to put greater emphasis on the individual, and see the individual self as a constant "object of scrutiny, attention, and contemplation."[86] Scholars such as Gillian Brown have traced the emergence of a specific kind of "possessive individualism" to the nineteenth century, especially the new values placed on domesticity, privacy, and inner psychology—indeed, the term "individualism" itself was coined in this period.[87] Initially a critical term, the idea came to stand broadly for the notion that "men and women in the modern world were becoming more private, autonomous, and unique (or contrarily, apathetic, rootless, and estranged)."[88] In an individualistic society, individuals were considered to be worthy of more grieving and more memory work than in previous eras. Of course, this may be part of a much older and slower transformation—Ariès has noted that as early as the twelfth century, "the desire for commemoration spread from the great personages to include ordinary mortals, who very discreetly and gradually sought to emerge from their anonymity."[89] Nonetheless, although we have seen that the death of an individual family member or kinsman always posed a problem for the rest of a group, in more individualistic, industrialized societies such problems were viewed less as matters of group survival and more as tragedies in their own right.

The attempt to communicate with the dead was one way of alleviating the tragedy of individual mortality. Telegraphy's near-instantaneous communication across vast distances almost immediately inspired renewed efforts at bridging the divide between the living and the dead. Again, John Peters has provided the most expansive discussion of this period's technological dalliances with the afterlife:

> Spiritualism, the art of communication with the dead, explicitly modeled itself on the telegraph's ability to receive remote messages. Though the ambition of forging contact with the dead via mediums is ancient and widespread, spiritualism's birth as an organized practice dates to 1848, four years after the successful telegraphic link of Baltimore and Washington.[90]

The telegraph, the wireless, the telephone, and the radio all provided nineteenth-century spiritualists with inspiration and pseudoscientific justifications for how the living might contact the souls of the deceased.[91] Indeed, many scientific investigators who visited séances were hard-pressed to debunk the most talented mediums of the day.[92] Well-known figures of this period such as physicist Sir Oliver Lodge, author Sir Arthur Conan Doyle, and philosopher William James all experimented with or outright championed the possibilities of contacting the dead via psychic practices inspired by or utilizing these new technologies.[93] Though many spiritualists were exposed as frauds,[94] this period still shows how technological advancements can be part of a larger shift in attitudes about the presence of the dead in social life.

Speaking in terms of the affordances of new electric communication technologies like telegraphy and radio, it is clear that these afford—maybe even demand—new ways of thinking about the relationship between distance and time. This affordance has in many ways been a reenchanting force in Western culture, encouraging all sorts of possibilities to blossom in the minds of enthusiasts—including the possibility that tapping into electric waves floating through the ether might be a way to speak to the dead as well. Of course, the different time scales in which a technology emerges and gains cultural ascendance make a comparative historical discussion of affordances somewhat tricky. The longer the time scale, the easier it is to see how culture and technology influence one another and evolve together. As Lucas Graves put it, "When we move from talking about objects to talking about epic, decades-long industrial–technological developments like printing and telegraphy, obviously society is implicated in these."[95] It remains to be seen whether we can make the same bold claims about newer digital technologies with shorter histories.

Nonetheless, what has emerged thus far in our historical narrative are two ways of understanding the relationship between death and communication. On the one hand, the notion that the dead are not gone, that their souls may linger or may require assistance from the living through various ritual forms of technologically mediated communication and commemoration—this is truly ancient. In that sense, one can see Victorians commemorating the dead by posing their bodies in photographs as something akin to early Homo sapiens decorating bodies of their dead with red ochre. In both scenarios, the living are trying to say something about the dead and their relationship to the living, using whatever technological means are available. On the other hand, modern communication technologies come with a feeling of possibility, of newness, of real progress in the age-old battle against aging and death. This sense of progress is, after all, part of what is meant by the term "modern" itself. There is also a sense of the growing importance of individuals, and a break from the time-honored rituals and traditional mortuary practices to go along with it. Again, these are part and parcel of what it means to be living in modernity.[96] At the same time, the spiritualist movement has been described as a harbinger of secularization in the West—Christianity's hold on such populations was beginning to become less rigid, and new forms of belief were sprouting up as a result.[97] Moreover, this modern sense of progress against death was often the result of reenchantments unleashed by dimly understood new media.

This all added up to a new aesthetic in the Victorian era, in which language about death became more poetic and beautiful, cemeteries were transformed into wide open spaces and parkland, and individuals were encouraged or at least allowed to cultivate highly personal relationships with the dead via spiritualism or, more commonly, smaller relics like a lock of hair or a photograph.[98] These represented "both the desire for the loved one's 'soul' to live on, and a willingness to dwell on the moment of loss."[99] But this openness to public grief, and to technological experimentation around postmortem communication, slowed down in the twentieth century.

The Postwar Period and the Denial of Death

"It is immediately after World War I (and the 1918 influenza epidemic) when we enter the modern age of death," wrote cultural historian Lawrence Samuel. "The traditional ways of perceiving and coping with the end of life were left behind for good because of these two traumatic events."[100] Of course, the variety of Victorian-era cultural and technological innovations mentioned previously suggests that many "traditions" had already been challenged or transformed. But the postwar period has been viewed as one in which Western attitudes toward death changed again, quite markedly. The mass death brought forth by two world wars and a global pandemic certainly were major factors. Ironically, these were coupled with the increasing lifespans of average citizens who were lucky enough to avoid these calamities. New developments in medicine and public health, especially new drugs like penicillin, were part of the reason for the new kinds of taboos around death, mourning, and public emotion. For instance, British life expectancy, which had varied between thirty and forty years from the sixteenth century to 1871, increased to over sixty years by 1930.[101]

Taken together, this was a time of "a powerful reaction against Victorian ways of death after the Great War" and thus the start of "a deep chasm between the cultural norms relating to death and loss in 1851 and 1951."[102]

Geoffrey Gorer's study of English attitudes about death and dying in the first part of the twentieth century suggested that Western, Protestant society had lost its connection to time-honored mortuary rituals and social guidelines for grieving. People increasingly died not in the home but in hospitals, surrounded not by family and loved ones but doctors and nurses. In such a climate, many traditional mourning customs began to seem obsolete.[103] The result, as one of Gorer's reviewers noted, was that "most people must devise their styles of mourning on their own, without social support, and there is a tendency to shrink from the overt acceptance of death and expression of mourning."[104] As Philippe Ariès noted at the end of his own historical survey of Western attitudes toward death, "Mourning is no longer a necessary period imposed by society; it has become a morbid state which must be treated, shortened, erased."[105]

The postwar period in the United States and much of Europe fell in thrall to this dismantling of tradition and shunning of grief. "If there is one single idea that summarizes the literature devoted to death and dying in America over the last half century or so," wrote Lawrence Samuel, "it is denial."[106] As discussed in the previous chapter, the term "denial" references Ernest Becker's germinal 1973 text, *The Denial of Death*, which explored the psychological implications of modern societies' aversion to grief and mourning. Becker argued that much of human culture had been dedicated to controlling the anxiety brought forth from the notion that one's own death is inevitable, but that modern society and modern individuals had repressed death, and kept it buried in the unconscious. This, for Becker, had resulted in all sorts of unhealthy cultural adaptations—especially factions fighting against one another for the kind of "immortality" found in nationalism, religion, or ethnocentrism. The need for self-esteem, for a kind of heroism that denied one's own mortality, was a potential source of evil in the world.[107]

Popular media technologies of the era reflected this denial of death as well. Real, intimate encounters with death were quite scarce in cinema, radio, and eventually broadcast television. This was not due to technological limitations, but to the ascendance of a one-to-many broadcast model in which powerful companies came to monopolize control over these media. In so doing, they also acceded to the demands of government censors, ratings agencies, and advertisers.[108] Thus, for much of this death-denying period, death was mentioned in newspapers and television news programs, and depicted in action movies,[109] but there was little of the realism, the spiritualist innovation, or the democratizing impulse of death communication technologies from earlier eras. When real death did appear on radio or television, it was often because of an unexpected disaster or tragedy—examples include the Hindenburg disaster in 1937, the assassination of Lee Harvey Oswald on live television and the week-long mourning for President Kennedy in 1963, the explosion of the space shuttle *Challenger* in 1986, and the death of Princess Diana in 1997.[110] In a way, this was a sort of retrenchment of the populist, democratizing aspects of earlier death communication technologies, as only the deaths of important and powerful people, or those due to highly newsworthy events, were represented with any level of detail or intimacy via the most popular media technologies of the day.

In any case, Becker's work on the denial of death has inspired many—including the researchers behind the terror management theory mentioned earlier—but it has not been without its critics, as touched on in the previous chapter. The denial of death "may be an effect rather than a cause of inequality and competitiveness in modern culture"[111]—in other words, it may be that a materialistic, hyper-competitive culture is not caused by death denial but is actually what prevents people from adequately contemplating mortality in the first place. Moreover, although Becker's theory may accurately describe a certain moment in some Western industrial societies, the fear of death and its subsequent repression are often wrongly framed as cultural universals. If we are to believe that this is a truly global phenomenon, as one critic explained, "death attitudes in more secular societies need some comparison with societies where religious outlooks prevail in a largely uncontested social environment."[112] Yet at the very least, the *idea* of death denial has become a powerful force in the conversation about mourning and grief in Western societies.

The idea of secularization is an important part of this conversation as well. For over half a century, scholars have suggested that as modern, scientific, rational ways of viewing the world ascended, religiosity had begun or would soon begin to decline. This idea has been the subject of significant debate among social scientists and historians.[113] Philip Gorski and Ateş Altinordu summed up some of the evidence in their review of this concept:

> First, levels of Christian observance and belief in Western Europe are now much lower than they used to be. Second, the levels of decline vary considerably by country and religion, as do the patterns of decline, their onset and rhythm. Third, ecclesiastical organizations and elites throughout the West perform fewer social functions than they used to.[114]

These kinds of social transformations in the West have been particularly visible around death and dying. One can trace a kind of secularization around death and dying all the way back to the bubonic plague, through the Industrial Revolution and into the American Civil War, as Lydia Dugdale has done. For her, many of the "pivotal moments of the last two centuries" demonstrate a shift in which "religious, specifically Christian, dying edged closer to—and even transformed into—a secular medicalized dying."[115] In that sense, it is hard to know how much of death denial is unique to the modern era and how much can be traced far further back, but its constituent features are certainly still with us today. As Tony Walter summarized, "Modern death is characterized by secularization, and the related features of medicalization, privatization and individualism."[116]

It is undeniable, then, that the period following the First World War in many Western countries was one in which death became medicalized, grief and mourning became private, and an undercurrent of shame was directed at anyone who grieved too long or too intensely. By the 1950s, about half of Americans died in a hospital, and by 1970 that figure had risen to two-thirds.[117] At the same time, American life expectancy grew from sixty-eight years in 1950 to almost seventy-seven by the year 2000.[118] So death was, quite literally, a less visible presence in everyday life during this era. Even if one disagrees with the broader psychological presumptions of theorists like Becker, a society in which death becomes removed from everyday life is one that will almost certainly have a harder time dealing with grief. Joan Didion very movingly captured her struggles with these social mores around bereavement in her memoir

The Year of Magical Thinking, which detailed her mourning after the death of her husband in 2003. Self-diagnosed with "complicated grief," she struggled to find guidance on how to return to normalcy, moving from Freudian psychology to self-help books to etiquette guides, with very little to show for all of it.[119] Perhaps it is simpler to say, as the anthropologist Donald Joralemon did, that due to the changes in the nature of modern death described above, we find ourselves needing "new cultural scripts for dying and death."[120]

The End of the Denial of Death?

Beginning in the second half of the twentieth century, there has been significant public pushback against these supposedly unhealthy Western attitudes toward death. For instance, journalist Jessica Mitford penned a scathing exposé of the funeral industry, *The American Way of Death*, in 1963. And perhaps most famously, psychologist Elisabeth Kübler-Ross wrote the international best-seller *On Death and Dying* in 1969. Though she is best known today for the five-step model of grief that emerged out of this work, her larger goal was to normalize death and dying, and to restrain the impulse to hide these topics from view. In her book, like Becker, she wondered whether our increasingly technological, medicalized response to illness and death was "our own way to cope with and repress the anxieties that a terminally ill patient invokes in us."[121] Although further research has shown that grieving people rarely progress so neatly through a five-step model from denial to acceptance,[122] the general thrust of Kübler-Ross's work—to bring death out of the shadows and normalize mourning—has continued into the twenty-first century.

Whereas grief in the twentieth century was often viewed as something pathological, especially if the bereaved were not able to quickly accept and move on from the loss, today psychologists speak of the therapeutic benefits of "continuing bonds"[123] between the living and the dead. The rise of home-based hospice care has also meant that in 2019, for the first time in half a century, more Americans died at home than in a hospital.[124] And whereas death and mourning were often seen as taboo topics of discussion in the previous century, today the Death Positive movement, led by people like Jon Underwood in Great Britain and

Caitlin Doughty in the United States, encourages people to talk about death both informally and in organized Death Salons or Death Café events, where experts on death-related topics are brought in to lead such discussions.[125] Yet as we will see in the book's conclusion, there is also reason to believe that the COVID-19 pandemic may be shifting social mores around death and bereavement again.

In any case, this is the social and historical context for the Internet's current engagement with death, especially as mortality has grown more publicly visible and more widely discussed in the 2010s. Millennials now comprise a generation of adults less attached to older taboos around death and dying and more open to new forms of ritual and mortuary practices. Entrepreneurs have taken note of these changing mores; one can now have one's body turned into a diamond or into compost after one is dead, or use a host of different apps to engage in the kind of end-of-life planning that members of older generations sometimes eschewed.[126] Moreover, the circulation of the dead on social networking sites—be they intimate friends or celebrities with whom masses of people feel a kind of para-social bond—marks the Internet as a public space in which the dead are once again a vital kind of social presence. These processes are not confined to the young, however. Digital technologies appear to be responding to secularization and filling a gap among the aged as well.[127] The ramifications of these changes will be explored more fully in the coming chapters.

Conclusion

"How do the dead survive?" asked Tony Walter. They "survive" by either (1) becoming ancestors, (2) achieving immortality, or (3) simply remaining in the memories of the living. These are "three of the more significant answers that have gripped human imagination and characterized particular cultures over millennia."[128] This seems true on its face, and yet where does little seven-year-old Nayeon fit into this framework, or rather, where does her digitally reconstituted avatar fit in? Is she achieving a new kind of digital immortality, with the help of her family, or is this simply a more sophisticated form of memory work, like a Victorian postmortem photograph? By bringing her back to life in virtual reality, are her family members denying death, or embracing it with a newfound positivity?

A reconsideration of our prehistoric roots may offer some answers. Despite a tremendous variety of mortuary practices over time and across cultures, burial "in the general sense of a ritual caretaking of kin after death" has always been a fundamental part of human life.[129] But the notion that ancestors actively intervene in affairs of the living is much less common in hunter-gatherer religion than the overall belief in an afterlife.[130] The time-honored practices of venerating the dead and ancestor worship involve a much less individualistic or therapeutic orientation to what constitutes communication with the afterlife, or social responsibilities between the living and the dead.

Today, by contrast, the dead themselves can return to care for the living thanks to a host of digital technologies. After all, Nayeon's digital resurrection at the start of this chapter was clearly not for Nayeon's benefit. It was meant to help her family, especially her mother, come to terms with and heal from her passing. It was also meant as a test of the technical capacities of virtual reality designers, and as a means for a Korean television station to garner ratings and thus advertising dollars. None of these have to do with any obligation to care for the dead themselves. But they do speak to the fact that the dead have had new possibilities opened up to them as new communication technologies have emerged throughout the last several centuries. These range from simply telling the living how to distribute their property through a written will, to posing for a postmortem photograph, to being digitally reincarnated as a salve for a mother's grief.

Of course, Nayeon was also not the one steering her own resurrection. But as we will see in the coming chapters, there are a variety of online platforms and applications that aim to allow the dying to direct their own sorts of resurrections, from postmortem messaging services to mind uploading research to AI chatbots and avatars made from one's digital data. One AI avatar start-up was called Eternime, and when I interviewed its founder, Marius Ursache, via email in 2017, he made some of the same points about the desire to extend one's digital existence. "When we asked people why do they want to use Eternime," Ursache explained, "the most common answer was that they want to be there for their loved ones even long after they pass away." As we have seen throughout this chapter, technologies as old as alphabetic script have already been used for this very purpose, but in this case for Ursache, the interactivity of an AI avatar was qualitatively different than what had come before. "Unlike diaries or photo albums, in the future Eternime will allow . . . family, friends and other people to interact with your avatar through natural conversations," he wrote to me.

However, just as Jang Ji-Sung's hands could not actually grasp her virtually resurrected daughter, there has always been something ineffable about the dead with whom we seek to communicate, something always just out of reach, slightly more than we can grasp. Homo sapiens have always cared for the dead, but we could never be entirely certain that our mortuary rituals had worked as intended. Technologies as different from one another as the written word, photography, and telegraphy have all promised new forms of communion with the dead of one sort or another, but we can still never be sure that the message has been received as intended, or that we are correctly perceiving the signals coming back to us. This is a fundamental problem of communication between living people as well, as scholars like John Peters and Stuart Hall have long understood.[131] To resolve this problem, we have either had to rely on faith in time-honored social practices or put our hope in cutting-edge technologies.

The situation is not so different today, despite the reenchanting promises of the digital afterlife. "No one believes any longer, if anyone ever did, that 'if it's on the Web it must be true,'" wrote historian Jill Lepore, "but a lot of people do believe that if it's on the Web it will stay on the Web."[132] In actuality, the Internet is not nearly so permanent. Digital data decay, links rot, spaces go empty and are forgotten, and much of it is never archived or backed up in any form. One study found that 25 percent of all the links to a specific web page in the *New York Times* were inaccessible, meaning that the target page no longer existed. This got worse over time, too, such that 43 percent of links from 2008 and 72 percent of links from 1998 were rotten.[133] In a similar vein, the massive virtual world Second Life, which once had over a million very active users, became a digital ghost town in a matter of years.[134] Along those lines, the social networking platform MySpace accidentally deleted twelve years' worth of user uploads in a matter of moments due to a server migration issue.[135] Even the Internet Archive, a nonprofit that uses web crawlers to archive as much of the public Internet as possible, misses between 10 and 65 percent of web pages—a range so big it suggests that we don't really know how much of the web is archived at all.[136]

The larger point is that no media can really fulfill the promise of posterity. Web pages get deleted today just like photographs have faded over time, letters have gotten lost in the mail, and diaries have been discarded. Even the red ochre markings that have survived on cave walls and at burial sites for tens of thousands of years are likely just a fraction of what was produced but did not survive. Impermanence is the rule governing both human lives and the artifacts we leave behind, whether analog or digital. This ought to remind us that affordances are really a product of imagination—many expectations for technology are "not fully realized in conscious, rational knowledge."[137] In sum, our digital afterlives depend on the same kind of imaginative relationships with the dead that have always been a part of human culture, even though the social and cultural milieu around these relationships does change over time, and the meaning of new technologies can vary based on all of this.

Moving forward into the digital era, then, we see five themes coming into focus. First, absent presence has been an effect of all media technologies around death and dying, though the degree to which this was seen as a feature or a bug has varied considerably. Second, the technologies generating these varied senses of absent presence throughout history have afforded new ways of thinking about time, memory, and mortality. Third, new technologies have often democratized access to the kinds of individualized commemoration that used to be reserved for elites. Fourth, attitudes toward death and dying have varied across cultures and time periods, and this dialectically relates to the imagined affordances of the death-related media in those times and places. Finally, although the living have always used media like red ochre to commemorate or commune with the dead, newer communication media appear to have opened up opportunities for the dying and dead themselves to steer these processes. What this will mean for larger notions of the soul and transcendence remains to be seen.

3

Suffering, the Self, and Narrative Freedom in Blogs of the Terminally Ill

On July 30, 2012, a twenty-seven-year-old woman posted what would be the final entry to her blog called *Holy Crap I Have Cancer!!! . . . now what.* For the past year, she had kept a record of the physical and emotional strain of managing a terminal diagnosis while raising her three-year-old daughter on her own. She had grown exhausted. In a 796-word post, she reminisced about her life and her goals just before her cancer was diagnosed, then turned her attention to her current state: "Right now it's probably the worst time of my cancer journey. The doctors are using the strongest pain medications, chemo is every week, radiation in between, scans . . . what if we run out? That's what I'm asking myself every day." She continued, "I know those 700 pills a day is what keeps me running. It also gives me horrible side effects. I'm not myself anymore, I lost the real me somewhere on the way. Now I'm just here, trying to survive. Trying to get into my child's memory so she won't forget her mother."

Five years later, *Holy Crap I Have Cancer!!!* was still online. This final post was still there at the top, and only in the comments section of that post did an anonymous visitor let the reader know, five comments down, that the author had passed away in hospice care a little less than a month after those words were written. As of October 2017, there were twenty-three comments left by readers of this final blog post. The four comments from before the author's death was announced contained words of encouragement for her, while eleven comments after her death contained messages of condolence. Several of these appeared to be from people who had never met or even interacted with the author online during her lifetime. The remaining seven posts consisted of spam messages peddling alternative cancer remedies.

What to make of this blog post, and the other posts on this blog, and the many other blogs like it from other terminally ill authors suffering through a variety of ailments? Certainly they are a function of the increasingly lengthy experience of dying that has accompanied improvements in modern safety, sanitation, and medicine. As sociologist Karla A. Erickson has explained, longer, slower ailments like cancer and heart disease have replaced sudden killers like strokes and accidents as the most prevalent causes of death, with the result that "contemporary humans can now see their own death coming."[1] In a digitally saturated world, this means that many terminal patients have the time and technology to share the experience of a serious illness online. This sort of peer-to-peer sharing of health information has become quite common—as early as 2012, one survey found that one in four American Internet users had read about or watched someone else's health-related or illness-related experience online.[2] Indeed, medical institutions are increasingly encouraging their patients with terminal diagnoses to blog about those experiences, as discussed in a 2013 National Public Radio report. One hospice director quoted in that piece explained that "as more people tell their story of dying with a terminal illness, we're seeing a change in how we look at illness and mortality. . . . Illness and death are still so technically driven, or medicalized. So getting a safe space, like a blog or social media, to talk about it can be very empowering."[3]

Yet a term like "empowering" conceals as much as it reveals. Sharing is something humans tend to value for its own sake, but the so-called "sharing economy" is often predatory and unequal as well.[4] So is sharing one's experience of a terminal illness simply a means of personal empowerment, or is it violating norms about privacy and publicity? *Guardian* columnist Emma Gilbey Keller and her husband, *New York Times* editor Bill Keller, took the latter view in 2014 when they attacked another prominent terminally ill blogger, Lisa Bonchek Adams, in a pair of editorials. For Emma Keller, there was something unseemly about Adams's prolific accounts of her treatments across her blog and her Twitter account, and the almost addictive quality they possessed for readers. Bill Keller, on the other hand, took issue with the false sense of hope and the valorization of needless suffering that he believed Adams's blog promoted. Both Kellers' pieces were resoundingly criticized online, by Adams herself as well as many of her supporters, resulting in the *Guardian*'s removal of the initial offending story.

Adams passed away in May 2015, yet her blog remains, and the practice of end-of-life blogging continues. Though concerns about the ethics or propriety of sharing one's experience of terminal illness seem over-blown, commentary like this suggests that the intimate discussion of pain and dying in these blogs has the potential to unsettle many read-ers. These blogs do not always appear on the surface to be spaces for empowerment, either. They frequently detail in stark terms the terrible symptoms, grueling treatments, and harsh side effects associated with terminal diseases, as well as their often crushing emotional toll. As the author of *Holy Crap I Have Cancer!!!* put it toward the end of that same, final blog post, "I hope everyone learned how strong cancer can be. I was a very strong person but it broke me down."

As sociologist Kathy Charmaz has noted, many terminally ill indi-viduals "claim uniqueness in the face of their dying." However, in her 1980 study, *The Social Reality of Death*, she also wondered "how long their special selves and statuses are maintained? Do these terminally ill also sink into silent obscurity in their final phase of dying? And are they not only able to sustain their newly achieved identities but also continue to *control* their dying processes?"[5] We have already seen in chapter 1 how online spaces can be a force for the reenchantment of the digital self, and how that reenchantment connects to a kind of limited vision of immortality through the digital texts we leave behind when we die. And in chapter 2 we learned that communication technology has always been ineluctably bound up with human desires to understand mortal-ity and to speak with the dead. But how do these issues play out in a specific genre of digital engagement with death and dying? With these and Charmaz's questions in mind, we might wonder what terminally ill bloggers are getting out of all of this. What meanings are constructed as these authors share their experiences online? What types of senti-ments and information are they most willing to share, and what remains undisclosed? What function do they themselves appear to impute to their blogging? How do these bloggers confront the end of corporeal life while affirming social ties that will persist beyond death? And what do the answers to these questions tell us about life, death, selfhood, and transcendence in the digital age?

To answer these questions, this chapter performs a discourse analysis of twenty blogs of the terminally ill. It focuses on the ways that self-hood gets constructed and reconstructed in the face of a terminal illness via the act of blogging, and compares those processes to earlier forms of life-writing. Ultimately, this chapter hones in on a key affordance of blogging—*narrative freedom*. As sociologist Robert Zussman explained, this term refers to "the ability to tell stories about our-selves in the ways we want, not simply to muster particular facts and events but to draw meanings and morals about our own lives."[6] The chapter argues that blogging encourages a kind of narrative freedom for terminally ill authors, which helps them come to terms with the physical and emotional pain to which they are subject, and to assert agency over their sense of self in the face of impending mortality. In this way, terminally ill blogging makes suffering legible and understandable, in ways that not only help to reconstruct a new sense of self, but even imbue these digital texts with a kind of soul as well.

The Affordances of Blogging

Blogs grew out of online diaries that early Internet users kept on their personal web pages in the early 1990s. These pages were created by hand, so to speak, written in HTML code by their authors. Indeed, the term "weblog" itself was not coined until December 1997, and at first it referred to lists of links with very little accompanying text. It was not until 1998 and 1999 that free tools like Open Diary, Pitas, and Blogger began to appear, allowing those who could not code to create online diaries for themselves.[7] Blogs have evolved today to the point where the term typically refers to a set of episodically structured personal narratives or commentaries hosted in a public, online space.[8]

Blogs have clustered around discrete topics like political commentary,[9] food,[10] and in many cases motherhood.[11] Indeed, the phenomenon of "mommy blogging" has generated a host of commentary in the press and a wide range of academic scholarship. Although many bloggers struggled against this "mommy blog" label,[12] many others found that blogging allowed them to push back on stereotypes of good or bad mothering[13] and to form supportive communities with other women.[14] One survey of 250 blogging mothers showed that the practice of blogging created "strong bonds of trust and support that bloggers characterize as meaningful friendship within a community."[15]

The gendered nature of blogging is worth dwelling on especially because, as will be discussed in more detail shortly, a large percentage of the bloggers in my sample identified as women, and among those, a majority were mothers. Technological affordances can be gendered because, as Davis has explained, "a person may recognize what a feature does (*perception*), and have the skill to use it (*dexterity*), but face formal or normative barriers that *refuse* or *discourage* enactment."[16] The simple fact that "men have been cast as more technologically inclined than women" often renders women's presence in some online spaces illegitimate.[17] But blogging—especially around issues related to parenting—became a gendered activity in the other direction, such that women were encouraged to "explore the self as fluid and plural and from multiple perspectives," as well as to "reclaim the *I* from patriarchy" via blogging.[18] Indeed, Kara Van Cleaf has described a "digital maternal gaze" at work in mommy blogs based on "an economy of connection, recognition, and pleasure women find online."[19] She explained that the digital maternal gaze allowed bloggers to "challenge ideals of competitive, hyper-individualism and the neoliberal imperative to brand the self," and to focus instead on "disrupt[ing] the status quo" by showing the value of "new connections to objects, bodies, and pleasures" rooted in motherhood.[20]

Of course, the pre-digital reference point for the blog as a genre is still the diary, where one's innermost thoughts and feelings were made legible at regular intervals with the passage of time. Blogs are personal artifacts that, like diaries, tell us something about the authors themselves, while allowing authors to refine their conceptions of self. The key difference between paper diaries and blogs is of course the public nature of the blog post, written as it must be with one's regular readers in mind, and relatedly, the possibility of a blog post's circulation across links and networks and platforms to a larger and largely unknown audience. These are key affordances of blogging, then: blogs encourage regular reflection and public dissemination of these reflections, and they also encourage connections between the writer and her readers. These connections to an audience—both real and imagined—also suggest that blogs discourage playing around with multiple identities and personas, at least in a single blog. They are much more suited, due to a combination of the technology and the cultural norms about how it should be used, for the development of a coherent perspective over time—a narrative of the blogger's life built publicly and incrementally. In addition, the fact that they often persist after the authors have died means that blogs allow readers to engage with them as postmortem memory objects or legacies, because this seems neither particularly encouraged nor discouraged by the technology or practice of blogging. With these features in mind, this chapter will focus primarily on the narrative construction of the self as it plays out for terminally ill bloggers.

Analyzing Blogs of the Terminally Ill

This chapter is built around a discourse analysis of twenty blogs from terminally ill authors who passed away.[21] Fifteen out of the twenty bloggers in my sample were women, and five were men. Their ages ranged from twenty-one to sixty-four, with a median age of forty-two at time of death. The most recent blog post in the sample was from April 2016, while the earliest post was written in November 2004, though the remaining eighteen blogs were composed between 2008 and 2015.[22] I performed a discourse analysis of the fifty most recent posts from each of the twenty blogs in this sample. Because of the retrospective nature of blog posting, this meant starting with the most recent blog post written by the author, usually just before death, and working backward to fifty.[23] The end result was a sample of 927 blog posts. I coded these 927 blog posts based on eleven thematic categories, which emerged from an initial read-through, and each post was potentially included in as many categories as fit. The most frequent of the eleven themes occurred in 60 percent of the posts, while the least frequent occurred in only 2 percent. Taken together, this coding produced a very robust picture of what these terminally ill individuals shared on their blogs.

Finally, in order to understand the way that terminally ill bloggers interacted with their readership, in October 2021 I returned to my sample of twenty blogs to analyze the comments on their posts. Three of the blogs were no longer online at that point, so for the remaining seventeen blogs, I returned to the ten oldest posts from each author in my initial sample, and this time read each of the comments from readers and any replies that the bloggers had made to these comments. This added up to 1,566 comments and 146 replies. These data helped me to understand how the blog posts themselves were received, how often people posted comments, and the extent to which bloggers engaged in discussions with their commenters. In the end, I aimed to understand not only how the authors of these blogs wrote and rewrote themselves, but also the social context in which their writing was received.

Common Themes in Blogs of the Terminally Ill

As mentioned already, the sample of data on which this chapter is based consists of twenty blogs and 927 individual blog posts from terminally ill authors who have passed away. An initial read-through of these blogs and some preliminary coding generated eleven categories of posts, representing the most common themes or types of discourse to appear in the blog entries. The five most common categories of post consisted of (1) updates on the disease or medical procedures; (2) reflections on death, illness, or grief; (3) regular daily activities; (4) reflections on family; and (5) reflection on friends (see table 3.1).

The six other, less common categories consisted of posts about (6) culture, art, music, or literature; (7) politics; (8) personal memory or autobiography; (9) religious themes; (10) advice to other patients or caregivers; and (11) discussion of one's legacy, or how one would like to be remembered (see table 3.2).

At first glance, these rankings make some intuitive sense. Of course blogs authored by the terminally ill focus on the effects of the illness itself and its treatments, and of course they feature a great deal of reflection on that illness and the looming confrontation with one's own mortality that it presents. And it is not particularly surprising that blogs

TABLE 3.1. Most frequent themes in 927 posts from blogs of the terminally ill (%)

Disease update/ procedures	Reflection on death/illness/ grief	Regular daily activity	Reflection on family	Reflection on friends
60	41	24	24	17

TABLE 3.2. Less frequent themes in 927 posts from blogs of the terminally ill (%)

Culture/ art/music/ literature	Politics	Memory/ Autobiography	Religious themes	Advice to patients/ caregivers	Legacy: How to be remembered
12	11	10	5	4	2

of the terminally ill are less concerned with art or politics. Yet these blogs don't do some other things we might have expected them to. For instance, despite the fact that several of the blogs in the sample appeared to have fairly large readerships, there was very little in the way of concrete advice to other patients suffering from similar ailments or their caregivers. And unlike the suicide notes that will be discussed in chapter 4, these blogs contained very few mentions of any desire on the part of their authors to be remembered in a particular way, or efforts to define a particular legacy for themselves. But beyond the frequencies of the categories themselves, these blogs still have much to reveal about the kinds of selfhood they afford and the narrative freedom they represent. This section of the chapter will detail the kinds of posts that made up each of the eleven categories above, beginning with the less frequent themes and working upward toward the most frequent.

To begin with, the idea that these blogs ought to serve as a legacy for their authors did surface a few times in the sample. For example, one terminally ill fifty-five-year-old woman wrote in her February 3, 2012, blog post,

> My sister Theresa died 21 years ago. I'm pretty sure I have seen every picture that was ever taken of her. I'm also pretty sure I've heard every story about her. And believe me, there were quite a few pictures and plenty of stories, but after 21 years without any new material created, I believe we have exhausted them all. There are no new memories and no new pictures. What I wouldn't give to see a video of her. I think I have forgotten the sound of her voice. I think her daughter has also forgotten. That is sad. So . . . I want to make sure there are plenty of memories of me to tap into for many years to come. I want my grandchildren to know who their parent's mother was. I want to leave a legacy. So . . . I make sure I get in to lots of pictures. I believe this blog could be a good legacy.

Quotes like this were exceedingly rare, however, appearing in only 2 percent of the sample.

Blog entries like Martin Manley's suicide note, mentioned in the book's introduction, that featured extensive autobiographical content were also somewhat rare, appearing in only 10 percent of the sample. By "autobiographical" I refer to posts that are explicitly looking back at older events in one's life, prior to one's struggle with a serious illness. The posthumous effect of all of the blogs in this sample may be to provide a kind of ad hoc autobiography, but as they are written and published they are typically about events in the present or very recent past, not about one's memories from other times. One example of an autobiographical post came from a thirty-nine-year-old mother, as she reflected on the care she was receiving in the hospital. "I used to be a nurse," she wrote. "I was attracted to the field because I was social and, honestly, young girls in Northeast Philly didn't set their career ambitions too high. Surrounded by so many loving nurses here, I have started t think back to my nursing days. Sometimes I wonder if I was a bad provider. Did I dismiss my patients concerns? Was I rude and uncaring? Was I indifferent to their suffering?" She continued by describing her memories of dressing the bedsores on two patients who were close to death from cancer:

> I think of those two patients now and then. They must have felt so alone in that room with me as I changed their dressings like some mindless robot. I was trying to be professional; I knew the last thing these patient's need was to comfort a young nurse. Now I think to my self, "Would it have been so bad to cry?" or to say, "This is not fair." I wish that I had had the maturity and strength to look these patient's in the eye, hold their hands and say, "I'm sorry for what you are going through." I wish I had pulled up a chair and given them the opportunity to share their grief and anger and sadness. But I was too young and stupid and naïve to know how awful it is to be sick and suffering and facing your mortality. I try and remember that when I experience the callousness of providers. I try to remind myself that they don't understand or know what to say, so they say nothing. Just like I did 16 years ago.

A fifty-year-old science fiction writer whose blog predated his terminal diagnosis helped explain why terminally ill authors might have avoided such memory work:

> I find lately that old hurts have been resurfacing in my thoughts. There's precious little point to that, and it's not the least bit constructive, but here I am. Like the chowdered dreams, my mind is trying to put things in order. I've gone through life not making enemies, though a few people

have certainly gone out of their way to make me their enemy regardless of my actual words and deeds. But in this case I'm talking more about the usual hurts of life, lost friendships and fractured loves and "whatever happened to . . ." moments. Really, I don't need these trips down memory lane amidst everything else that's going on.

When one is embroiled in a struggle to survive, distant memories can be painful or at least, an unwelcome distraction from the matter at hand. Most terminally ill bloggers in my sample were keenly focused on the present. As Lisa Bonchek Adams put it, "Everything is an equation now. Everything is a calculation. Everything has a cost. I try to balance risks. I study statistics and results. But in each equation I calculate, the result is always time. Nothing is more valuable than time that I am able to enjoy the world and those around me." Such an attitude does not seem to lend itself to many reminiscences of better days from years past.

Although the authors of the blogs in the sample spent much time reflecting explicitly on mortality, they mostly did so from a secular perspective. Explicitly religious messages appeared in only 5 percent of the sample, and even these were often speculating about religious matters rather than making concrete claims about god or the afterlife. For instance, one twenty-one-year-old woman wrote,

> I am very happy with my spirituality. Am I religious, no, but I do have my own thoughts about what happens after death and I like to pick and choose different things to believe in. I believe that everyone is entitled to believe in what they choose as long as it does not hurt anyone else. If you believe in God, Allah, Buddha, etc, ok. If not, ok. Nothing is going to convince anyone one way or the other. I guess what I love so much about religion and spirituality, is that it is so unknown and there is no proof one way or the other. I think that is one of life's great mysteries that is one that should never be solved, people should have some sort of hope one way or another of what lies beyond. I DO appreciate it when people say that they pray for me, hope for me, wish for me, anything positive that kind of shows that they do care about me and think about me.

It is likely that people with a strong set of religious beliefs and a close connection to a community of coreligionists would feel less inclined to blog about a terminal illness in the first place. The blogs sampled here were largely a tool for making sense of the senselessness of a terminal diagnosis—something religion has traditionally done for us. As one author explained, "I find myself entering the last phase of my life and there are no rituals for the dying. I'm just sort of 'winging it.'" Such a sentiment would be less apt for a person with strongly held religious beliefs, embedded in a devout religious community.

Indeed, the blogs themselves, and their network of readers, were not usually discussed as any kind of "community," at least not on the surface. Although the authors occasionally referred to their readers in a general sense, and although they occasionally expressed the hope that others suffering from the same disease or condition might find their blogs useful, the blogs very seldom offered advice to other patients or their caregivers—only 4 percent of the entries contained this. One example came from a forty-nine-year-old Canadian breast cancer patient, who advised her readers, "If you have any hidden medical devices like a breast prostheses or a port and are planning to fly, you may want to read this post. Canadian airports have full body scanners and pat-downs but not the issues found in the US. So when you're traveling south of our border, beware of what's happening and prepare yourself." A sixty-four-year-old cancer patient also offered this helpful and humorous tip: "One piece of advice I will pass along is take care of all personal care needs BEFORE beginning chemo . . . especially cut your toe nails!!! . . . there are days I can barely lift my feet to get socks on or tie shoe laces . . . as the weeks wear on it all becomes beyond embarrassing and I find myself stuck on the bathroom floor having fallen off the commode trying to cut my toenails."

Much of the academic literature about blogging alludes to the sense of community that blogs can establish among authors and their readership. When I analyzed the comments and replies attached to a sample of ten posts from seventeen of my sampled bloggers, I found that the median post had 2.7 comments from readers and .3 replies from the bloggers to their readers. Essentially, a few of the more popular blogs with large readerships had many comments per post, but most of the blogs had only a few comments or less on each post. Many posts went uncommented upon, and authors infrequently replied to the comments left by their readers. One gets the sense on most of these blogs that, as far as establishing a sense of community, a little went a long way: a few reader comments may have called to mind for bloggers a larger, imagined community of supportive audience members. Nonetheless, it is also clear that direct conversations with readers and interactivity between authors and their audiences were not the primary functions of these blogs.

The blogs were also not particularly focused on art, music, literature, and popular culture, or on politics, as these topics appeared in only 12 and 11 percent of the blogs, respectively. Moreover, these numbers were skewed by the presence in the sample of several blogs that had begun long before their authors were ill, and thus had a predetermined repertoire in which such topics were fairly common. These several bloggers thus tried to continue to blog about some of their old topics, even while the blogs became more and more focused on their illness and treatment. Occasionally the politics of funding for disease research or proposed legislation about euthanasia were discussed, especially on the blog of a fifty-seven-year-old Australian man who used his site as a platform to argue for pro-euthanasia legislation. At other times, bloggers purposefully steered clear of these things, as when one fifty-year-old man wrote, "I have some political and cultural posts I'd like to make, but as I'm under a lot of medical stress, I don't trust myself to be as nuanced and focused as I need to be in those cases. If I'm going to be inflammatory, I'd strongly prefer to do so on purpose." Art and popular culture would also occasionally work their way into larger reflections on death and illness, as in this post from a thirty-six-year-old mother of two, who wrote,

> I'm not afraid. Not for me, anyway. But I think about [children's names] all the time. How robust their little bodies seem, but how much they already understand . . . How little we know about the future and what it will bring for them, for me, for [husband's name]. And this is where what I read and watch seems give me an outlet for my worry, a cartoonish way to imagine the unimaginable of leaving them. Will I end up like Mufasa looking down over my little Simbas from the starry heavens? Will [children's names] turn out wild like Peter Pan's lost boys? Or starved in an attic by some evil school master like Sara Crewe? Perhaps I could come back as the family Patronus (a lioness, natch) to protect the brood forever?

However, references like these were, again, still somewhat rare in the overall sample.

So what did feature prominently in these blogs? That same thirty-six-year-old woman discussed her friends in several blog posts, and indeed reflections on friends featured in 17 percent of the posts. She wrote that "whilst other relationships might define us more—with our parents, partners, or children—for me female friendship has been the steady tick-tock of adult life, the oil in the engine, the ink in the pen, the wind in my sails: all those clichés and more." She continued by describing the changes in these friendships that her illness had brought:

> We have conversations which play in my mind for days afterwards. Interesting, funny, profound discussions about how to live, perhaps the sort only prompted by not knowing if you will. We make new memories; now in my back garden, but soon, we plan tentatively, AWAY in foreign places. I lean on them when I feel lonely and anxious about the future, and promise to do the same for them when they need it . . . This might not be how I planned my friendships to go, but it's not so bad.

More prominent than reflections on friends, however, were the reflections on family that appeared in almost a quarter of the entries. This too, is not surprising, given that most of the authors in the sample had children and spouses. Still, the depth and power of these reflections are often staggering. For example, one of the final blog posts from another thirty-six-year-old woman was a reflection on living a year longer than she was supposed to when initially diagnosed.

"So what have I learnt from this bonus year?" she began.

> I've been here for teeth to fall out, bikes to be ridden without stabilisers, both the kids to ski and become more confident in the water. I have received hand-written birthday cards and plaited L's hair whilst together singing 'Do you want to build a snowman?'. R and I have celebrated our 8th anniversary and I've excelled my optimistic survival stats. I have loved, laughed, travelled, cherished my Mummy memories, but perhaps most importantly realised the amazing value a few people have put on my life. Spend as much time as you can with your children. You may take being able to read 'apple juice' for granted, but the first time your

child realises they can read is a huge moment for them. Don't take it for granted. Create magic for them. From Father's Christmas' frosty footprints dotted around the house on Christmas morning, to a letter from the tooth fairy, these are massive occasions your kids will remember from their childhood.

Other posts in this category were, of course, less upbeat. One woman diagnosed with terminal cancer worried quite a bit about her three-year-old daughter, in a post that combined both religious themes and reflection on family:

> As for me I'm not scared anymore. I'm just heartbroken and so sad for my child. I just don't understand it. I will never question god. He made us and he has the right to take us but it seems so cruel. I know it will break her little spirit forever. I grew up without a dad but I could not imagine it without my mom. And she is a mommy's girl. Don't get me wrong, she loves her daddy but at the end of the day she comes back to the one she loves the most. We have a bond that I can not describe. It started before she was born. It's a bond nobody could ever replace. So what will happen to her.

These discussions of children and motherhood were not, then, always joyful. Indeed, as Carsten Stage has noted, "Social media cancer narratives do not only produce a sense of relief, but can also play a role in the production of negativity, anger, irritation, sorrow and loneliness."[24] The authors of these blogs were not afraid of dealing with negative emotions or poking around in areas of deep ambiguity.

For instance, some women in the sample reflected on their spouses' lives in the future without them. One author wrote of her husband,

> He's such a good man: loyal and steadfast, loving and dependable, witty and affable. He will find someone new to love. I truly want that for him, but laying in my hospital bed with him as we inched closer to the end of my life I finally felt the very natural sadness that comes with the realization that someone will take my place at [my husband's] side. He will share the remainder of his life with another woman who will run her hands through his wavy hair, keep him from getting lost, and act as tour guide on trips to foreign lands.

As one might expect, given the episodic nature of blogging, mundane details of life also featured prominently in these blogs. Going out to lunch, shopping, travelling, getting the kids off to school in the morning—these appeared in 24 percent of the entries. Of course, even the most normal daily events carry added weight in the context of a struggle with a terminal illness, as in this post from a sixty-four-year-old tech journalist who described a small moment of peace amidst rapidly declining health: "It's just me, and my [wife's name], and some organ music. Gentle, pale sunshine reflects off the terrace opposite, fluffy clouds float in the delicate blue. The wind outside is cold, but [wife's name] and I got out for a visit to the Farmers' Market in Stoke Newington, bought some nice sourdoug bread, wild green salads, Russetts (apples) and fig-and-ginger cake." The post quickly turned, however, to weightier reflections: "It is so good, just being here with my girl. We recall memories and smile. Life has had its struggles, but overall, we've been together for 40 good years, and there's little we don't know about each other now. Suddenly, I'm overwhelmed by pure happiness."

At the same time, there was a great deal of pain and suffering contained in these blogs. This was most frequently manifest in the category of updates on the disease and medical procedures. Of the posts in the sample, 60 percent contained these updates—they were the primary function of these blogs, at least in terms of frequency. Sometimes the updates were about relatively minor changes in one's condition or small new procedures. "Time for another MDA update," one blogger wrote. "I schlepped all the way to Houston on Wednesday for my 3 month check-up. My borrowed immune system is still up and roaring, and presently doing what immune systems are supposed to do, except for the whole attacking my lungs thing. It still thinks my lungs are the enemy."

At other times, these posts went into more specific details about the severity of a condition or its symptoms:

I have trouble concentrating. I have problems forming complete thoughts some days. I'm tired in a way that only weaning off of steroids can leave you. I've put on 20 pounds since starting steroids last July. My hair has fallen out, grown back in, and fallen out again. I've developed cushingoid features. The muscles in my lower body have deteriorated significantly.

I have general muscle weakness. My adrenal glands aren't functioning properly. I shake uncontrollably some days. The list goes on.

Bloggers such as this one often discussed the emotional toll of their symptoms: "Right now we spend most of my waking hours preparing me to eat, tricking me into eating, calming me down when I react to food, and planning how I will eat. It is a freaking misery." Another blogger shared a similar rundown of side effects and their emotional toll:

> Today was depressing. My pain increased again this morning, and I was forced to stick an extra Durogesic plaster. The strength in my right arm and hand is going much faster than I have feared. I am clearly getting clumsier by the day. It's so bad now that I have decided to use my feeding pump to inject my food into my stomach catheter instead of just by hand. I now wonder which new problem I'll wake up with tomorrow. It is so tiring having to watch your body break down like this, and knowing that the worse is yet to come.

Perhaps the most harrowing posts were the ones relaying particularly bad news, ones where the authors had to come to terms with a particularly grim outlook. One author wrote, "last week's scan shows that the good news is really good, but limited to 'No more chemo for me!' And the reason is 'it isn't working.' Sorry guys, but I'm off. Hopefully, my last few weeks will be fun, and at least, more comfortable than the last few weeks have been." Another explained more matter-of-factly, "On Monday my oncologist brought up the topic of 'hospice' for the first time. Once a patient decides to stop curative treatment, they transition to hospice. As I understand it, insurance officially stops paying for anything meant to cure the person and instead focuses on what's needed to provide comfort and symptom relief." Two days before passing away, a twenty-five-year-old woman with cystic fibrosis wrote, "the medications have been piling up. they are taking their toll. i am supersaturated with medications. i've been medically missing in action for two days. the docs started taking me off some of them to see how i would manage. and i am not managing. not managing at all. i'm drowning in the medications. i can't breathe. every hour. once an hour. i can't breathe. something has to change."

The author's bodily discomfort was drawn into stark relief in posts like this. Tamara Kneese has reminded us that both physical pain and relational labor undergird these digital narratives[25]—behind the texts themselves there are not only bodies in agony but networks of affective labor in the form of nurses, doctors, family, and friends who are physically caring for the ill authors. In my sample these interactions with caregivers were fairly well documented, especially as part of this larger theme of disease updates and medical procedures. Indeed, in addition to functioning as a way of marking time and controlling the rhythms of daily life,[26] such updates rendered the self visible through these descriptions of suffering. As classics scholar Judith Perkins has pointed out, there is a long history, dating back to early Christendom, of people coming to understand the self by detailing bodily afflictions.[27] Though the physical pain of others is notoriously difficult to fully understand,[28] rendering one's own bodily pain legible is an important locus of control for those suffering deeply from it.

Of course, physical suffering and mental anguish often go hand-in-hand, and this was certainly the case in the blogs that I read. For instance, one author reflected on the moment of her terminal diagnosis by writing,

> It now seems that my story isn't going to have a happy ending. The cancer is back. It's back like one of those horror movie villains you think you've killed, but who rises from the dead and scythes you down. Back in my colon, back in my liver, and now also in my bones. This, my friends, is it. The news you fear the most, the phone call you can't bear to make, the words it hurts to write. For those of you not in the cancer-know (you lucky buggers), once it spreads to the bones it is pretty much incurable. You can live with it, sometimes for a long time, but once it's got a hold on the bits of your body that make you tick, as mine has, we are talking a year or two if I'm lucky and months if I'm not. So, I return to my half-life in January. Back to chemo, and this time it's the really baldifying one. So I expect I will die bald, which because I am nothing if not vain seems spectacularly cruel.

The sly, self-deprecating humor with which this blogger addressed her terminal diagnosis is not necessarily unique. In fact, what makes the final category of posts surprising was the frequently positive spin put on these most dire of circumstances. Of the entries in the sample, 41 percent contained reflections on death, illness, and grief, and, as one would expect, many were filled with pain, worry, and anguish. One author wrote, "With each treatment, a clip of ammo is emptied, a bridge is crossed and burned. Slowly, I am being forced through a labyrinth which will result in the same dead end (pun intended) no matter which path I take. So completing a treatment is bound to be at least a little depressing, even when the treatment itself was terrible." Another blogger explained this pain thusly:

> Sadness is such an overwhelming emotion. It has a way of derailing all your plans for the day, and snuffing out your energy. Sadness plants itself in the centre of your consciousness, and dictates you from then on. It spreads itself out through your spirit so that you leave a trace of it in everything you do or say. I've just finished baking a tray of sadness-flavoured cookies. I'm now listening to some of the cheeriest sad music. I guess sometimes you just have to drown yourself in sorrow. I'm drowning . . .

Yet surprisingly, many more attested to the positive value of the experience of a terminal illness, for the way it brought them closer to loved ones and especially for the wisdom it generated. Consider the following quote:

> It turns out that no one can imagine what's really coming in our lives. We can plan, and do what we enjoy, but we can't expect our plans to work out. Some of them might, while most probably won't. Inventions and ideas will appear, and events will occur, that we could never foresee. That's neither bad nor good, but it is real. I think and hope that's what my daughters can take from my disease and death. And that my wonderful, amazing wife . . . can see too. Not that they could die any day, but that they should pursue what they enjoy, and what stimulates their minds, as much as possible—so they can be ready for opportunities, as well as not disappointed when things go sideways, as they inevitably do.

Another blogger made a similar point:

> If I can somehow stay positive throughout facing my mortality at such a young age, then I believe others should stay positive too. We are all given difficult cards in life, in one way or another, but we must survive and adapt to them. Part of adapting is taking change in stride and keeping a smile on your face. Since my life will most likely be cut very short, there is no reason for me to waste my time feeling bad.

Lisa Bonchek Adams similarly wrote,

> I was originally diagnosed with early breast cancer on December 20, 2006. That anniversary approaches. I search for the beauty each day. I make myself find it. I won't give up these days even when they are so hard. Today as I drove the kids to school the full moon sat above the horizon. It was beautiful in the blue sky after our gray day of snow and rain yesterday. We all looked at it. And I was glad to be able to see it with them.

Indeed, a very common sentiment within this category was that the authors were actually, in a way, grateful for the changes that their illnesses had brought about—grateful for the ability to fashion a new kind of self out of the chaos and anxiety of a fast-approaching end date. As one author explained,

> So in some ways I am far more confident now than I ever was before my diagnosis. Cancer has changed my life completely and the road from rock bottom to where I am now has been a bumpy one, but I am glad I have managed to stick with it and not let the horrendous situation I find myself in depress or isolate me socially. I am lucky in so many ways to have such a supportive network of wonderful people around me who have all played their part in rebuilding almost my whole sense of 'me'.

Another blogger put his newfound appreciation for life succinctly, and humorously: "Each and every morning since being told my lung cancer staging had rocketed form Stage 1 to Stage 4 with brain metastasis has been a Stage 4 morning and believe me there ain't no morning like a stage 4 morning." And this remark was perhaps the most poignant of all in the sample:

Despite all this gloom, the truth is there is a best thing about having—or having had—cancer. What it has stolen is the normality I took for granted. But I have taken from it, too. For starters, there is a feeling of being alive, awake, which reasserts itself so strongly after illness that you can't help but feel joy . . . Then there is the way I feel about the people in my life. [Husband's name] and I have grown a love known only in power ballads, a depth of understanding and companionship which in any fair world would last us both a lifetime. My parents, always such dear friends to me, now closer physically as well as emotionally since their relocation to the flatlands. And friendships which survived on the leftover bits of time after real life was done have had a renaissance . . . And whilst the world may have lost a future stateswomen, I have, at least, found my voice. And with my voice, an intellectual and spiritual hinterland which had been too long lost between the answering of emails and the wiping of tiny bottoms. I am woman, hear me roar. I am not sure whether what is lost is greater than what has been found. Perhaps I should simply celebrate the fact that I can ask that question at all.

Such quotes hint at the therapeutic qualities of blogging, but also at the ways that the confrontation with mortality affects the very essence of selfhood. Certainly, the affordances of blogging outlined earlier, its encouragement of regular periods of introspection amid a supportive audience, have much in common with more traditional forms of therapeutic encounter. Moreover, reframing terminal illness as something positive could be a way to combat the many stigmas associated with death and dying. Yet very few of the blog posts in the sample discussed such stigmas directly. Instead, what became clear again and again in these blogs was the transformative capacity of blogging a terminal illness. It was not just that anxieties were salved in the process of writing them down, or that order was made out of the chaos of a terminal diagnosis by creating these narratives, though undoubtedly these were important effects. The capacity to craft a new self was an even more powerful factor.

Blogs as Technologies of the Self and Soul

As mentioned in chapter 1, social networking profiles of the recently deceased were initially treated as ad hoc spaces for mourning and commemoration, in ways that occasionally presented challenges to family members and friends looking to moderate content posted there.[29] Today Facebook has rules in place that allow surviving loved ones to transform a deceased profile into an official kind of memorial. Profiles of the dead tend to elicit messages of condolence and remembrance, and researchers have found that mourners return over time just as they would a tombstone or other kind of spontaneous shrine in the physical landscape.[30] But as I will explain, the blogs of the terminally ill in my sample did not end up functioning in the same ways as social networking sites once their authors had passed away.

Most scholarship on blogs in this context has been concerned with the social consequences of illness in general, rather than looking specifically at bloggers' considerations of their own impending mortality. Some scholars have focused on the integration of social media practices into traditional hospice wards.[31] And one study did include terminal illness blogs in its study of end-of-life narratives dating back to the 1950s. It found that there had been a general increase in the frequency of end-of-life narratives over time, and that such narratives increasingly focused on the therapeutic benefits of this kind of writing.[32] Yet this work was still not focused on the specific affordances of blogging or the narrative construction of the self in the face of mortality.

Carsten Stage and Tamara Kneese are two of the few to study blogs of the terminally ill from these kinds of perspectives. Kneese examined the "process of turning individuals' dynamic illness narratives into interactive digital heirlooms."[33] She focused on the ways that the affective labor of grieving spouses or other family members was necessary in order to maintain blogs of the terminally ill once their authors had died. Stage studied three specific blogs of the terminally ill, and examined the ways that readers continued to interact with these blogs after their authors had died. Influenced by actor-network theory, he argued that such interactivity destabilized boundaries between the statuses of living and dead, and suggested instead that such blogs were better understood as existing in a state of what he called "permanent changingness."[34]

These two perspectives on terminal illness blogs reflect two of the frameworks discussed in chapter 1: either the blogs are heirlooms/artifacts or they are selves/ghosts/souls. But these frames both focus on what happens to blogs after the death of their authors, rather than looking at the process of coming into being as a dying self, which is what the authors themselves wrote about and grappled with throughout the blogs that I read. Additionally, only a few of the blogs in my sample demonstrated any prolonged period in which they were used by friends, family, or even Internet strangers as tools for grieving, mourning, or commemoration. The most dramatic example of post-mortem interactivity between a blog and its mourners was the one where my sample of twenty and Stage's sample of three overlapped. Eva Markvoort died in 2010 and her family continued to use her blog after the fact to promote a documentary film about her life and to support cystic fibrosis charities. But eventually this activity slowed down and stopped as well. The last post on her site by her family was from 2014, with three comments on it. The second-to-last comment commemorated what would have been Eva's thirty-first birthday, in 2015. The final comment came after five years of inactivity on the site, in 2020, and it simply read, "I'm cleaning up my livejournal. Could you please remove/defriend me?" The example from *Holy Crap I Have Cancer!!!* mentioned at the start of this chapter also reaffirms that the comments from readers of such blogs tended to dry up fairly quickly after the author's death, while spam messages having nothing to do with the author's life or ailment became more common. These were generally not spaces where the living engaged in prolonged forms of commemoration, grief, or mourning, at least not in any way that showed up on the sites themselves.

The point of drawing attention to this is simply to show that post-mortem interaction was not the norm here, and that even the few blogs in my sample that did serve as a kind of interactive memorial to the deceased for some time eventually became static. Furthermore, as this chapter's analysis has shown, these authors did not consider their own legacies or how they would like to be remembered very often. As we will see in chapter 4, there are indeed genres of death-related communication that make such legacies a more explicit part of their textual strategies. But the research in this chapter suggests that blogs are a particularly powerful tool for the digital construction of the self, and that this process of self-construction may take on its most interesting, urgent, and profound form in terminal illness blogs. Yet such suggestions require some historical context.

Jean-Jacques Rousseau's *Confessions* is one prominent example of an early modern view of the self—one that was achieved through the kind of life-writing we take for granted in autobiographies, memoirs, and even blogs today. "I know my own heart and I understand my fellow man," wrote Rousseau. "I am made unlike any one I have ever met; I will even venture to say that I am like no one in the whole world. I may be no better, but at least I am different."[35] Though the notion that each of us is in some way unique is essentially conventional wisdom today, in Rousseau's day this was a radical proposition. "Great numbers of people, like Kant, saw Rousseau as the harbinger of great possibilities for human growth and freedom."[36] Indeed, Rousseau's *Confessions* signaled a variety of key features of the modern self: "hidden inner depth, self-creation, uniqueness, authenticity, the affirmation of intimate life, self-determining freedom, and moral inwardness."[37] Rousseau insisted upon presenting an unflinching look at his past, through major events and minor ones, happier times and many dark ones as well. In so doing, "Rousseau creates the Romantic paradigm: the recounting of the history of the self so that the self can concurrently create itself in writing and affirm that self it has created."[38]

Of course, Rousseau's work is not without its critics. Some have pointed out that it is filled with anti-feminist sentiments that reaffirm traditional gender roles,[39] and *Confessions* in particular casts various women in Rousseau's personal life as his shadowy persecutors.[40] At the same time, "Rousseau's blurring of private and public realms . . . does have a parallel in feminist theory." Given that feminist theory "challenges the traditional separation of private and public[,] whatever Rousseau's reputation as an antifeminist, in relating intimate life to the political community he anticipates aspects of feminist theory."[41] Freudian psychoanalysis can similarly be viewed as a "search for a lost self" that is "shaped by powerful precedents out of the past."[42] It is clear, then, that this Romantic vision of a self achieved through careful reflection on one's past has remained a potent influence on a variety of modern intellectual currents.

As discussed in the previous chapters, early social scientists understood the self to be a product of social relations, rooted in our imagination of others, rather than their physical bodies or geographical presences, and to potentially extend to the dead inasmuch as they continue to take hold of our imaginations.[43] Yet from Rousseau we understand the self also as the product of deep, internal reflection on one's life, especially one's misdeeds or misfortunes. The self is one who has not only suffered but reflected on that suffering as part of an internal dialogue and, in Rousseau's own paradigmatic example, done so in writing. But the possibilities afforded by the practice of blogging have altered both the reach and the nature of the relationship between suffering and selfhood today.

In these ways, blogs constitute a unique technology for the production and circulation of personal narratives, or what Foucault might have labelled a "technology of the self." Technologies of the self "permit individuals to effect by their own means or with the help of others a certain number of operations on their own bodies and souls, thoughts, conduct, and way of being, so as to transform themselves in order to attain a certain state of happiness, purity, wisdom, perfection, or immortality."[44] Foucault traced the roots of such technologies to Greco-Roman philosophy and early Christian spirituality, in particular the ways in which notions about knowing oneself and caring for oneself intertwined in these periods.[45] Though self-knowledge and self-denial became deeply intertwined in the medieval period, Foucault concluded that by the eighteenth century, "techniques of verbalization" had become means "to constitute, positively, a new self."[46]

This "verbal" constitution of the self, exemplified by Rousseau and identified by Foucault as a new kind of self-generating technology, is certainly a feature of personal blogging as well. In fact, some scholars have analyzed blogs using Foucault's framework. Ignacio Siles noted that early bloggers "turned to online diary writing as a means of introspection. Daily events thus provided an occasion for exploring what users constantly referred to as their 'inside' or 'inner world.'"[47] He argued that "online diarist" became "the singular kind of being produced through these techniques"—a new social identity defined by the practice of daily, public writing about the self provided by this new digital technology.[48] Maria Bakardjieva and Georgia Gaden have applied the term "technology of the self" to more recent "Web 2.0" platforms like Facebook and other social networking sites as well.[49] To give a specific example, Barbara Schneider has examined the ways that the blog of a homeless man acted as a technology of the self, and a means for the ethical care of that self, because the author used his blog to become "the best possible version of himself" in the face of social estrangement and drug addiction.[50] Tanja Bosch has similarly applied the term to the use of social media on mobile phones by young women in South Africa.[51] Agnès Rocamora has even shown how fashion blogs can document the process of self-construction through clothing choices.[52]

In these ways, technologies of the self like blogging are part of what Russell Belk called the "extended self." Belk coined the term to refer to the ways that even material possessions can "provide a sense of past and tell us who we are, where we have come from, and perhaps where we are going."[53] Later, he applied the term to the digital world, and found that although much of what we value in the digital era is, obviously, dematerialized, the "digital extended self" is produced when we use our digital data and networks to craft or refine our sense of who we are. As he put it, "Anyone who has built up an elaborate Facebook presence has experienced the illusion of an evolving coherent core self. . . . The sense of self changes as it did in predigital days, incrementally as we progress through life."[54]

While one might quibble with the term "illusion" above, what we see in Belk's vision of a self constituted through both material and digital objects is a kind of dialectical relationship between self and technology. Such a perspective is similar to that of Donna Haraway and her famous figure of the cyborg as well. Haraway's "Cyborg Manifesto" pointed out the variety of ways that boundaries between human and machine had blurred in the modern world, and urged readers to take pleasure in these boundary confusions.[55] Though it is dangerous to summarize such nuanced work too broadly, and risk glossing over the finer points of each piece, it is clear that a wide variety of thinkers have envisioned the self or the individual or the human as mutually constituted through technologies and the social relations in which those technologies are embedded. This is true whether those technologies are paper and pens or ones and zeroes. Affordance theory is a way of applying these sorts of insights,[56] while still retaining the ability to hone in on particularly important elements of the technologies in which our selves are enmeshed.

Ultimately, then, what terminally ill blogging affords is a type of *narrative freedom*. With this term, Robert Zussman was referring to "the processes of selection and connection, the acts of imaginative construction that are basic to narrative."[57] Such narrative construction of one's personal life "does not simply reflect a self but creates one, does not simply report an identity but claims one, does not simply claim an identity but transforms that identity."[58] As we have already seen, blogging encourages this sort of writing by combining the personal reflections of diary writing with the public, networked audiences of online communication in ways that can transform one's sense of self—and even the relation to one's own physical being.

To say that blogging constitutes a technology of the self makes clear that this "new" digital technology has a philosophical lineage that goes back many centuries. But one overlooked element of selfhood—as it is narratively constructed today in blogs or as it was in years past through letters and diaries—is the relationship between selfhood, bodily suffering, and the soul. I have already argued in chapter 1 that despite the cleavage between these concepts in modern philosophy, notions of the self and the soul tend to intertwine again in digital spaces. But the deep history of "technologies of the self" shows suffering to be a clear link between these two. Foucault mentions how, in the sorts of early Christian confessions on which he focused, the body was a focal point for discourse about oneself. The classics scholar Judith Perkins has traced this idea out further.[59] In the early Roman empire, "narratives were projecting a particular representation of the human self as a body liable to pain and suffering," which she labels the "suffering self."[60] We can see a kind of "suffering self" at work in blogs of the terminally ill as well, which often detail the pain and misery of a terminal condition in harrowing detail.

Thus, not only is the networked, relational, curated self that we cultivate on social media, in blogs, and elsewhere imbued with a feeling of transcendence by many friends and family members when we die, but blogs of the terminally ill demonstrate a further sense in which the self and the soul merge, through the association of suffering with soulmaking. As the English poet John Keats put it in an April 21, 1819, letter to his brother, "Do you not see how necessary a World of Pains and troubles is to school an Intelligence and make it a soul? A Place where the heart must feel and suffer in a thousand diverse ways!"[61] This remark inspired the theologian John Hick to envision an alternative Christian theodicy where the mysteriousness of evil and suffering is the point of human existence. The question of why suffering exists in a world supposedly created by a loving God is answered by the notion that humankind is "still in process of creation."[62] The world is thus a "sphere of soul-making" because the seemingly random, undeserved, and unjust nature of our human miseries is necessary so that "true human goodness . . . and loving sympathy and compassionate self-sacrifice can take place."[63] This perspective—that the soul fully flourishes only through suffering—has achieved "a certain pre-eminence . . . among the various theological responses to the problem of natural evil."[64] It is also on display in the blogs that are quoted throughout this chapter.

Here, then, is where the sociological self—narrative, relational, networked—and the theological soul—forged through moral grace in the face of suffering—become fused together. In other genres of personal blogging, without the prevalent physical and psychological pain of a panoply of medical treatments, without the specter of death looming so largely, perhaps this "soul-making" factor of these blogs would be less evident. But these are not ordinary blogs. In these blogs of the terminally ill, the self that gets reimagined in text and data is a soulful one. This is not the kind of "cruel optimism" discussed by Lauren Berlant, in which the attachment to and struggle for life itself might be seen as getting in the way of accepting a peaceful end.[65] What we see enacted here is the very same struggle for individual transcendence that animates some of our earliest human mortuary rituals, but directed by the dying themselves, and undergirded by a much more modern conception of what constitutes the self and mortality. One does not need to be religious to appreciate the crucible through which the authors of these blogs have been put, and to be amazed at the almost beatific nature of some of the insights that result.

Conclusion

Death has changed a great deal in the modern era, especially in the last century with the advent of medical technologies that prolong life and make it more likely that the end of one's life will occur in a hospital. "These days, not only are people dying more often in hospitals, they are seeing a lot more of the hospital in the time before they die."[66] This is true not just in the United States but in most other industrialized nations as well.[67] In such a context, one can see blogging as a reenchanting force in the lives of the terminally ill—something that turns the modern experience of dying into a means of reconnecting with friends and loved ones, or even making new friends as part of an expanding readership. And of course as we have seen, blogging enables those enmeshed in this kind of heavily hospitalized end-of-life care, who might normally find themselves losing their grip on their very sense of self,[68] to reassert and even reimagine that self for the better.

Of course, art and culture have always been based on what literary scholar George Steiner called the "gamble on transcendence" in which "the writer or thinker means the words of the poem, the sinews of the argument, the personae of the drama, to outlast his own life, to take on the mystery of autonomous presence and presentness."[69] But typically, throughout history, there has been a significant amount of gatekeeping at work determining who even had the chance to tell their story in poems, arguments, and dramas. Indeed, creative industries like publishing remain a largely closed, elite arena today.[70] Rousseau himself was a famous author and philosopher when he wrote his *Confessions*—many others might have suffered like him and lived similarly eventful lives, but without his combination of luck, talent, and eventual privilege, they were never given the chance to fashion a self in writing.

Terminally ill bloggers, on the other hand, craft new selves using the affordances of digital blogging platforms that are typically free and public. Of course, a significant amount of cultural capital is likely still a factor in one's disposition and ability to create such a blog, just as it is with any digital content creation.[71] At the same time, these blogs have opened up space especially for women and mothers to engage in this particular form of public, networked introspection. As such, the selves called forth on these blogs—those who craft detailed records of their physical suffering over tens or hundreds of posts, who describe friends and family with love and tenderness, who ruminate on the meaning of life and death with humor, apprehension, and deep, abiding wisdom—speak to the transcendental qualities of this particular technology of the self.

Two affordances of blogging help call this new form of digital selfhood into being. First, blogging's encouragement of regular reflection and introspection helps draw out the new qualities of the dying self, often in ways that are positive or therapeutic for these authors. Blogging provides a kind of narrative freedom that allows for precisely this kind of self re-creation. Second, the resulting selves are public, shareable, and networked, such that this is not a purely palliative phenomenon to make people feel better while waiting to die. Rather, it is an emphatically social experience of broadcasting to the larger world—to friends, family, and strangers alike—a sense of the new person that illness and impending mortality have helped create. "Here is who I have become," these blogs seem to say, "this is the person I have made in the face of suffering and through much perseverance. Here is how I felt about my life as it came to an end."

In sum, these blogs offered more than just lessons about coping with illness—they provided a means of personal transformation. Even the author of *Holy Crap I Have Cancer!!!*, who felt so disconnected from herself by the end, had also written, "When you read through my posts you will notice that I came a long way. I became a complete new person. And I'm so proud of that. I finally found myself." Blog posts like this functioned as both technologies of the self and technologies of the soul—a means to catalogue and reflect on the physical and psychological suffering of the self, and a tool to demonstrate to oneself and others the transformative, "soul-making" power of such experiences.

4

Self-Destruction as Self-Commemoration in Digital Suicide Notes

Early in the morning on his sixtieth birthday, August 15, 2013, sportswriter and statistician Martin Manley fatally shot himself. Later that day a website called MartinManleylifeanddeath.com went live. Manley had quietly been creating the site—which described his life in exhausting detail as well as his rationale for ending it—for months prior to his suicide, and he had paid in advance to keep it hosted for five years. Although Yahoo initially took the site down, other mirror sites had already been created.[1] Today, Manley's family, friends, and a host of curiosity-seeking strangers visiting one of the remaining mirror sites can still read his musings and recollections about travel, music, basketball, his parents, his marriages, and of course, his suicide. On that last topic, he wrote, "I'm sure there are people out there who study suicide that would like to study mine—so I've left nothing to the imagination. It's all here."

Manley is not alone in the creation of such an elaborate digital suicide note. Sixty-three-year-old television producer Joe Bodolai posted a three-thousand-word suicide note listing his greatest accomplishments and biggest regrets to his personal website before killing himself in 2011. Thirty-five-year-old Mitchell Heisman made available online his 1,904-page treatise on sociobiology and liberal democracy, entitled *Suicide Note*, before shooting himself on the steps of Harvard's Memorial Church in 2010. Transgender teen Leelah Alcorn killed herself after posting a note to Tumblr in 2014 claiming that "the only way I will rest in peace is if one day transgender people aren't treated the way I was, they're treated like humans, with valid feelings and human rights." Her death, and her note, "sparked a nationwide debate about how families should react when a child comes out as transgender."[2]

These notes have contributed to a growing interest in suicidal expression online. In 2009 public attention was drawn to two suicides where notes were left on social networking sites, yet none of their many readers intervened to help.[3] By 2011, the press had noticed that "there have been a growing number of suicide notes appearing on Facebook"[4] and that "the number of people who post the equivalent of a suicide note online . . . appears to be a growing trend."[5] That year, Facebook instituted an initiative, updated again in 2015, to connect potentially suicidal users to counselors.[6] Other websites have since followed suit.[7] Yet although these online suicide notes have engendered significant public concern, little scholarly work has been done to understand them.

Of course, online suicide notes have much in common with the suicide notes from pre-digital eras that have been studied by psychologists for decades.[8] But a peculiar sense of novelty emerges in Manley's claim that his extensive note was "something to be entered into the Guinness Book of Records," or in Heisman's challenge for readers "to resist public and political pressures and confront this application of sociobiology to politics on the basis of its scientific merits." In both cases, these notes spoke to their authors' desire to control how they and their life's work would be publicly remembered after death. This desire stands in stark contrast to conventional views of suicide as either an "escape from self"[9] or a response to a loss of self.[10] Instead, online suicide notes often function more as a means to cement a particularly authoritative narrative about oneself than as a testament to the self's disappearance or undesirability. In that way, online suicide notes reflect some core sociological concerns about self-presentation and cultural memory, while raising new questions about the way these can be managed online—even after death.

To better understand the changing narrative construction of selfhood in online suicide notes, this chapter is built around the results of a comparative discourse analysis of 163 suicide notes divided among roughly three different time periods and written in two different formats. Included in the data are paper suicide notes from 1945–1954,[11] 1983–1984,[12] and 2002–2017,[13] as well as online suicide notes from 2004–2015.[14] This chapter examines the common themes that emerged in all of these notes, the changes in frequency of these themes across note format and time period, and the themes that were unique to the digital notes. The aim of this comparison is to understand the affordances for self-presentation and self-commemoration that online notes provided to suicidal individuals.

In the previous chapter, we saw how blogs of the terminally ill encouraged a kind of reconstruction of the self. The blogs' incremental reflections on family and friends, mortality, and physical and mental suffering added up over time to a kind of soulful, almost beatific perspective on the lives and deaths of their authors. I argued in chapter 3 that these blogs afforded a kind of "narrative freedom"[15] that enabled users to craft the sorts of self-representations that could make meaning out of the senselessness of their suffering. But we also saw that the authors of these blogs were mainly focused on the present. They used the admixture of technology and mortality to come to terms with what was happening to them, with little regard for their legacy or how they would be remembered. In that way, they differ greatly from the digital suicide notes that are the focus of the present chapter.

This chapter shows that online suicide notes contained narratives of self-commemoration that were a largely new feature of suicide notes in the digital era. This self-commemoration allowed their authors to resolve a tension in modern life surrounding death, namely, the difficulty of accepting the cessation of one's self. Whether or not one agrees that Western or American culture has engaged in the kinds of wholesale denial of death discussed in previous chapters, coming to terms with one's own death as an individual is certainly a terrifying prospect for many today, as it has been for millennia.[16] And research has shown that an individual's own sense of self-identity can affect the extent to which they fear death.[17] It makes sense, then, that the curated, public, and seemingly permanent character of online communication has opened up new possibilities for those contemplating ending their own lives.

In fact, the authors of 43 percent of the digital suicide notes analyzed here sought to preserve a favorable version of themselves in their online notes, even in the face of the significant amount of stigma that accompanies ending one's own life. Building on Zussman's notion of "narrative freedom," then, this chapter argues that digital suicide notes enact a kind of *mnemonic freedom*: freedom to have the stories we tell about ourselves get remembered in the ways that we intend. This appeared to be an especially important function of the websites and platforms with which these authors confronted the end of their own lives at their own hands. In sum, these online suicide notes enacted a kind of digital self-commemoration to accompany their authors' corporeal self-destruction.

Studying Suicide

The importance of Émile Durkheim's *Suicide* to the discipline of sociology can hardly be overstated. Though the book's status has grown to almost mythical proportions over the years, it remains true that by taking a phenomenon that was considered highly personal and individualized, and showing how it was actually a social fact, Durkheim helped establish the validity of sociology as a field of study.[18] Of course, many of Durkheim's contemporaries had been studying the social factors behind suicide, and many suicide researchers of the time were also making use of the same sort of comparative statistical methodologies as Durkheim.[19] But the strength of Durkheim's work, as Giddens contends, was in its ability to craft "a consistent framework of sociological theory which could bring together the major empirical correlations that had already been established."[20]

Durkheim's comparative study of suicide rates led him to theorize that there were four types of suicide, influenced by the amount of social integration or moral regulation facing individuals. And yet even here, Durkheim's work has been criticized for overly complicating the correlations between these factors,[21] or for ignoring some non-Western cultural meanings around suicide.[22] Durkheim himself found that two of his own four types of suicide—fatalistic and altruistic—were very rare, while the two types on which Durkheim focused—egoistic and anomic—were similar enough that many scholars consider them almost identical.[23] Viewed in this light, Durkheim's findings boil down to the still very significant conclusion that those more isolated from society are at greater risk of committing suicide. This conclusion has been challenged but largely confirmed in many subsequent decades' worth of research,[24] and is reflected in the Centers for Disease Control's focus on promoting "connectedness" as a means of suicide prevention.[25]

Coincidentally, concern over the problem of social isolation online has been a consistent feature of Internet research. Scholars who focus on digital culture have been engaged in a long debate about the potentially alienating or enriching effects of the Internet on social life.[26] These issues have made their way into studies about the effects of the Internet on suicide ideation and attempts as well, but the closest to a scholarly consensus on the topic is that "more research is needed on the degree and extent of social media's negative and positive influences."[27] Certainly, high-profile cases of cyberbullying and resultant suicides are enough to establish that such bullying is a negative feature of online life,[28] and the Internet obviously makes information on specific techniques for killing oneself easier to obtain.[29] There is also evidence that exposure to suicidal behaviors in friends may influence similar suicidal thoughts in adolescents[30]—a problem long associated with traditional media,[31] but one that online suicide notes could conceivably exacerbate. Yet current research shows that even among youths who seek out self-harm and suicide websites, many use these sites for social and emotional support, and to provide coping strategies during difficult times.[32] All of this suggests that suicide in the digital age, and the online suicide notes that accompany it, raise questions beyond just the Durkheimian focus on social isolation or integration.

It is worth pausing to point out that this chapter cannot solve the question of why individuals commit suicide, or why suicide rates change over time or from place to place. What it can do, however, is examine the possibilities that emerge when suicide notes are composed in new, digital spaces. What are the connections between the things people say in suicide notes and the technologies that are used to produce those notes? If, as discussed in other chapters, there exists a dialectic relationship between the self, communication technologies, and the social and cultural context in which these are apprehended, then we should expect to find some differences in the ways that suicidal people explain the decision to end their own lives depending on the time period in which these notes were composed and whether they were written on paper or online.

Indeed, this chapter presents a test case for the idea that technological affordances ought to be studied from a more comparative perspective, when possible. Affordances are often perceived in relative terms, after all. A variety of tools may be able to help a user accomplish a specific task, but often a particular tool is perceived as being more suited to the task than others. A bigger hammer may be perceived as more appropriate than a smaller one to strike a nail into a hard surface, for instance. Or an electric nail gun may be more appropriate still. These examples of affordances in comparative perspective are easy enough to see, but when scholars have turned to more complex technologies, especially communication technologies, often the comparative element has fallen by the wayside. Internet studies using affordance theory have often focused on one social media platform or one application and the ways it affords a variety of outcomes or practices for its users. There are of course exceptions to this generalization: one interesting piece of scholarship on death and digital media compared the affordances of three different platforms for death-related communication,[33] and the emerging methodology of "app feature analysis" is often based on comparisons.[34] Still, investigations of communication technology affordances typically have not made the kinds of cross-media comparisons that might really allow analysts to hone in on how certain media are perceived relative to one another, and why one medium was chosen instead of another. In the case of suicide notes, each of the authors in my digital sample could have chosen to write a note on paper, especially considering the fact that paper suicide notes are a time-honored means of postmortem communication. The fact that they sought out instead an online space, platform, or app already begins to point us toward the particular affordances of digital suicide notes.

This chapter thus investigates why the digital suicide note might tend to emphasize different themes than other forms of death-related digital communication like blogs of the terminally ill, for instance. More than that, the comparative discourse analysis at the heart of this chapter helps us understand why the genre of the suicide note might take on different functions depending on whether the note was written on paper or posted to the Internet. In so doing, it helps sketch out the range of possibilities that the Internet provides for our engagements with our own mortality, and shows how the kind of timeless elements of an act like suicide might be affected by the technologies of the digital era.

Studying Suicide Notes

Psychologists have undertaken research on the content of actual suicide notes for over half a century. Edwin Shneidman's 1949 discovery and subsequent analysis of hundreds of suicide notes in the Los Angeles coroner's office established the modern field of suicidology, as he and others searched these notes for clues to the inner workings of the suicidal mind.[35] Early on, these studies showed that suicide notes contained a range of affective tones and a wide variety of reasons and rationales.[36] Yet theirs remained a very individually focused exploration of the psychology of suicide notes, one that shied away from sociocultural analysis.

Beginning with a 1967 article, sociologist Jerry Jacobs sought to move beyond the Durkheimian statistical approach to suicide. Jacobs critiqued both Durkheim and the suicidologists for trying to "infer . . . the 'real' meaning of the suicide's story, either by superimposing upon the data an unconscious irrational explanation or some other such synthetic system."[37] Jacobs also turned to the study of suicide notes, because in suicide notes "we have available, after all, the best possible authority on the subject—the suicide himself."[38] His phenomenological approach to the study of 112 notes led him to conceive of suicide as the result of a relatively logical thought process that allowed one to rationalize the violation of social norms against suicide by constructing a view of the absolute necessity of one's own death that "remove(s) all choice and with it sin and immorality."[39]

Yet the phenomenological analysis of suicide notes was hardly exhausted by Jacobs. The meanings behind the act of killing oneself are themselves socially and culturally constructed. Rather than reflecting a bank of unchanging psychological states or social conditions, new motives for suicide are likely to be expressed in suicide notes as social norms change. New scripts or twists on conventions are likely to reveal themselves via new technologies of writing and publishing—these are the affordances that online communication offers to suicidal individuals. These new or emergent conventions can be examined through comparative content analysis of suicide notes from different eras.

Indeed, the public availability of online suicide notes allows us to understand suicidal individuals on their own terms, and in intimate detail. It offers the kind of opportunity to "more thoroughly investigate the social meaning(s) of suicide" and "the contexts from which these meanings are derived" for which many scholars have advocated.[40] After all, researchers have already shown that culturally specific patterns of meaning affect the suicide rates of various demographic groups.[41] Thus if "the sociocultural milieu greatly shapes the meanings people carry about suicide, its viability as an option or solution to coping, and the moral directives guiding action,"[42] then one would expect to see changes in the thematic content of suicide notes over time, and especially as they shifted from paper to digital media. In that sense, comparing analog and digital suicide notes can reveal the affordances that digital technologies provide to those contemplating suicide, and the way such individuals seek to control the meanings that others might assign to their deaths with these new tools.

There are a few studies that have explored the subject of online suicide, but rather than focus on documented cases and specific examples of suicide notes, they have typically used large data sets culled from publicly available blogs or social networking profiles of the general populace, and scanned these with content analysis software in hopes of identifying statements and messages with *potentially* suicidal content.[43] This approach is a promising one for public health researchers who hope to find new methods of suicide prevention, but no studies appear to exist that focus on a corpus of specifically online suicide notes from people known to have killed themselves. For instance, the only academic paper I could find that attempted to study a corpus of online suicide notes culled fifty notes from a website called the Suicide Project.[44] That site urged users to "share your *suicide* story, either as a person contemplating it, or someone who has survived it." As such, that paper was not able to confirm that any of the authors of those purported digital suicide notes had actually committed or even attempted suicide—they may very well have been fictitious or fantastic, and in important ways, very different from genuine notes.

Of course, compiling a corpus of genuine suicide notes online is not a simple task.[45] I initially found ninety-two cases where I could confirm that an actual suicide had left an online note. I then excluded any cases where the text of the entire note was not available.[46] I also selected only notes that the suicide had posted in a public site or had requested be made public, which meant that I excluded several notes from the sample that had been made public after the fact by family members of the deceased. I was left with fifty-one online suicide notes for my sample. It is safe to assume that other online suicide notes have been quickly removed by family members in the wake of a suicide, since social networking platforms now all have ways for loved ones to take control of the profiles of those who die, and since suicides in general are often kept quiet by family and friends. Thus, the sample of online suicide notes analyzed here likely represents only a portion of the actual online suicide notes that had once existed, but were eventually made private or erased.[47] Thus, while it is impossible to know how representative these notes are of the larger universe of digital suicide notes, there are enough here to allow us to see a variety of ways that online, digital affordances were identified and put to use by the notes' authors. In addition, the comparison to three other collections of paper notes, while admittedly imperfect, allows us to treat the affordances of the Internet as a key variable.

Previous studies of suicide notes have been made by those with access to coroners' offices or other official agencies.[48] More recently, John Pestian has engaged in a study that solicited notes from family members of suicides as well, resulting in a collection of 1,278 notes.[49] Most studies of suicide notes have worked from much smaller corpuses, however, and none of these have been collected through any kind of random sampling.[50] Indeed, small sample sizes are often a hallmark of discourse analytic work in general.[51] In any case, this chapter's comparison of 163 notes is comparable to the sample sizes of other work with this type of data, though the present work appears to be the first to compare notes from three distinct time periods and across paper and digital note formats (see table 4.1).

The digital suicide notes in the 2004–2015 sample came from a variety of online spaces. Twenty-one of them were posted to Facebook, nine on personal websites, six on MySpace, five on Twitter, three on Tumblr, three on LiveJournal, two in chat rooms, one on YouTube, and one on the website of a university newspaper. The oldest note was from a suicide in September 2004, while the most recent came from February 2015, but thirty-eight of the fifty-one notes were written between 2010 and 2014. Thirty-eight of the notes were from men and thirteen were

TABLE 4.1. Age, gender, and length in four samples of suicide notes

	Age range	% Men	Median word length	Mean word length
1945–54	25–59	100	79	109
1983–84	25–59	63	115	154
2002–17	11–80	80	175	213
2004–15 digital notes	14–63	75	177	675

from women, which is not surprising given that men are more likely than women to kill themselves.[52] The average age of the suicides was twenty-nine, and the ages ranged from fourteen to sixty-three. The average length of the notes was 676 words, but this statistic is skewed by the presence of longer notes, even though the two longest notes—Heisman's and Manley's—were so extensive that a word count was not included, so as not to further skew these data. Many of these notes were much shorter, with a median length of only 177 words. This brevity is actually normal for suicide notes in general,[53] so it is not surprising to find it online as well.

The notes in the 1945–1954 sample came from a collection published in Shneidman and Farberow's *Clues to Suicide*.[54] The authors of these thirty-three notes were all men between the ages of twenty-five and fifty-nine, though ages for individual authors were not provided. The mean word count was 107 and the median was 79. The notes from the 1983–1984 sample came from a corpus published in Leenaars's *Suicide Notes: Predictive Clues and Patterns*, which aimed to explore cultural and historical differences in suicide notes since the era of Shneidman's original collection.[55] That sample also consisted of thirty-three notes from men aged twenty-five to fifty-nine, but added an additional twenty notes from women in that same age range, though again the individual ages of note authors were not supplied. The mean word count was 154 and the median was 115. I culled my corpus of twenty-six paper suicide notes from 2002–2017 by combining two sources of notes. Five of the notes were given to me by the coroner of a small suburban county in the midwestern United States. I found the remaining twenty-one notes in the sample by looking at coverage of particular suicides on the websites of news organizations. In the course of reporting on these suicides, these news organizations saw fit to publish images of the suicide notes or full transcripts of them. So even though I eventually found them online, these suicide notes were all originally written on paper. The authors of these paper notes ranged from ages eleven to eighty, and 75 percent were men, with a median word length of 175.

The four samples are thus demographically similar, though not identical, due in part to the exclusion of women from the initial 1945–1954 sample and the wider age range in the 2002–2017 and 2004–2015 samples. There are also other demographics that could not be identified in most of the notes, including the race or ethnicity, sexual orientation, and socioeconomic class of the authors. However, studies have shown little difference in the content of suicide notes based on gender, age, or method of suicide.[56] It is worth noting that selecting twenty-one of the 2002–2017 suicide notes from news reports meant that, to an extent, that particular segment was skewed toward suicides deemed "newsworthy"—either because the suicide himself was a somewhat notable public figure or because the suicide was involved in a violation of norms significant enough to be seen as worthy of public attention. Thus, one might have expected the notes in that sample to be more likely to express themes of reputation management and self-presentation, but this was not actually the case, as will be discussed shortly.

Common Themes

Table 4.2 shows the ten most common themes in the sample's 163 suicide notes, divided across four samples. The first seven of these themes contained at least 25 percent frequency in at least one of the four samples. The final three thematic categories were found mainly in the digital notes. Organizing the data this way reveals some common attributes of suicide notes across all samples regardless of time period or note format, some features of the notes that seem to vary by time period, and some

TABLE 4.2. Frequency of themes in four sets of suicide notes (%)

	1945–1954	1983–1984	2002–2017	2004–2015 digital notes
Apologies	45	36	73	43
Family/loved ones	92	60	73	53
Mistakes	30	24.5	27	18
Mental health	15	18	42	31
Lack of love/connection	12	11	23	33
Property/money	30	41.5	38	8
Addressed to someone	88	49	65	31
Creed/beliefs/views	0	0	4	20
Legacy	0	0	11.5	27
Autobiography/narrative	0	2	0	31

themes that seem to occur almost exclusively in the digital notes. Thus, although the samples are not representative, we can still see in miniature the somewhat "universal" features of suicide notes, some cultural changes over time in how suicidal ideation is expressed, and the affordances of digital communication for new themes in suicide notes.

For instance, among these categories, "apologies" figured prominently in all four samples, and indeed, apologies have been shown to be a very common feature in other collections of suicide notes.[57] Similarly, a small but relatively constant percentage of notes in all four samples discussed specific mistakes that the suicide had made in their life. And the most common theme across all four time periods was the discussion of one's relationship with family members and loved ones, though this was most prominent in the 1945–1954 sample. In addition to making intuitive sense, the focus on family and loved ones in all four samples lines up with the prominence of interpersonal relationships in other content analyses of suicide notes.[58]

In other categories, one begins to see differences between the notes in different time periods, perhaps representing cultural shifts in the reasons for suicide or at least in the ways individuals feel enabled to understand and describe their suicidal motivations. This was the case with mental health. Though the notes in all four samples occasionally made explicit reference to mental health issues, this grew more pronounced in the samples from 2002–2017 and 2004–2015. One author of an online note exclaimed, "I don't mean to sound self pitying; I've suffered from mental illness and have spent most of my life in deep depressions, so it's natural that I would view the world that way." By contrast, the language around mental health was less explicit in the earliest sample, with statements like "I'm all twisted up inside" hinting at serious mental health issues, yet steering away from clinical terminology. This may simply reflect the growth of psychological language in everyday life,[59] but in any case the explicit references to mental health increased in both of the more recent samples.

This was true as well of the theme of lack of love/lack of connection. This theme did certainly exist in the paper notes, occurring in 12 and 11 percent of the 1945–1954 and 1983–1984 samples, respectively, but it jumped to 23 and 33 percent for the two more recent samples. For example, one author of a digital note explained succinctly, "I don't feel like I'd be particularly missed." While this does suggest a kind of Durkheimian lack of social integration, it doesn't necessarily mean that these individuals were actually less socially integrated than their earlier counterparts. It may simply be that social norms have shifted such that expressions of isolation are more acceptable and more common now. What is clear, in any case, is that the discourse of isolation itself figured more prominently in the two more recent samples.

On the other hand, some themes of the notes were clearly more prominent in paper notes, regardless of time period, than in digital ones. For instance, the online notes were much less frequently addressed to specific persons than their paper counterparts. The earliest set of paper notes were almost always addressed to particular people, with opening salutations such as "Dear Mary" or "Honey." These greetings were present in almost half of the 1983–1984 notes as well, and in 65 percent of the 2002–2017 paper notes. But only 31 percent of the 2004–2015 sample directly addressed specific people, and even when they did, only six of the online notes began with a direct salutation such as "To All my Family and Friends."

Along those lines, the theme of money and property figured prominently in all three sets of paper notes, but almost disappeared in the online sample. The 1945–1954 sample contained simple instructions about personal property such as "my phonograph records, now in storage with my parents, I give to my former wife." A 2002–2017 paper note expressed similar instructions about money to loved ones: "There is a little surprise waiting for you in the BOA account. Please use the monies for final arrangements and various account settlements." By contrast, such sentiments were expressed in only four of the online notes, a sign that the digital notes' authors had very different conceptions of the audiences and purposes of their notes.

Taken together, these different frequencies of features in the online notes reflect the publicness of the media in which they were composed. This on its own is a significant shift—a genre of fundamentally private writing reimagined as a form of public communication in this digital context. Online suicide notes tended to be aimed to a broader audience than just the immediate friends and family who might have gotten access to a paper suicide note. This is why the digital notes were less frequently addressed to specific people and were less likely to discuss financial matters or the dispersal of personal property. These were public declarations of suicide intended to address other people beyond one's immediate geographic or familial circles, and as such, they dealt with some largely new themes appropriate to this wider public audience.

New Themes in Digital Suicide Notes

Three themes appeared fairly regularly in the digital notes but almost never appeared in the paper notes from any time period. Online notes featured statements of the authors' personal creeds, beliefs, or political views in 20 percent of the sample; were explicitly concerned with their authors' legacies in 27 percent of the sample; and provided substantial autobiographical details in 31 percent of the sample. In all 112 notes across all three paper samples, only one note provided the kinds of autobiographical narrative found frequently in the digital notes. Similarly, only one note in all the paper samples—from a disgraced priest who had been accused of sexual abuse—spoke of the author's personal beliefs and spiritual creed. Three notes in the 2002–2017 paper sample did speak somewhat to the author's legacy, with the aforementioned priest joined in this reputational work by a police officer who had killed a man in custody and an executive embroiled in an accounting scandal. In those three notes, each author sought to refute the characterizations of wrongdoing to which they had been subjected, as when the executive wrote, "I have always done my job honestly and with the highest level of integrity." Beyond those few exceptions, the digital notes made public declarations about their authors' lives, beliefs, and legacies in ways that were different from anything else in the paper notes. In all, 43 percent of the digital notes in the sample contained one or more of these forms of narrative self-commemoration, while only 4 of the 112 paper notes exhibited anything like these.

The autobiographical details in Joe Bodolai's note were quite extensive, for example. It was primarily a bullet-pointed list of four categories, the most extensive of which was titled "Things I am Proud Of." There he described professional successes and personal triumphs like "writing the first draft of Wayne's World with Mike Myers" and "helping my mom to read and write English after my dad died when I was ten." Alcorn's note also detailed her tragically short life story, of feeling "like a girl trapped in a boy's body" since age four, finding out what "transgender" meant at age fourteen, and being taken to hostile counselors and cut off from friends by parents who would not accept her identity.

Indeed, these personal histories could be quite dark and shocking. A former prisoner wrote before killing himself, "There are some people who go through prison and find religion—literally or figuratively. They find some value in the experience: they got off drugs; they realize the mess they made of their life, etc. That was never me." In another case, a graduate student began his note with the admission that "My first memories as a child are of being raped, repeatedly. This has affected every aspect of my life. This darkness, which is the only way I can describe it, has followed me like a fog." The note then ran through the events of his life from kindergarten to dating to his decision to commit suicide, and explained how this sexual assault—which he had never revealed to anyone—had such profoundly negative consequences in each instance.

The authors of these online notes were also more concerned than the rest of the sample with discussing their legacies. These included a somewhat famous outsider in the field of artificial intelligence, who reminded his readers,

> Oh and BTW, the mind is a maximum hypersurface and thought a trajectory on it and the amygdala and hippocampus are Hopf maps of it. No one knew this before me, and it seems no one care. So be it. My time will come in a hundred or a thousand years when the idea again returns.

A man who set himself on fire as a form of political protest was also understandably concerned with the way he and his actions would be posthumously labelled: "Am I therefore a martyr or terrorist? I would prefer to be thought of as a 'spiritual warrior'. Our so-called leaders are the real terrorists in the world today, responsible for more deaths than Osama bin Laden." The aforementioned graduate student also worried about how he would be remembered, and concluded his note with the following postscript: "Please save this letter and repost it if gets deleted. I don't want people to wonder why I did this. I disseminated it more widely than I might have otherwise because I'm worried that my family might try to restrict access to it." Even the former prisoner also mentioned, "I do like to think in the end that this site actually contributed a little something and may have fostered a little debate here and there."

The online notes were also the only ones to feature political statements and personal or philosophical beliefs. Leelah Alcorn's note ended with this now-famous plea for transgender rights: "My death needs to be counted in the number of transgender people who commit suicide this year. I want someone to look at that number and say 'that's fucked up' and fix it. Fix society. Please." And the aforementioned protester complained of the war in Iraq that "Our interference completely destroyed that country, and destabilized the entire region. Everyone who pays taxes has blood on their hands."

Digital Suicide Notes and Mnemonic Freedom

The distribution of these ten themes across four categories of notes can reveal some of the constant features of all suicide notes, as well as the historically or culturally contingent ones that change to match evolving social norms. Yet for the purposes of this chapter, the most illuminating distinctions are between the digital notes and all the other sets of paper notes regardless of time period. These distinctions show that the narrative content of suicide notes can change as communication technologies offer new affordances for transmitting those notes to others. Indeed, the present work suggests that more consideration ought to be made for how "the so-called 'eternal' motivations to suicide—including physical suffering, financial distress, mental illness, romantic disappointment and social disgrace—are mediated through the social milieu of the time."[60] But more than time, particular affordances of new communication and social networking technologies appear to be enabling new kinds of self-presentation in suicide notes, which were much less feasible in the paper notes of the 1945–1954, 1983–1984, or 2002–2017 samples.

Although this likely varies from app to app or platform to platform, in general the publicness of social media allows or encourages suicide note authors to move beyond simply personal matters and discuss themselves in more detail. Social media is, after all, a venue in which the self is constantly curated for a set of shifting audiences, so it makes sense that suicide notes on Facebook or Twitter or even Blogger would focus on the qualities of the dying self. Along those lines, the sense of limitlessness of online communication encourages digital note authors to go into more detail about themselves, to branch into more topics, to explain themselves with more nuance than they might in a paper note. Conversely, those public and limitless qualities seemed to discourage the discussion of interpersonal matters and things that would have been considered private. Anyone who really only wanted to communicate to a small circle of close family or friends would likely have opted for a paper note instead of a digital one.

Similarly, the perception that the Internet is a space of posterity and permanence likely allows or encourages suicidal individuals who are looking to cement a legacy or reputation to post online. In the end the Internet is not necessarily any more permanent than a scrap of paper might be, depending on what company is hosting the data and what its policies are about the accounts of the dead. One's postmortem absent presence has no guaranteed right to remain online. But as discussed in chapter 2, it is still the case that people imagine that the Internet never forgets. For those who were committing suicide hoping to be forgotten due to great personal shame or self-loathing, an online note would seem to be anathema. But for those invested in preserving a narrative about themselves, repairing a reputation, or establishing a legacy, online suicide notes offered new possibilities.

Indeed, in my own survey of Internet users, there was general agreement about the value of the Internet for remembering the dead. When I asked my respondents, "Do you think that digital technologies like blogs or social networking profiles are a good way to remember a deceased friend or loved one?," 53 percent said yes, 29 percent were not sure, and only 19 percent said no. When I pushed further and asked, "Do you hope that your friends and loved ones will use *your* blogs or social networking profiles as a way to remember you when you are dead?," the percentages shifted only slightly: 44 percent said yes, 30 percent were not sure, and 26 percent said no. So while there was a little more unease about one's own digital remains being used as a memory device, in both scenarios my respondents tended to support the idea of remembering the dead, and being remembered themselves, in online spaces.

Thus, the opportunity to publicly present a lasting account of one's self to a wide range of others is clearly an affordance of Internet technologies, even for the dying and the dead, and this affordance is worthy of more discussion. While it is true that, in the eighteenth century, newspapers and magazines sometimes quoted suicide notes, this was up to the discretion of editors, and was certainly not the norm.[61] Suicide was still officially repressed in that period through a variety of civil and religious penalties.[62] Today's online suicide notes reflect very different views about suicide notes and their audiences. Previously, the private status of these notes had been so taken for granted that even suicide researchers like Antoon Leenaars had to argue against the notion that studying suicide notes constitutes "invading the person's private life, something the person never intended."[63] But this notion of suicide notes as private documents is simply not compatible with the public qualities and broader sense of audience demonstrated in the online notes found here.

It is partly this public quality that allows the online notes to serve new functions surrounding the suicide's reputation. By crafting these notes in online spaces, and in ways that sought explicitly to secure a legacy for themselves, the suicides whose notes were studied here became, in a sense, "reputational entrepreneurs."[64] But rather than serving as custodians of the reputations of others, these suicides were trying to cement a reputation for themselves. The need for such public, online statements about one's identity, especially in conjunction with an event that is likely to bring oneself under increased public scrutiny, seems especially clear given the fraught nature of the self in online spaces. Though many users manage the tensions of online selfhood through skillful exhibition of digital content in their personal online spaces,[65] social media are typically "sites of struggle between users, employers, and platform owners to control online identities."[66] But the public nature of these digital notes, and the likelihood of them remaining public for some time after their authors had died, attested to a kind of *mnemonic freedom* at work here. Any paper suicide note might have also called forth the uncanny sort of absent presence of a dead loved one, for the few who had access to that note. But these digital notes cemented a final *public* narrative about who their authors were and how they ought to be remembered, one that would likely not have been possible had these notes not been created and published online.

Online suicide notes thus provided the opportunity for the suicidal individual to combat the stigma attached to suicide.[67] This stigma is strong enough that medical examiners investigating suspicious deaths often ponder "whether the deceased could have intended to commit suicide *in spite of* the stigma,"[68] and that friends and family members will often attempt to steer medical examiners away from this verdict. Being dead typically means that the suicide himself or herself is powerless in these matters, and even traditional paper suicide notes that might help cast a definitive account of one's actions are often withheld by family members or are difficult to contextualize.[69] The public nature of the online suicide note served as a way for suicidal individuals to assert agency in these matters, to mitigate their stigmatization by crafting a narrative explaining their fateful decisions and fashioning their own niche in cultural memory.[70]

Egyptologist Jan Assmann divided cultural memory of the dead into two types: retrospective and prospective. The retrospective form is the more natural or universal one, in which "a group goes on living with its dead, keeping them present, and thereby building up an image of its own unity and wholeness."[71] This is the form of memory that dates back to the Paleolithic burials discussed in chapter 2. The prospective element, on the other hand, "consists in 'achievement' and 'fame'—the manner in which the dead have rendered themselves unforgettable."[72] Assmann noted that in ancient Egypt, these two forms of memory were combined, because those who achieved high office were able to commission monuments commemorating themselves. But historically such prospective memory has been out of reach for those outside the ranks of the powerful or the widely renowned. This is one of the things that make these digital suicide notes so noteworthy: these are not just acts of self-presentation, but self-commemoration. Their authors sought the mnemonic freedom to control the narrative surrounding not only their deaths, but their lives and legacies as well.

For example, four of these suicides sought to focus attention on the physical or sexual abuse they had suffered. This reputation management was explicit in the notes of two disgraced figures in the sample as well, who created personal websites that both contested the charges against them and showed the miserable effect those charges had on their lives. Even the suicides in the sample with less traumatic life circumstances seemed to be aiming for a similar narrative closure and reputational control. One man in his early thirties remarked,

> I've done my best to be a good person, and I feel that my existence has been an overall benefit for the world . . . I hope . . . that when you think back on me you are mostly filled with good memories and are happy to have known me.

Such themes were found even in very brief notes as well, such as a Facebook status update that read in its entirety, "Was born in San Francisco, became a shooting star over everywhere, and ended his life in Brooklyn . . . And couldn't have asked for more." This small act of self-commemoration still hints at a desire to positively control the public narrative surrounding this man's life and to combat the stigma that might be attached to his death.

Martin Manley wrote that "the thought that my memory or legacy would come to an abrupt end was unacceptable to me—and in my opinion, it *should* be unacceptable to anyone in my situation." These lines begin to make explicit what is at least an implicit or latent feature of many of the other online suicide notes studied here—the desire to exert agency over one's posthumous legacy. Of course, many paper suicide notes may also contain implicitly performative characteristics, designed to impress a certain sense of self in the memories of the suicide's friends and family.[73] After all, so-called deviant acts, "even suicide . . . may have the primary function of affirming, in the language of gesture and deed, that one is a certain kind of person."[74] But many of the digital notes examined here do more than this. Not only do they seek to cement the reputation of their authors, they make the case that the author is worth remembering, and suggest in some small way that the author will live on, online, after their corporeal body is gone.

In that sense, the online suicide note resolves a long-standing tension in modern life, discussed in earlier chapters in connection with Ernest Becker, Anthony Giddens, and the scholars behind "terror management theory."[75] Edwin Shneidman referred to this as the problem of "naughtment" or "being oblivionated,"[76]—these were his names for the stark reality of ceasing to exist that confronted all writers of suicide notes. David Stannard has called this the fear of "death as cessation of self,"[77] and as discussed in chapter 2, it is something that religion has historically helped to suppress with promises of an afterlife for the devout or the chosen. As the pioneering sociologist Harriet Martineau once wrote, "Suicide is one thing to a man who is certain of entering immediately upon purgatory; and to another whose first step is to be upon the necks of his enemies; and to a third who believes that he is to lie conscious in his grave for some thousands of years; and to a fourth who has no idea that he shall survive or revive at all."[78] In a more secular, pluralistic society, without a strong set of religious mores, Stannard argued that American culture had returned to a more primal state of fearing death:

> Once again we are faced with the most fundamental human responses to death, the response that for several millennia has been suppressed by the coercive and imaginative power of religion—the response of bewilderment and fear before the prospect of emptiness.[79]

For Stannard, as well as these other critics, some have met this fear by denying death and cordoning off the dead and dying in ways that are potentially unhealthy. But the online suicide note provides an alternative—it allows the author to confront the certainty of their own death with a corresponding certainty that their memory will live on in the ways they intend.

What these online suicide notes offer, then, is mnemonic freedom in the face of impending death. Personal websites, blogs, and social networking sites make it possible to ensure the public reception of one's final words in their intended state, and in ways that present an authoritative version of the self that secures a particular narrative, reputation, or legacy. Though this struggle to positively represent the self has been a feature of social life since well before the Internet, the online suicide note is a powerful tool in this regard. After all, "we tend to read with special reverence and awe *any* words, however banal, that are part of a death-oriented document."[80] The digital notes studied here blended the authenticity and authority of the traditional suicide note with the public qualities and imagined posterity of online communication in order to broadcast a final and lasting sense of self to the world. These were self-made monuments enshrined not in stone, but in code.

Conclusion

In an 1844 edition of the *New Monthly Magazine and Humorist*, one essay entitled "The Duty of Self Commemoration" commented sarcastically on the case of a man whose last will included the bequest of a large sum to be used for the creation of a statue in his own honor:

> Some people leave the care of their reputation to their children, some bequeath it to their executors, others entrust it to the public. There is no small hazard in each of these courses. Children prove ungrateful; executors find "assets" deficient, and the public, although not always a great wit, is notorious for one attribute of that character—an exceedingly defective memory.[81]

This mindset, mocked in 1844, may strike the contemporary reader as quite reasonable. As Martin Manley put it, "After you die, you can be remembered by a few-line obituary for one day in a newspaper when you're too old to matter to anyone anyway . . . *OR* you can be remembered for years by a site such as this. That was my choice and I chose the obvious."

In the digital era, more of us have more of ourselves presented to a wider audience of others than ever before, so taking control of one's public legacy and crafting a final narrative for public consumption make some intrinsic sense. Yet beginning in 1990 with the work of social psychologist Roy F. Baumeister, suicide has often been conceived as a means to escape the self, or at least, a way to be rid of "meaningful awareness of certain symbolic interpretations or implications about the self."[82] While some of the suicidal individuals in my sample may indeed have been motivated by a desire to break away from negative emotional states, for the authors of many digital notes the act of suicide came with a sort of leaning into selfhood, a datalogical self-commemoration to accompany their corporeal self-destruction.

"Fame," wrote the cultural historian Aleida Assmann, "is a secular form of self-immortalization, and it has a great deal to do with the image a person creates of himself."[83] The authors of these digital suicide notes have found a way to enact a form of self-immortalization, but without achieving the fame that it used to require. This would appear to be a very populist, democratizing element of digital spaces—average people can now achieve a seemingly permanent place in public, cultural memory. Yet the Internet is not as permanent as we sometimes like to think; once a person is dead, they have no guarantee that their digital suicide note will stay online. Even Martin Manley's meticulous plans were almost thwarted when Yahoo initially took down his site. Nonetheless, the ability to commemorate oneself before death was clearly a perceived affordance of which these authors made use, a novel effect of the unique admixture of digital technology and death in the twenty-first century.

5

Race, Racism, and Mnemonic Freedom
in the Digital Afterlife

On April 15, 2017, the HBO network premiered a film by rapper and producer J. Cole entitled *4 Your Eyez Only*. Built around music videos for eight songs on his full-length album of the same name, the film also featured documentary footage of Cole returning to his hometown of Fayetteville, North Carolina, and travelling around the country discussing Black life in America and Black activism surrounding the Black Lives Matter movement. In one scene, Cole visited Ferguson, Missouri, and sought out the small memorial plaque that had been erected on the spot where Mike Brown was murdered by police in 2014. While there, Cole began talking to a man who identified himself as Mike Brown's cousin. He revealed to Cole that Brown had been recording music in the days leading up to his death, and that Brown had once told him, "I don't know what it's going to take but people are going to know my name." Brown's cousin then noted that "everybody knows his name now from coast to coast." After momentarily reflecting on this, Cole remarked, "What's happening right now, everybody being awake and being, like, fed up—he had a lot to do with that. So, like, his contribution, his life, sacrifice . . . look what he gave to the world." Cole concluded that "not only does everybody know his name, he's the reason why people are fighting . . . trying."

Though the tragic irony of Brown's posthumous fame was not lost on either Brown's cousin or Cole himself, it nevertheless raises many larger questions about how individual legacies, collective memory, and mediated forms of "immortality" play out under conditions of state racism and skyrocketing inequality. Fame obviously means much less when one is not around to experience it for oneself, and if the condition for achieving such fame or helping launch a vitally important social movement is being murdered by police, it's likely that most would choose to forgo that opportunity. Of course, Mike Brown was never given such a choice.

American public discourse is increasingly populated by names like Brown's. What these names have in common is that their deaths, or the moments surrounding them, were captured on video and eventually uploaded to the Internet. Eric Garner couldn't breathe beneath a police officer's chokehold. Walter Scott was shot in the back. Sandra Bland was pulled over for failing to signal and turned up dead in jail. Philando Castile was shot while his girlfriend filmed from the passenger seat and his young daughter sat in the back. Mike Brown's body simply lay in the street. The list, tragically, goes on. These digital videos, circulating throughout the Internet in the days, weeks, and years after each murder, have created a kind of legacy for these victims of police brutality. Such videos have become outsized parts of the collective memory surrounding each of these individuals, who were doubly victimized inasmuch as they lost not only their lives but also the agency to define themselves and the ways they'd like to be remembered.

The concept of legacy thus remains a vital and complicated one in digital spaces, as evident in the previous chapter on digital suicide notes. And as we have seen throughout the book, individuals today are experimenting with the affordances of digital spaces to craft lasting narratives about themselves and to create a sense of self that transcends death in a variety of ways.[1] Indeed, technologists and scholars have been discussing the Internet as a kind of de facto digital afterlife since the late 1990s.[2] Today the term "digital afterlife" can refer to everything from Facebook memorials to digital estate planning to postmortem messaging services.[3] But the larger utopian undercurrent to this language about the Internet has been prevalent almost since its inception. As science writer Margaret Wertheim pointed out in 1999, "Cyberspace is not a religious construct per se, but . . . one way of understanding this new digital domain is as an attempt to realize a technological substitute for the Christian space of heaven."[4] This vision of a limitless expanse creating new forms of community and collectivity, and extending forever into posterity, has helped establish the Internet as a kind of reenchanted space for the living and dead alike.

At the same time, such a vision often obscures the questions of access and resource distribution that underlie much of its cutting-edge properties. So while the Internet is indeed an important frontier for experimentation with collective memory, individual legacies, and digital souls, the very notion of memory in digital technologies has already been racialized in a variety of ways. Digital spaces tend to privilege the memory and representation of some groups over others, often doing significant harm in the process. For example, given how much of our cultural memory is retrieved through search engines, Safiya Noble's work exposing the often violently racist and sexist Google search results for terms like "black girls" has raised many alarm bells.[5] The mainstream depiction of victims of police violence has faced similar scrutiny. As Ruha Benjamin put it, "Racism runs all the way through the visual representation of crime and victimization."[6]

As such, the victims of police violence are often memorialized today on hashtags devoted to celebrating their lives, combatting negative media portrayals, and advocating for social justice or police reform. This is obviously a far cry from being able to advocate for oneself and craft a lasting narrative about one's own life. But a handful of innovative hashtags have begun to address the tension between combatting racist state violence and commemorating the lives of those under its threat. This chapter engages in a discourse analysis of two Twitter hashtags that do precisely this: #IfTheyGunnedMeDown and #IfIDieInPoliceCustody. I argue that these two hashtags, but especially the latter, collect the digital claims to *mnemonic freedom* of thousands of Black people. As discussed in the previous chapter, mnemonic freedom refers to the ability to ensure that the stories people tell about themselves get remembered by others in the ways they want. More than simply that, however, these hashtags show how mnemonic freedom might be achieved collectively rather than individually. They afford a kind of communal imagining built on both the dread of racist violence and the hope for a future without it.

The Internet, Memory, and the Black Lives Matter Movement

Many early adopters of the Internet viewed it as a potential utopia, one where "all may enter without privilege or prejudice accorded by race, economic power, military force, or station of birth," as John Perry Barlow put it in his 1996 "Declaration of the Independence of Cyberspace."[7] Barlow's paean to digital libertarian self-governance, discussed briefly in chapter 1, was premised on the idea that the Internet was a space of "transactions, relationships, and thought itself," not, as he put it, "where bodies live."[8] But this expansive notion of the virtual, when married to such an extremely limited vision of property and the law, overlooked the many ways in which cyberspace had always been a creation of economic power and military force, and how race and station of birth did in fact conspire to limit access to the Internet from the moment it was created.

In response, digital social scientists like Lori Kendall and Lisa Nakamura detailed the various ways that online spaces did not erase race, class, and gender but often actually relied upon conventional or stereotypical views of them.[9] This insight has been largely confirmed in over a decade's worth of studies.[10] At the same time, the growth of the Internet has indeed created new spaces for play with identity, and new possibilities for disruption of essentialist notions around gender, sexuality, and race.[11] Today, access to the Internet is wider than ever before, because even those without an Internet connection at home can use an inexpensive cell phone to log on. Whereas in 2000, 52 percent of Americans used the Internet in some capacity, that number was up to 90 percent as of 2019.[12] However, such forms of access often limit lower socioeconomic-status users to merely consuming online content, while making it much more difficult to actually produce content of their own.[13]

Within this changing digital landscape, Twitter has become home to its own vernacular Black culture—known as "Black Twitter"—that exerts a powerful influence over the rest of Twitter and the entire Internet.[14] Hashtags are a major component of Black Twitter and beyond, because of their ability to link individuals interested in a common issue to one another. Hashtags like #MeToo or #BringBackOurGirls have become catalysts for widespread social movements around sexual assault and gendered violence, for example. And the so-called "Blacktags" emerging out of Black Twitter have often functioned as a kind of interruption of the whiteness of the overall Twitter network,[15] a way to disrupt mainstream discourse and raise attention to the concerns of Black people in the United States and throughout the world.

Perhaps the most widely known activist hashtag has been #BlackLivesMatter, which galvanized the American population and the world in the wake of Mike Brown's 2014 murder and the subsequent protests in Ferguson, Missouri. Created by activists Alicia Garza, Patrisse Cullors, and Opal Tometi in the wake of George Zimmerman's July 2013 acquittal for shooting and killing unarmed Black teenager Trayvon Martin, it was not immediately very popular. But its use skyrocketed when Mike Brown was killed, and it has remained active during many subsequent incidents of police violence, fatal or otherwise, against Black people.[16] The phrase "Black Lives Matter" has come to stand not only for this hashtag, but the organization it spawned, and even "the sum of all organizations, individuals, protests, and digital spaces dedicated to raising awareness about and ultimately ending police brutality against Black people."[17]

What the preceding paragraphs have mapped out, then, are two forces at work on the Internet today that might affect the way that digital legacies and online collective memory play out in an America that remains suffused with racism and state violence. On the one hand is an emergent Black digital culture that exerts a tremendous influence on all of the Internet, from humorous memes to viral trends to social justice activism. On the other hand is the Internet's stubborn tendency to reproduce and even magnify existing inequalities, as discussed by scholars like Ruha Benjamin, danah boyd, Jessie Daniels, Safiya Noble, and Jen Schradie.[18] As we will see, this tension was reflected in the varied ways that both of the hashtags analyzed here engaged with what is known as "respectability politics."

That said, it is worth momentarily comparing Mike Brown's unintentional digital legacy to some of the others profiled in this book, most of whom have been or at least appeared to be white. Lisa Bonchek Adams wrote of her experiences with terminal illness for eight years on a blog that captivated thousands of followers and was even turned into a book entitled *Persevere: A Life with Cancer*. Martin Manley's lengthy suicide note, which extensively documented his life, personal philosophy, and professional achievements, is still available online, many years after his death, and has been the subject of a host of news coverage in a wide variety of outlets. Though death can leave us with many mysteries, it is fair to say that there is little mystery surrounding these two figures. Adams and Manley had the agency to leave anyone who might be curious with a voluminous textual legacy attesting to precisely who they were in life and how they ought to be remembered in death.

Brown's image and legacy, on the other hand, have been heavily contested. After his death, police, lawmakers, and their conservative allies in the press all cast Mike Brown in the familiar role of a menace. As with so many other young Black men, Brown's criminality and ill-intent were often simply assumed, including by the *New York Times*, which infamously described him as "no angel" in a story about his final days.[19] The assumption of coverage like this was that Brown must be at least partly responsible for his own death, despite the hazy facts of the case. This sort of news coverage was often accompanied by a particular photo of Brown, taken from his Facebook page, in which "the low camera angle made Brown look particularly large and, to some, menacing—especially since he was holding out his right hand in an ambiguous three-finger gesture."[20]

This choice came under heavy scrutiny, especially online, and after receiving numerous complaints many news outlets switched the photo on their websites to a more neutral one. But the damage had been done—the press had helped to cement a racist stereotype of Mike Brown, which also added to the defense of the white officer who murdered Brown that he had a "reasonable fear for his safety when he fired the fatal shot."[21] It was this constellation of events that led to the creation of the Twitter hashtag #IfTheyGunnedMeDown.

#IfTheyGunnedMeDown was started by criminal defense attorney C. J. Lawrence, who posted a tweet containing two photos of himself on August 10, 2013. One was a picture of himself delivering a speech at the graduation ceremony of Tougaloo College, where he had been student government president, with former president Bill Clinton smiling and laughing just behind him. Just below this was another photo, of Lawrence dressed like Kanye West for Halloween, with a bottle of Hennessy cognac in one hand and a microphone in the other. The caption reads, "Yes let's do that: Which photo does the media use if the police shot me down?" followed by #IfTheyGunnedMeDown.

The hashtag took off quickly, and by the end of the day it had been viewed over 100,000 times.[22] Many subsequent contributors to this hashtag tended to recreate this initial dualistic framing by posting one "socially acceptable" picture—usually from a graduation ceremony, in a military uniform, or as part of some other formal event or ceremony—and juxtaposing it with a second "socially problematic" photo of the variety initially used to demonize Brown.[23] In her excellent study of this hashtag, Nora Gross argues that #IfTheyGunnedMeDown posts "embody the twin consciousness Du Bois argued Black Americans were both blessed and burdened with."[24] These contributors were engaged in an act of solidarity that acknowledged "that anyone could be represented as either respectable and innocent or violent and criminal—depending on the photo."[25]

A similar hashtag emerged on Twitter in July 2015, when twenty-eight-year-old Sandra Bland was found dead in a jail cell in Waller County, Texas, after being pulled over in her car for an initial failure to signal, and eventually for assaulting an officer. Bland was booked on July 10, spent three days in jail, and then was found dead of an apparent suicide. Bland's family and friends refused to believe this version of events, as Bland had just interviewed for and gotten offered a job there in Texas, and was scheduled to post bail the following day. Bland had also been a Black Lives Matter activist, making her death in a county that had once been called "the most racist in Texas" doubly suspicious.[26] Public outcry eventually pushed the FBI to join the investigation into the circumstances leading up to Bland's death. Though the notion that Bland was the victim of foul play was never substantiated in court, Bland's family was awarded $1.9 million in a civil suit against the Waller County jail, and the arresting officer was eventually fired after being indicted on perjury charges.[27]

Bland's tragic and highly suspicious death inspired the hashtag #IfI-DieInPoliceCustody, which began on July 16, three days after her death. The first tweet, composed by someone with the handle @GregariousAli, read, "#IfIDieInPoliceCustody raise hell. Just know I didn't resist nor was I armed." By the end of its first week the hashtag had been used over 16,500 times,[28] and as with #IfTheyGunnedMeDown, contributors quickly began to contest the racist notions of Black criminality that animate so much state violence against African Americans in the United States. But many of these contributors made more explicit what had been a sort of latent set of themes in that earlier hashtag concerning commemoration, digital selfhood, and online legacies.

As Nora Gross noted about #IfTheyGunnedMeDown, "The young people posting their dueling self-portraits seem to be aware of their own mortality and concerned about the way they might be remembered if they die young."[29] This element of that hashtag, and of #IfIDieIn-PoliceCustody, is the focal point of this chapter. In essence, these two hashtags demonstrated the affordances of Twitter for experimentation with new forms of collective identity and memory. Of course, as discussed in chapter 3, cultural norms and institutional codes affect the way affordances are perceived and utilized.[30] "While users may have a range of interpretations and functions available to them when they are engaging with [information and communication technologies], that range is not unlimited. Technologies are designed with preferred users and interpretations in mind, though users, in turn, may use and interpret technologies in unexpected ways."[31] Twitter hashtags encourage a kind of "momentary connectedness"[32] that brings people together around a common issue, but for Black Twitter such connectedness occurs within and as a form of resistance to larger social contexts of racism and exclusion—both online and off.[33] Especially in comparison to the lack of agency experienced by the victims of police brutality that inspired these hashtags, we can see how Twitter has allowed its users to fight back, and to map out a new sense of subjunctive collective memory at the intersections of race, technology, state violence, and Black death.

Analyzing Hashtags, Digital Videos, and Collective Memories of Anti-Black Violence

This chapter is thus built around a discourse analysis of tweets from both #IfTheyGunnedMeDown and #IfIDieInPoliceCustody, as well as an examination of videos of people of color killed by police. My aim is to understand the ways in which digital activism, digital legacies, and the digital afterlife combine in these hashtags. To fully grasp those themes, I also needed to understand the digital videos of police killings that inspired the hashtags in the first place, which comprise a very well-known type of digital legacy in their own right.

As opposed to other hashtags that are more narrowly focused on particular victims of police violence, like #mikebrown, #sandrabland, or even the Bland-inspired #SayHerName, these two hashtags asked users to put themselves in the shoes of those victims, to go beyond confronting the deaths of others and instead imagine their own deaths. The responses to such a prompt can tell us about how people of color have used digital spaces to think about memory and mortality. For both of the hashtags, I wanted to know not only what kinds of images were shared, but also what sorts of textual messages were relayed.[34] I unsystematically read through the top tweets from the first three days of both hashtags, as a way to get an overview of their most common themes. I then reread and systematically coded the themes in the text itself at each hashtag. Since #IfTheyGunnedMeDown was very popular, I coded only the textual themes in the top tweets.[35] In a separate spreadsheet, I also coded the types of "socially acceptable" images that were shared.[36] All in all, I analyzed 380 tweets from the first four days of this hashtag, August 10–13, 2014, 102 of which contained the acceptable/problematic image pairings.

Because #IfIDieInPoliceCustody took longer to reach the kind of popularity that #IfTheyGunnedMeDown attained almost instantly, I did not utilize the "top tweets" function when coding this second hashtag. Instead, I read and coded all 209 tweets from the first day of the hashtag and then added 401 tweets from part of the second day, when the hashtag began to gain popularity, making a total of 610 tweets from the first two days of the hashtag, July 16–17, 2015. All told, between the two hashtags I read and analyzed 990 tweets. I collected these data in September 2019 and January 2020, which was the same time period in which I viewed the videos as well.

An April 19, 2018, web article in the *New York Times* entitled "Black Lives Upended by Policing: The Raw Videos Sparking Outrage" was my main source for videos of police brutality against people of color.[37] The piece began by noting, "Raw videos that show officers shooting and beating unarmed black people have stirred outrage and prompted disbelief. Captured by cell phones or police cameras, footage has spread through social media, shining a light on disturbing police encounters."[38] It suggested that the point of collecting all these videos in one place was "to provide a record of the raw footage that has sparked a national conversation about race and policing."[39] The *Times* article ultimately featured thirty-two embedded YouTube videos, some containing multiple video sources edited together—i.e., cell phone footage and police body camera footage of the same killing—and some containing images of police brutality that did not end in death. I focused on the eighteen cases in which the target of police violence did die. These ranged from well-known victims like Mike Brown and Tamir Rice to less well-known victims such as Antonio Zambrano-Montes.[40] As mentioned, in several of these cases, multiple videos were included in the embedded YouTube.[41]

In all, I watched twenty-three videos of people of color—mainly Black men—recorded just before, during, or immediately after they were killed by police.

In the book's introduction, I discussed the ethics of qualitative social research using digital data, including blogs of the terminally ill and suicide notes, and on platforms like Twitter. The ethics of watching videos of people of color being murdered by police are in many ways more dubious. The videos I watched are, of course, already publicly available and easily accessible, having been viewed millions of times already. Yet personally, I had previously avoided viewing all such videos from murders that happened after Eric Garner's and Tamir Rice's, because I already agreed with the political uses to which such videos were being put—it didn't feel necessary to digitally witness anyone else's death in order to further convince myself of the problems of systemic racism in the criminal justice system. But in order to understand the concepts of digitally mediated legacies and online immortality as they manifest for people of color in America, and in order to understand the context in which the hashtags I studied had arisen, I felt it necessary to more systematically watch these videos as part of my research. In the end I decided that my ethical responsibility, while watching these videos, was to keep in mind the full humanity of the victims—the lives and loves and families they must have left behind—in the face of the very dehumanizing ways in which their deaths played out on screen.

As mentioned, I viewed a total of twenty-three videos concerning the final moments of eighteen people who died at the hands of police—or under mysterious circumstances in police custody, as in Sandra Bland's case. Of those eighteen people, eleven had videos that showed their deaths on-screen, while the deaths of seven others were not shown. The sources for thirteen of the twenty-three videos in this corpus were police—either body cameras, dashboard cameras, or surveillance helicopters. Only eight of the videos came from cell phones, five of which belonged to bystanders, two belonged to a wife or girlfriend, and one was taken by the victim herself. The final two videos were taken from the surveillance cameras of a business and a public park.

What these numbers attest to is the detached, dehumanizing quality of most of these videos. Viewers are placed in the position of police officers, either chasing after victims or simply watching from squad cars, more often than any other position. The viewer's identification with the camera is a long-standing element of cinema studies,[42] which might help explain why these videos are often used to exonerate the officers involved when such matters go to trial. On the other hand, identification with the camera is never a given, and is sometimes actively resisted by viewers from marginalized groups.[43] In any case, the only empathetic, or even very explicitly emotional, videos in this corpus were those filmed by loved ones like Philando Castile's girlfriend, Diamond Reynolds, who spoke into her cell phone and narrated the events leading up to the shooting from inside the car, pausing to reassure their daughter in the backseat or to tell her bleeding, quietly groaning boyfriend, "Stay with me." Similarly, Keith Lamont Scott's wife, Rakeyia Scott, pleaded with the police officers surrounding her husband in his car, "Don't shoot him, he has no weapon" and screamed, "Did you shoot him?" at the officers moments after they fired several fatal shots.

This gut-wrenching dialogue is rare, however. In most of these videos we are privy only to the voices of police, or are unable to hear any words at all. We watch Alton Sterling accosted by police in a parking lot, from the vantage of a bystander hiding with a cell phone camera in a nearby car. We hear almost nothing from Sterling and see only his red sweatshirt in the grainy video, though the two police officers yell loudly and frequently while pinning Sterling to the ground, then firing the fatal shots. We watch Tamir Rice executed in silence, via surveillance footage from the park he was playing in, two seconds after a police car pulls up next to him. He crumples to the ground in a glitchy, pixelated heap. Laquan McDonald is similarly silent as we watch him shot to death from a police car dash cam. He walks along a highway surrounded by other police cars, and the first shot spins him around as he too lands on the asphalt, twitching for a moment before a final, steamy breath leaves his lungs.

As Jennifer Malkowski put it in her book *Dying in Full Detail*, "Digital technology takes us nearer to death than film technology ever could, but perhaps in the end the idea of proximity is less important to understanding these images' appeal than the idea of control."[44] For her, control refers to the viewers of digital death videos, who can "tailor death's progression to their whims" with the "click of a mouse" or the "tactile slide of a finger on a touchscreen."[45] But somewhat obviously, videos of Black people killed by police remind us that victims and their families have no control over these processes. Although victims' families and community organizers have pushed for the release of many of these videos in order to expose the unjust, capricious, and racist nature of these arrests and killings, the perspective of the victims we get in the vast majority of them is an alienated, degraded one, which in many ways lends itself to the kind of stereotyping and character assassination implied in the news coverage of these victims. Such news coverage is precisely the target of the hashtags analyzed here.

To begin my analysis of these hashtags, I coded the types of "socially acceptable" images shared in the tweets at #IfTheyGunnedMeDown. As Gross noted, the "problematic" photos shared there tend to "depict either informal situations or the contexts are unclear."[46] By contrast, the socially acceptable photos in these dyads are typically taken from formal settings. Partly to see for myself, and partly to check the reliability of my own sample against Gross's, I coded 102 of the socially acceptable images and found the breakdown, listed in table 5.1.

Over 80 percent of the sample was made up of images in these four narrow categories: adorning oneself in academic regalia; wearing suits, ties, or formal dresses; donning a military uniform; or wearing some other uniform denoting gainful employment. These comprised the small handful of ways that an overwhelming number of Black users imagined they might appear less threatening or more sympathetic to a white audience, and especially white police officers. As Gross put it, "There are many ways to be problematic but not as many to be seen as socially acceptable."[47]

The point of this hashtag, as *Time* magazine quickly commented, was that "so many ordinary people . . . could be made to look like a public

TABLE 5.1. Most frequent subjects of socially acceptable photos at #IfTheyGunnedMeDown

Subject of photo	Percentage
Academic regalia/graduation	35
Well-dressed/formal clothes	31
Military uniform	13
Other uniform	10

menace with one photo dropped in a particular context," and that "it's so much easier, given our culture's racial baggage, for a teenager of color to be made to look like a 'thug' than a white teen showing off for a camera the exact same way."[48] That said, the images alone don't tell the whole story. The hashtag was also a venue for discussion and debate. In fact, the commentary accompanying these images spoke to more than just pushback against media stereotypes and racist policing.

To better understand this commentary, I coded the text of 338 of the "top tweets" on the hashtag over its first three days. The majority of the top tweets did not, in fact, include the photo pairings that initiated the hashtag. Given Twitter's well-publicized problems with harassment and trolling,[49] it makes sense that many people would not want to post such pictures of themselves. Yet many still wanted to discuss these images and the larger themes of race and representation that they called forth. In cases such as this, Twitter acts as a kind of public sphere, or a multiplicity of public spheres,[50] and Black Twitter specifically forms a kind of "counterpublic," where there is "not just a different perspective on issues, but different issues [are] discussed altogether."[51] Thus the tweets at #IfTheyGunnedMeDown were more about the discussion surrounding these images than the actual sharing of them.

As table 5.2 shows, the hashtag was a venue for sharing news articles and commentary about race, racism, privilege, and police violence in America. This amounted to a kind of digital "consciousness raising."[52] It was also, even in the first few days, a place where trolls attempted to derail the discussion, and where users pushed back against such efforts. In this way, hashtags like this are not only attempting to contest "African Americans' ongoing experiences of abject inequality in an age of

TABLE 5.2. Most frequent themes in #IfTheyGunnedMeDown

Theme	Percentage
News/links	29
Photos	23
Signal boost/praise for the hashtag	21
Comment on racism/police/privilege	10
Fighting with trolls	9
Trolling/satire	8

alleged colorblindness,"[53] but are themselves contested spaces that need to be guarded from those who would undermine their messages or dilute their impact.

Many authors used the hashtag to confront the issue of respectability politics. One user wrote, "Are black people meant to wear a graduation gown everyday to avoid being unlawfully murdered by the police?" Another said, "Regardless of if I'm in a Suit or I'm a Thug MY LIFE MATTERS." A sociology professor writing on the hashtag said, "#IfTheyGunnedMeDown reminds us that #RespectabilityPolitics will come back to dehumanize us even after death. Our choices are erased." Contributors mentioned Du Bois's concept of double consciousness explicitly, and were also quite explicit that the hashtag formed a kind of counter to mainstream reportage. "In order to have our own narrative correctly reported," one author wrote, "we have to do the reporting ourselves." And indeed, users would write things like "White people need to stop appropriating and making fun of #IfTheyGunnedMeDown" when such satire and trolling came to feel noticeably intrusive.

But people went beyond simply discussing and debating these issues. Some of their tweets also provided tiny autobiographical details, both to accompany their photo dyads or in many cases without photos. One such tweet read, "#Iftheygunnedmedown would they even mentioned I taught kids for 12 yrs. Mentored 7 boys in the projects of SF for 5 yrs. Would I just be blk." Another asked, "#IfTheyGunnedMeDown was I another Black gang affiliated teen or a honor student who recently came back from Paris?" These sorts of posts suggest that, in a very small way, this hashtag also functioned as a commentary on the preservation of individual legacies and the presentation of digital selfhood.

Consider, as well, the following quotes: "#IfTheyGunnedMeDown I would just be a number." Or "another nameless faceless African American victim of this crooked nation." These tweets speak to more than just the news media's tendency to support racist narratives of Black criminality, they depict the injustice of dying in such a depersonalized way. Other users made these sentiments even more explicit, such as one who wrote, "If this is the only representation left of me #iftheygunnedmedown my fam can rest assure that my authentic voice is all thru my fb/tweets." Another wrote, "make sure they tell the truth #iftheygunnedmedown." In fact, the desire to control the images and narratives around one's specific, hypothetical demise at the hands of police went even further. One author wrote, "#IftheyGunnedMeDown Why would they need to talk about my degrees? My honors. Organizations I started? Charity I do?" Another commented, "#IfTheyGunnedMeDown, man. I already know what pictures . . . Tweets . . . Songs they would choose . . . Just know I wanted to live." Still another wrote, "#IfTheyGunnedMe-Down I am pretty certain I would be made into a radical racist who hated white people." Some users even moved away from the dyadic acceptable/problematic format and posted a single, "acceptable" photo, with directions that this was the specific photo they'd like used if they were killed, posting captions like "#IfTheyGunnedMeDown Use this pic to remember me." Moves like these shifted the hashtag from a critique of the media to a thought experiment about how one would like to be remembered in a context where racism and inequality may make it impossible to be the author of one's own final narrative or legacy.

Having noticed this small theme in my coding of #IfTheyGunnedMe-Down, I wanted to see whether it showed up in a later hashtag around a similar case, so I coded tweets at #IfIDieInPoliceCustody. As mentioned previously, this hashtag was made in the wake of Sandra Bland's death in 2015, and although it was not built around a specific photographic/visual form of messaging, it was an otherwise very similar instance of hashtag activism.

Understandably, given the circumstances surrounding Bland's death, the most frequent type of tweet was one declaring that the author would never kill themselves (see table 5.3). These sentiments were often coupled with comments about how the tweet's authors would or do always interact with police. Some representative examples include the following: "#IfIDieInPoliceCustody Please know damn well that I did not commit suicide. I didn't react violently. I would not take deadly risks." "#ifidieinpolicecustody I want all of my friends to know that I didn't kill myself. Don't let the media portray me as some thug." "Know that I'm not stupid enough to have been combative or 'reaching for something' #IfIDieInPoliceCustody." "I wasn't armed. I have never owned gun legal or otherwise. I ABSOLUTELY did not 'reach for his/her weapon.'" "I hate running and Im non confrontational. Just plain happy go lucky jokester. #ifidieinpolicecustody."

TABLE 5.3. Most frequent themes in #IfIDieInPoliceCustody

Themes	Percentages
I did not commit suicide	19
Interaction with police (e.g., didn't resist, wouldn't be violent, etc.)	17
Protest my death	15
Signal boost/retweets	14
How to be remembered	10
Family/friends	8
Commentary on racism/policing	8

As one journalist put it, "That people even feel the need to make these kinds of advanced directives in case they're detained shows just how deep distrust in the police runs, particularly in minority communities." He continued, "These concerns aren't necessarily new in Black communities, who have complained about mistreatment by police for decades. But over the past year, stories such as [Freddie] Gray's, Garner's, Brown's, Scott's, and now Bland's have elevated these issues to the forefront of conversation in the US, which is why a hashtag like #IfIDieinPoliceCustody can go so viral so quickly."[54] "Advanced directives" is a particularly interesting way of framing these tweets, one that some of the hashtag's authors themselves picked up on. One contributor to the hashtag explained it simply enough by writing, "This is the only will some of our children will ever have."

Indeed, the tweets often moved beyond the comments about suicide that were a direct response to the circumstances of Bland's jail-cell death, and instead mimicked some of the elements of a living will, including instructions related to the care of family members. One author wrote, "My son has Aspergers, take care of him. Somebody care for my Mamma. Know good &damn well I didn't commit suicide. #ifidieinpolicecustody." Tweets about family and friends in general comprised 8 percent of the tweets in this sample, many of which consisted of statements like "#IfIDieInPoliceCustody let my mom know I'll visit every so often when she needs me" and "#IfIDieInPoliceCustody my greatest accomplishment was being a mom. My kids were the very best thing that ever happened to me."

The advanced directive character of the hashtag played out in other ways as well, as authors left fairly detailed instructions for loved ones in the event of their hypothetical deaths. One such instruction was "#IfIDieInPoliceCustody fight for a rape kit to be done look for videos on my phone/dropbox." Another was "#IfIDieInPoliceCustody break my phone, hard drive & laptop -and pay my podcast monthly fees so it can live forever." Other authors frequently asked that their loved ones use their hypothetical deaths as a subject for renewed protests. One tweet read, "#ifidieinpolicecustody rise up, take to the streets, shut shit down . . . do whatever it takes." Another said, "Make my name a hashtag. @ all major news networks. Protest in my name. Hold the police accountable."

This idea that one's own name might become the tragic inspiration for one more hashtag dovetailed with one additional, prominent theme. Ten percent of the tweets in the sample consisted of statements about specific ways their authors wanted to be remembered. Some echoed the concerns of authors on #IfTheyGunnedMeDown by posting a photo they wanted to be used if they were killed, often stating things like "#IfIDieInPoliceCustody Don't let the media post up a ratchet picture of me." Others posted similar remarks like "#IfIDieInPoliceCustody they will find a high school pic of me with braids and a du-rag and suggest I was a 'thug.' You know better." That same author also shared a variety of autobiographical details about his life on the hashtag. In one tweet he wrote, "#IfIDieInPoliceCustody know that I graduated from one of the top undergraduate business schools in the country and work for a Fortune 500." Other contributors similarly mentioned elements of their personalities and biographies that they wanted remembered. One tweet read, "#ifIdieinpolicecustody tell them I was strong, outspoken, a faithful believer in God's word, & that I would N E V E R interrupt his will for me." Another said, "#ifidieinpolicecustody flood the Internet with all the positive things I've done in the world." Still another said, "#IfIDieInPoliceCustody Make sure the world knows my story" and included a link to a personal blog. Yet another author wrote, "#IfIDieInPoliceCustody I would want my name to go around the world as a symbol of the countless people that have died at the hands of the [police emoji]." Such tweets speak to a desire to have a sense of one's individuality, one's selfhood, or one's legacy preserved as part of this larger digital struggle against racism and media misrepresentation.

Mnemonic Freedom and Immortality in the Digital Public Sphere

Twitter in general, and especially the hashtags through which digital activism takes place on Twitter, can be thought of as a kind of public sphere, in as much as they provide "space for people within a nation-state to exchange ideas outside of state control."[55] Hashtags like #BlackLivesMatter or #Ferguson can quickly stitch together "counterpublic networks" or "digital counterpublics" that shape public debates about racism and policing in America,[56] and that contest the rigidity of respectability politics.[57] Hashtags like the two analyzed here— #IfTheyGunnedMeDown and #IfIDieInPoliceCustody—reveal the digital phenomenology of Du Boisian "double consciousness" at work.[58] This is the sense, as Du Bois himself put it, "of always looking at one's self through the eyes of others, of measuring one's soul by the tape of a world that looks on in amused contempt and pity."[59] Or as André Brock explained, "The libidinal tensions powering Black online respectability can be understood as despair—despair over the perceived pathologies of Black morality intertwined with fears of being left behind in Western technoculture through 'inappropriate' digital practice."[60]

But amid all the scholarship on Black Twitter and digital activism, hashtags like these have rarely been analyzed as a form of struggle over collective memory, or an expression of a desire for a kind of digital afterlife. And yet that is what so many of the tweets quoted in this chapter have suggested. They were a way of criticizing white supremacy, media stereotypes, and state violence, but also a way of demanding to be remembered on one's own terms, to live on in the memories of others in a manner that reflects one's deepest sense of self, one's full humanity. They made this demand in what media scholar Barbie Zelizer called "the subjunctive voice" or "the 'as if.'" This mode of representation "offers a way of transforming the relationship between the possible, probable, impossible, and certain by accommodating contingency, the imagination, and the emotions."[61] The tweets at these hashtags form something like a subjunctive demand to be remembered, a plea for collective caretaking of one's legacy based on the imagined likelihood of being murdered by police.

When sociologist Robert Zussman initially coined the term "narrative freedom," he identified the roots of such narrative self-invention in "the long tradition of African-American autobiographical writing," which "both claims blackness and attempts to transform its meaning."[62] Such writing can significantly refashion selfhood and identity. The posts at #IfTheyGunnedMeDown and #IfIDieInPoliceCustody both aim for a kind of narrative freedom, the freedom to tell a story or invent a self outside the racist and violent discourses perpetuated through the mainstream media. But the retrospective and subjunctive or conditional character of these tweets—the requests to be remembered in particular ways after one's hypothetical death—suggests that we ought to see these as demands for mnemonic freedom: freedom to have the stories we tell about ourselves get remembered in the ways that we intend. Like the authors of the digital suicide notes discussed in the previous chapter, the contributors to these hashtags wanted to be the ones to control their own legacies in the event of their deaths, without the stereotyping and racism of news outlets and police spokespeople interfering.

Of course, the individual tweets at these hashtags are not particularly robust representations of any single person's life or legacy. But the concept of mnemonic freedom still makes sense in this context, given the complex realities of digital Blackness. The essayist Aria Dean explained that

> as black people, we are constantly grappling with this question of collectivity. Where do you end and the next person begins? Faced with the immense pain of watching other black people die on camera, our sense of autonomy is thrown. When we speak of "we need," "we grieve," "we hope," "we demand," and so forth, we speak of something beyond a collection of individuals and something beyond a community.[63]

We can see, then, the hashtags #IfIDieInPoliceCustody and #IfTheyGunnedMeDown as a different kind of memory project. They aggregate many individual, *collected* memories and, in so doing, transform them into a narrative of truly *collective* memory.[64] They blur the distinctions between individuals and create a sense of community in this subjunctive, conditional voice.

Zygmunt Bauman's book *Mortality, Immortality, and Other Life Strategies*[65] stakes out some of the same philosophical ground as the work by Becker and Giddens mentioned in previous chapters.[66] In it, he argues that human culture is composed of simultaneous efforts to give meaning to life and to suppress the certainty of death. As he put it, death "is the ultimate condition of cultural creativity as such. It makes permanence into a task, an urgent task."[67] Historically there have been two paths for achieving the kind of immortality that culture can actually grant: individual achievement captured in art, literature, or monuments—which is usually the domain of elites—and "collective destiny," which refers to the sense of group transcendence allotted to the masses through things like war, nationalism, or xenophobia. As Bauman put it, "With their private hopes for transcendence doomed from the start and thus seldom consciously entertained, the perpetuity of the group is the masses' only . . . chance of immortality."[68]

What we see at these hashtags, in the hundreds and thousands of tiny acts of narrative self-assertion, of pushback against racist stereotypes, of demands for mnemonic freedom under the ever-present threat of police violence, is a grasping at a kind of hybrid form of immortality. Bauman's notion of collective immortality for the masses presupposed that individuals remained anonymous—"The future of the group . . . will not have their names engraved on it," as he put it.[69] But in these hashtags we see the sum total of countless "micro-narratives of suffering"[70] that forge community and demand empathy while maintaining some kernel of the individual's biography. Of course, this all depends on the imagination of one's own death, which marks such hashtags as in some ways different from many of the other practices described in this book. On the other hand, the notions of digital permanence upon which so many digital death practices depend are also largely imaginary. The digital soul is always, in some ways, narrated in the subjunctive voice.

In any case, it must be acknowledged that police advocates and other opponents of Black Lives Matter find it easy enough to deny the empathy that such micro-narratives of suffering demand. "We know that, as far as images of Black people are concerned, in their circulation they often don't, in fact, do the imaging work that we expect of them."[71] This is what collective immortality feels like "in the wake," as Christina Sharpe so powerfully named it. "Living in the wake means living the history and present of terror, from slavery to the present, as the ground of our everyday Black existence."[72] In such a context, demands for the freedom to write one's own narrative, to control one's own legacy, are necessarily heavily constrained. That fact alone makes them all the more urgent.

Conclusion

"First of all, I hope you're up and at them, kings and queens, out there doing something to establish your kingdom and queendom, your legacy." This is how Sandra Bland began her April 7, 2015, YouTube video, one in a series of videos she called "Sandy Speaks." Bland began most of those videos with a similar affirmation to her "kings and queens," but the use of the term "legacy" in this particular entry is eye opening. As it turned out, Bland's own legacy was as a tragic victim of police violence whose death inspired #IfIDieInPoliceCustody, as well as other hashtags and many other acts of protest. But the "Sandy Speaks" videos are also part of her digital legacy, albeit much less well known than the videos and events leading up to her death. She posted twenty-nine videos to YouTube between January 15 and April 8, 2015, broadly themed around the Black Lives Matter movement but also focusing on religion and self-empowerment. Bland's YouTube videos, which have been viewed between 1,000 and 15,000 times, give us a vision of her as a full human being, not just a name in a hashtag, even as their intimacy reinforces the tragedy of her untimely demise.

Yet for most of the victims of police violence, and even for Bland, the digital images that others produced surrounding their deaths have dominated collective memory. While the most-watched "Sandy Speaks" video tops out at 15,000 views on YouTube, the most-watched version of her arrest footage has been viewed 1.1 million times on that site. What does it say about American culture when bystanders' cell phones, dashboard cameras in police cruisers, police officer body cams, and surveillance tape tell such important and gut-wrenching stories about Black life? In an age where the digital presentation of self is an increasingly fundamental part of social life, for people of all backgrounds, how might people of color secure control over such self-presentations under threat of state violence? Can Black people, as individuals, push back effectively against narratives of Black criminality that are so deeply rooted in mainstream media? How can the power to represent, to narrate, and to commemorate be wrestled away from those with a vested interest in the denigration of Black lives?

The kinds of collective narratives composed at #IfTheyGunnedMe-Down and #IfIDieInPoliceCustody offered one possible answer to these questions. As Aria Dean put it,

> The 20th century taught us that one of our rights is a right to representation, not only politically but personally—that we have a right to be represented as we are, for our images to hold true. But what if one says to hell with that? Blackness . . . is a copy without an original. There is no articulable ontology of blackness, no essential blackness, because blackness's only home is in its circulating representations.[73]

These hashtags served as a kind of amalgamated narrative of Black suffering and Black empowerment. They afforded something Bauman thought was incompatible—collective immortality and individual immortality, existing uneasily, hypothetically, electronically together. They held thousands of individual micro-narratives, and legibly combined them into a collectively composed story affirming the value of all Black lives and legacies.

As the Internet comes to envelop most of social life, the tales we tell ourselves and the ways we make the world meaningful may be changing too. Indeed, "there is already little we can do in society that stands apart from this new growing digitalism. Narrative life, its stories, imaginations, and realities are transforming under the rule of digitalism."[74] We need to understand the hashtag as its own kind of collective narrative, its own sort of claim to a digital legacy. The particular examples of this new narrative form that were analyzed in this chapter were created in opposition to white racism and police violence. They were formed in a new verb tense, as a kind of conditional commemoration for lives that had not yet been lost, for lives under the ever-present threat of racist violence. They presented a demand for mnemonic freedom in the event of a scenario that was still only hypothetical and yet, tragically, felt almost certain to many of these contributors. As one such contributor wrote, "#IfIDieInPoliceCustody Know that I had a feeling I would. We all do." In such a context, the struggle to define one's digital self and defend one's digital legacy is not just a matter of personal interest. It is part and parcel of the collective struggle for Black lives.

At the same time, this struggle takes place on vastly unequal ground. As this book has shown, the digital traces, remains, or "footprints" we leave online when we die are an increasingly important means of grieving for our loved ones, and an increasingly important means of establishing a sense of legacy or transcendence. But "digital footprints" themselves vary tremendously based on socioeconomic class,[75] and those with less economic and cultural capital are likely to leave behind less digital material to work with. That sad fact is coupled with the sense among people of color—so palpable in the hashtags analyzed here—that one's legacy may be wrestled completely out of one's own control in a single violent instant. Ending up as the inspiration for a hashtag protesting one's death, or as the victim in a viral video of police brutality, is as much a form of digital damnation as immortality. Thus, sadly, the digital afterlife remains plagued by the same racism and inequality that haunt so much of our time among the living.

6

The Reenchantment of Technology and
the Quest for Virtual Immortality

Waves crash on a pristine beach lit by a hazy orange sunset. A middle-aged man with graying hair and white stubble sits on a blanket, his eyes gazing thoughtfully toward the water. There, near the water's edge on this otherwise empty beach, his son and daughter play peacefully. They are not yet teenagers. Armed with pails and shovels, they build a sandcastle in front of a jetty. The only sound is the crashing of the waves upon the shore. The man nods contentedly, then picks up an iPad that has been sitting beside him. Piano music begins to swell, and with a suddenly wistful and slightly worried countenance, he pushes his hair back from his forehead, takes a deep breath, looks directly into the iPad, and begins to record a message. "Hey Princess . . ." A young woman in a wedding dress gazes into a mirror as she applies a few final strokes of mascara. A bridesmaid enters, champagne flute in hand, and reacts with glee to the sight of the bride-to-be. "Oh my god, it's absolutely perfect," she beams, as they embrace. A diamond engagement ring is visible on the bride's left hand as she glances again at her reflection. Suddenly, the familiar digital tone of a new text message rings out, diverting her attention away from the mirror and toward an iPad. She sits down and pushes some hair away from her face as she concentrates on the device. We hear the voice of the father from the beach, seemingly picking up right where he left off: "I know you've probably been dreaming about this day for pretty much your entire life." We see the device's screen—it is the father on the beach. This is the message he recorded there, many years earlier, for his daughter to receive on her wedding day. "And if you want to know the truth, I have too."

This is the beginning of a video that greets users upon clicking the "Learn More" button on the website of a company called SafeBeyond. As the video continues, more family members preparing for the daughter's wedding receive messages recorded by the father that day on the beach.

His wife stops in her tracks to view her message amidst rows of evenly spaced, white wooden folding chairs in a lush garden. His son pauses with a tuxedo slung over his shoulder. Each message offers words of encouragement and reassurance from the father, who, we gather, is no longer living. He tells his wife to be proud of the job she has done raising their daughter. He tells his son to keep taking care of the family. He tells his daughter, "I just want to say I love you. I want you to go out there and have a great wedding, and a great rest of your life, all right?" We watch the wedding taking place as the father's words proceed in voice-over—the daughter being walked down the aisle by her brother, the mother watching joyfully as her daughter says, "I do." And then we return to the beach, where the father has just finished recording these postmortem messages while his young children play. He runs off screen to join them near the water, but the camera remains focused on the landscape, the ocean lapping onto the wet sand. A tagline emerges: "Be there when it counts." Then the SafeBeyond logo appears, along with another tagline: "Life continues."

SafeBeyond offers what it calls "emotional life insurance." In addition to digital estate planning or digital legacy services in which passwords and other sensitive information get transferred, upon one's death, to one's heirs and next-of-kin, SafeBeyond is one of a number of companies that will store personal messages to be sent to family and friends in the event of one's death. SafeBeyond allows users to not only schedule such messages for up to twenty-five years in advance, but also to create messages for specific milestones in the lives of loved ones, such as weddings, graduations, or the birth of a child. It can even attach messages to particular geo-tagged locations, so that attending a game at Yankee Stadium or visiting a national park might trigger a new message from a deceased parent, friend, or spouse. Of course, as SafeBeyond founder and CEO Moran Zur explained to me, these messages will not come as a "total shock" the way they did in the video. Instead, recipients are typically informed ahead of time that they can view new messages, rather than being surprised mere minutes before a wedding ceremony. Nonetheless, this powerful promotional video offers a provocative glimpse at the way new digital technologies may allow us to extend our intimate, emotional interactions into a new kind of digital afterlife. But some organizations have begun to push this idea even further.

For example, Lifenaut is a project financed by the Terasem Foundation, an organization devoted to the principles of a philosophy called transhumanism. Lifenaut allows people to create a free database "of personal reflections captured in video, image, audio and documents about yourself, that can be saved, searched, downloaded and shared with friends. Each account comes with an interactive Avatar that becomes more like you the more you teach and train it to think like you."[1] In addition to these elements of the digital self, collected in what Lifenaut calls a "Mindfile," Lifenaut also offers to collect and store users' biological specimens as part of a "Biofile," available for a onetime fee of ninety-nine dollars. The idea is that one's DNA might be kept alongside this voluminous information about one's personality, until such time that these things might be used to recreate or reanimate oneself. Indeed, Lifenaut will even "Spacecast" your Mindfile, beaming it out into the universe "at the speed of light." As it explains on its website, "The purpose of Spacecasting your personal auto-biographical information . . . is to ensure that some aspect of you can survive any catastrophe that might befall earth. We hypothesize that advanced technology that is capable of recovering the Spacecast signal will also most likely be capable of reconstructing yourself from the information in the Spacecast by future generations or even ET's."

Although the technology and scope of these two services differ, there are clear similarities. Both envision a world in which a dead individual can have meaningful interactions with others by using digital technology. Both rely on the perception of digital permanence; their users must trust that their data can be stored safely for many years and then put back into circulation at the appropriate time. Both invest online, digital texts and technologies with a kind of reenchanting power to cheat death, in ways both big and small. And both depend on assumptions about the user's place in their social world, that their continued presence for years or decades or even much longer after they have died is important, and worth taking measures to ensure.

There are differences as well, of course. SafeBeyond's technology is a reality today, in the here and now, while Lifenaut is based on imagining a distant future in which the data it collects now can be fully put to use. SafeBeyond's messaging is firmly rooted in attachments to the living, whereas Lifenaut bills itself as a "long-term computer science research project that explores how technology may one day extend life." Both can collect the same kinds of images, text, and messages, but Lifenaut asks for lots more of it, and while SafeBeyond can store messages for up to twenty-five years, Lifenaut plans to hold its data in perpetuity. SafeBeyond posits that the self is best captured by the affective power of a thoughtful, personal message, delivered to one's closest friends and loved ones. Lifenaut attempts to archive and eventually recreate the self through the curation of a much larger amount of personal digital data.

In either case, both SafeBeyond and Lifenaut provoke visitors to their sites to consider the possibility of digitally extending themselves into a future in which their corporeal presence is no more. And they are not the only companies and organizations working on such digital self-extension—there appear to be a growing number of scientists, foundations, and start-ups working on mind uploading in some capacity, and SafeBeyond is only one of a number of postmortem messaging services on the market today. In fact, despite the differences between them, in the popular press these sorts of companies are often blurred together. Headlines like "Technology Now Lets You Speak from Beyond the Grave,"[2] "Web Immortality: The Social Media Sites That Keep You Alive in the Digital World,"[3] "Digital Messages for Loved Ones from Beyond the Grave,"[4] and "8 Digital Legacy Apps That Can Make You Immortal"[5] have been commonplace in news coverage of what are actually fairly simple postmortem messaging services. This sort of hype was significant enough that in 2020 a fictional postmortem messaging service called "The Forever Social," with a slickly designed fake website, turned out to be a successful viral advertising campaign for a dramatic podcast—it fooled several news outlets into covering the company as if it were real.[6]

Regardless of the hype, these two sets of digital technologies bring together a variety of themes that have surfaced throughout the book, while raising new questions about those themes. We have already seen how loved ones are apt to use social media profiles of the dead as a way of continuing their bonds with the deceased. We have examined the long history of using new communication technologies to transcend death. We have read detailed examples of the ways that blogs offer a kind of narrative freedom for the terminally ill to reconstruct a sense of self. We have seen how the seeming permanence of the Internet allows individuals to craft digital suicide notes that commemorate their preferred version of themselves. And we have witnessed the creative ways in which collective narratives about users' imagined legacies take shape on Twitter hashtags in order to combat racism and inequality. These same social and philosophical undercurrents connect us to postmortem messaging and mind uploading as well—the desire to continue bonds after death, the need to fashion a compelling vision of oneself and one's intimate relationships that will outlast one's physical body, the longing for a digital legacy that will span into the future, and the technological reimaging of previously metaphysical forms of transcendence. Yet postmortem messaging and mind uploading add some new wrinkles to this mix as well. As such, I have engaged in multi-modal qualitative research consisting of digital discourse analysis, interviews with the founders of some postmortem messaging companies, and interviews with the creators of a handful of foundations and companies working in and around the field of mind uploading.

My research for this chapter began when I sought to learn more about postmortem messaging. Although I was never able to gain access to a corpus of actual postmortem messages—the companies providing these services were understandably very careful about the privacy of their users—I was able to interview the founders of seven postmortem messaging services. These were Moran Zur, of the aforementioned SafeBeyond; Tamar Goudsmit from Afternote; Peter Barrett from Gone Not Gone, Aristotelis Zournas from Knotify.me, Tim Hewson from Parting Wishes, Nicola Piccinini from Postumo, and John Thornton from Wishes Keeper.[7]

I also felt that I could not examine postmortem messaging without comparing and contrasting it to mind uploading, a more cutting-edge and future-oriented technology that seems to be increasingly dominating the conversation around digital death and postmortem communication. To understand public opinion around mind uploading among a segment of the public that had already familiarized itself with this prospective new technology, I engaged in a discourse analysis of Reddit posts devoted to the topic.[8] I ended up reading and coding the 977 top Reddit comments about mind uploading from the ten most-commented-on posts. I supplemented this analysis by interviewing four people associated with mind uploading and the transhumanist movement. These were Bruce Duncan, the managing director of the aforementioned Terasem

Foundation; Eric Klien, the founder and president of the Lifeboat Foundation, an organization devoted to "safeguarding the future" from technological threats; Robert McIntyre, the co-founder of Nectome, a company pioneering new methods of preserving the human brain; and Randal Koene, the founder of Carboncopies Foundation, devoted to promoting research into "whole brain emulation."[9]

As such, the chapter first explores the landscape of postmortem messaging using interviews with the creators of postmortem messaging services. Next it looks into the public perception of mind uploading by analyzing Reddit posts about that topic. Then it compares that discourse to the remarks of some prominent mind uploading proponents whom I interviewed. It then returns to the literature around death and dying, with a focus on existing scholarship around transhumanism—the common name for the philosophy undergirding mind uploading and some other technological efforts at extending human lifespans. Ultimately, the chapter argues that despite the somewhat fantastical rhetoric around them, postmortem messaging services largely represent the same impulses toward extending the self and exercising mnemonic freedom that have been discussed in previous chapters. They are rooted in connections to family and loved ones and are effective inasmuch as they continue the kind of reenchantment of the digital self associated with the everyday digital technologies discussed in earlier chapters. However, mind uploading represents a sort of boundary crossing, one in which the self is disenchanted and ties to family and community are downplayed. Instead, mind uploading acts as a reenchantment of science itself, where humanistic conceptions of the individual mean little but faith in algorithms and computation provide a new way for tech-savvy humans to combat death anxiety.

Understanding Postmortem Messaging

As mentioned earlier, postmortem messaging platforms have often been framed as a means of achieving some form of virtual afterlife for oneself, or digitally conquering death, but the rhetoric around these sites and services has often exceeded a much more mundane reality. Typically, postmortem messaging services store text, images, and/or audiovisual messages on servers until such time as they consider the authors of those messages dead. On some services this is because the authors failed to check in by responding to a certain number of automatically generated emails. In others, this is because a predetermined executor or trustee contacted the company to let it know that the author was deceased. Some of these services let their authors schedule messages for many years in advance. Some of them even combine other services, like online memorials and legal wills, with these messages.

But in point of fact, the hype surrounding these services in the middle part of the last decade never resulted in a robust consumer base. SafeBeyond founder Moran Zur told me that his service had twenty-five thousand users in 2017 when I interviewed him, but the six other post-mortem messaging services whose founders I interviewed several years later had far fewer. Their customer bases ranged from five thousand to as few as ten—several of the founders ran the sites more as a hobby, and all of them held other jobs in the tech sector, allowing them to continue supporting sites that were not profitable on their own. In fact, the brief history of this field, probably only a decade old, is already littered with companies that have not survived—an irony noted by one of the few other scholars to study them, Tamara Kneese.[10]

The difficulty of securing customers loomed large in all of the conversations I had with the founders of these companies. As John Thornton, creator of Wishes Keeper, put it,

I talked to people. Everyone was like, "Yeah, that's a great idea. That's awesome. That's a great idea." So I built it, and the idea was basically the majority of the features would be free, but then if you wanted some extra features you could pay for them. I released it and really a lot of people, even the people who were like, "Yeah, that's an awesome idea," they didn't do it. They didn't use it.

Tamar Goudsmit, the co-founder of Afternote, agreed:

A lot of people told us, "Yeah, what a good idea," and "This is something you need!" We also did a test with users before we went online, and people told us they really found it a good idea, but to actually sit down and actually fill out all these questions, that was the next step, and that was something you don't do so easily, and that takes a lot of emotions to do it, and sometimes you really don't know what you want.

The affective process of creating messages for loved ones, of sitting and thinking so hard about one's own demise and the effect it would have on one's spouse or children, also ended up being more significant than many creators had envisioned. Nicola Piccinini of Postumo admitted, "Doing it is really emotional, writing it is really very tough, and for the person who received it, it could be even worse." Tamar Goudsmit mentioned similar feedback from a customer: "One guy told me that, he said, 'I was crying constantly, I was writing these letters to my children,' and he said it was so wrecking in the end." But Peter Barrett, the founder of Gone Not Gone, found the process of creating postmortem messages quite rewarding. "It's actually therapeutic, to a certain extent," he told me. "I've got an eleven-year-old and a seven-year-old, and I know they're going to receive messages from me, whatever happens to me. If I get hit by a bus tomorrow they'll still get messages from me. So that's good, and actually when you've finished it, it's a really good feeling."

Along those lines, each founder had deeply emotional reasons for creating a postmortem messaging service, usually built around a personal experience with loss. Moran Zur explained to me that he had founded this business partly because his own wife was diagnosed with brain cancer, and "knowing, hey, she can be there for my son, even when she's gone, has been very hopeful" for her. Similarly, Aristotelis Zournas of Knotify.me was moved to create that service by thinking about what his own wife and child would think if he died. Peter Barrett was spurred by finding a second-long clip of his deceased father's voice on a videocassette. Tim Hewson was moved to start Parting Wishes after attending a colleague's funeral that didn't seem to match well with the colleague's actual personality. Afterward, at a bar with other attendees, "there were fifteen people around the table and somebody was saying that they needed a will and they hadn't written one, and we went around the table and not one person around the table had a will. And we were all in our thirties and forties, we had kids and houses and everything else." He continued,

It was around the dot com boom where everybody was trying to put everything online. So we thought, hey, that's a natural fit. We'll put will writing, funeral wishes online. And then it was this sense of at that time, people were starting to prepare their own blogs and pages for themselves, and we thought it would be kind of cool to have a blog that could last forever, even after you died, and then people could write on it and memorialize you and things like that.

These entrepreneurs found themselves caught in a moment of shifting cultural norms around death and dying. On the one hand, some spoke of a change in our sense of obligations between the living and the dead. Tim Hewson explained,

> I think this sense of "I don't care. I'm going to be gone anyway," I think that's a dated view. I don't think many people express that as much now as they used to. You used to get people saying, "Why do I care?" and I think, maybe people are more connected [today]. I'm not sure, but I do get a sense that people do feel more of a responsibility to loved ones.

John Thornton's remarks partially confirmed this point of view. He suggested that "as we age, as a society, and people are more comfortable with applications and the web . . . you probably will have an increased usage then." However, a larger obstacle loomed in his mind:

> I think you're still going to have that similar boundary. I don't feel, I never got any pushback that "Oh, it's on the web" or "its technology, the technology's too hard . . ." So I think the big barrier is, you know, just death. We're not comfortable talking about it. We're not comfortable with our mortality.

Although critics have questioned the extent to which death anxiety and death denial are fundamental parts of modern life,[11] the creators of these postmortem messaging services still felt that an inherent fear of death posed a problem for their business models. Thornton suggested that "if I was better as a marketer I possibly could get some more traction, but I think the bigger issue is people don't like to deal with it. Yeah, you know, it's just something that, it's like, everyone admits they need a will. No one wants to do it." Peter Barrett made a similar point: "A lot of people don't want to deal with the fact that they're going to pass away at some point in the future, and due to that they don't want to get involved in some kind of service that has a degree of finality for them. . . . The whole thing about planning for death is very few people do it. You know, we all think we're invincible until it's too late."

These feelings were seemingly confirmed by my own survey of Internet users. Even though 61 percent of my respondents had viewed a social networking page of someone who was dead in the past year, only 22 percent said that they had discussed what would happen to their own social networking pages or other digital possessions after they died. I also asked them whether they would want to receive postmortem messages from a loved one after that person died; 41 percent said yes, 29 percent said no, and 30 percent said it depended on the loved one or the circumstances. Fewer people still said that they themselves would want to send such messages, even if the cost of doing so was not an issue. Only 34 percent of respondents wanted to, while 33 percent did not and 33 percent once again said it depended on the loved one or circumstances surrounding the message.

In the end, even though I prompted the founders of these postmortem messaging services to think philosophically about what it meant that people could now use digital technology to continue communicating to loved ones after they died, most eschewed the kind of overheated rhetoric associated with some of the press they had received. When asked about whether his service provided something akin to digital immortality, Zournas said flatly, "No. For me it's just a practical reason, nothing else. I don't believe that digital life can be continued just because you send something to someone like ten years later . . . Real life is real life." Goudsmit also pointed to the practical benefits:

> What I sense now, it's going so fast that you don't have the time to, really, what you record, all these pictures, all these movies, you don't have time to put them in order, and I think that's a shame, because I like to look at the [photo] books that my mother made when she was my age. . . . So you're not leaving anything to just grab or even go on your computer and have, like, an overview. No, it's like this big data of all these photos and it's not structured and that's something I miss. I think it would be a nice thought that you leave that behind.

But Tim Hewson was a bit more willing to think of the implications of our digital lives on history and memory:

We know very little about our great-grandparents, you know, and our grandparents; we know what we can get from census data and that's about it. And we're leaving now massive footprints of our lunch, the people we met, and what we did, and the latest meal I cooked. And yeah, you do wonder how much should we be leaving and how much of this information are future generations going to be interested in. . . . But I think it's very interesting to think that potentially our great-great-grandchildren are going to know an awful lot about some of us, and they may be really puzzled about us as a group.

Moran Zur also spoke about the changing nature of memory that apps like his foretold: "I think we all want to be remembered. The next generation will know their roots. They will know their great-great-grandparents. It will definitely change how we are remembered."

Comments like this bring us back to the concept of mnemonic freedom. It is clear to the founders of postmortem messaging sites that the digital ephemera of our lives will serve, in some capacity, as heirlooms or memory aids that end up defining our posthumous reputations. In that sense, leaving postmortem messages for them is a way of exerting agency over that process, of embracing the kinds of mnemonic freedom that digital culture provides. Moreover, the very possibility of postmortem messaging would seem to request that users think of their own deaths in relation to the networks of family and friends whom they would leave behind, and encourage imagining the kinds of things those people would like to hear from them in the future. In the process, one would seem to be reflexively engaged in a reassessment of self when creating a postmortem message—who have I been and what is the nature of my connection to others? Of course, mind uploading technologies also allow an individual to exert a kind of agency over their digital future, and to reflect on their own mortality, albeit with different affordances attached to them, built upon a fundamentally different view of self, memory, and transcendence.

Mind Uploading and Transhumanism

The contemporary concept of mind uploading is part of a broader intellectual movement called transhumanism. Put simply, transhumanism refers to the idea that human evolution can and should be actively steered beyond its "natural" biological course. Using a variety of scientific technologies—some of which are in development and some of which exist only in imagination at the moment—transhumanists hope to improve human capacities and eventually achieve immortality. As noted transhumanist Natasha Vita-More explained, "At the core of transhumanism is the conviction that the lifespan be extended, aging reversed, and that death should be optional rather than compulsory."[12]

Transhumanists trace their intellectual lineage back to the Enlightenment, framing their worldview as one that emphasizes individual liberty and a concern for the welfare of all of humanity.[13] Nick Bostrom, another well-known transhumanist, has located the roots of transhumanism in a 1923 essay by the biologist J. B. L. Haldane, in which Haldane argued that humans would someday be able to control our own genetics and drastically improve the course of our own evolution. Bostrom also credited Aldous Huxley's brother Julian Huxley as the one who actually coined the term "transhumanism" in a 1957 book.[14] But the contemporary vision of what transhumanism means probably began with the work of R. C. W. Ettinger, whose 1962 book *The Prospect of Immortality* essentially launched the modern cryonics movement. Writing in a 1972 follow-up titled *Man into Superman*, Ettinger explained that through cryogenic freezing, "you, personally, and your families have a genuine opportunity to prolong your lives indefinitely and outgrow the human mold."[15]

Cryogenic freezing certainly laid the groundwork for the notion that one could transcend death today because of scientific breakthroughs that were bound to happen in the future. Yet contemporary transhumanism is not solely focused on cryonics. Developments in computing, especially artificial intelligence, are often a focal point of this movement as well, which has coalesced around the work of Ray Kurzweil. Kurzweil is a computer scientist and entrepreneur who did pioneering work in the 1970s on optical text scanning and text-to-speech technologies, and who was eventually hired by Google in 2012 to work on machine learning and natural language processing. In addition to a variety of other entrepreneurial ventures, he began writing books on artificial intelligence in the 1980s. Kurzweil was convinced that human intelligence and machine intelligence would eventually become indistinguishable from one another.

In 2005, to describe this "impending merger of our biological thinking with the nonbiological intelligence we are creating,"[16] he wrote what has become his most famous book, *The Singularity Is Near*. Kurzweil defined the Singularity as "a future period during which the pace of technological change will be so rapid, its impact so deep, that human life will be irreversibly transformed."[17] He noted that while this rapid change would be neither inherently utopian nor dystopian, "this epoch will transform the concepts that we rely on to give meaning to our lives, from our business models to the cycle of human life, including death itself."[18]

Though he was not the first to use this term, with the publication of this book, Kurzweil became more or less the "unofficial leader and spokesperson" of a broad section of the transhumanist community called "Singularitarians."[19] *The Singularity Is Near* has sold hundreds of thousands of copies and has gained Kurzweil admirers worldwide. This is especially true in Silicon Valley, where the libertarian entrepreneur Peter Thiel, a PayPal co-founder and early Facebook investor, has given financial support to Kurzweil-allied concerns.[20] Indeed, other notable transhumanists occupy influential positions within US government agencies like the National Science Foundation and the Defense Advanced Research Projects Agency.[21] Although not all transhumanists venerate Kurzweil or believe in the Singularity, and although transhumanist beliefs vary quite widely across national contexts,[22] his work encapsulates much of the philosophical thrust of transhumanism in general, and of the spirit behind mind uploading in particular. Rather than see the ascendance of artificial intelligence as a threat to humanity, Kurzweil and his devotees tend to view this as "a final achievement of the project, an ultimate vindication of the very quality that has always defined and distinguished us as a species—our constant yearning for a transcendence of our physical and mental limitations."[23]

Still, writing about transhumanism is often very ideologically weighted—boosters such as Kurzweil, Bostrom, and Vita-More have been active in defining this movement in print,[24] yet other valuable works of analysis by Abou Farman, Susan Levin, and Mark O'Connell are highly critical.[25] Thus I needed to investigate for myself not only what some of the major proponents of mind uploading had to say about it, but how the larger audience for such claims thought of them. I wanted to know the concerns surrounding mind uploading expressed by everyday people. What parts of transhumanist philosophy did they espouse? Did they see mind uploading in a markedly different manner from the founders of mind uploading and transhumanist organizations? What were their most common concerns, what concerns were left out of these discussions, and what could all of that tell us about the perceptions of self and soul associated with these cutting-edge technologies?

Mind Uploading Discourse on Reddit

To begin to answer these questions, I analyzed comments on the top ten Reddit posts about mind uploading. I first engaged in an unsystematic read-through of some of the comments from some of the posts, in order to develop the official categories for my coding. I then categorized the discussion around some key themes—most were themes I saw in the initial read-through and a few were themes I was especially curious about, though those did not end up figuring heavily in these discussions. I ended up coding 977 comments based on eight central themes, with 1,056 total codes because some comments fit more than one category.

Redditors were overwhelmingly focused on debating the ontological nature of mind uploading: whether mind uploading would create an inauthentic copy of oneself or be indistinguishable from—or even superior to—the self associated with one's original body. It was the most frequent topic of conversation, appearing in 32 percent of the comments (see table 6.1). For instance, the initial post in a thread called "A small issue with mind uploading" on the r/singularity subreddit began by laying out the problem:

> There is a small issue with mind uploading: it duplicates your mind instead of transferring it. This means that if you want to be in a computer and only in a computer, you have to destroy (i.e. kill) the original version of you. That's quite inconvenient. If you don't, then there are now two versions of you. For one of them, the upload is a total success and you are now inside a computer, with extended cognitive abilities and the power to travel at will through the cyberspace at the speed of light. For the second version, the attempt completely failed. Nothing special happened, except that there is now a program in the computer, that claims he is you and keeps bragging about how cool it is now to be inside a machine.

TABLE 6.1. Mind uploading discourse on Reddit

Theme	Frequency (%)
Ontology of mind uploading—is it you or a copy?	32
Crosstalk—speaking to one another rather than focused on a particular theme	30
Technical possibility—will it happen/can it work?	17
Ethics—is it good/right, do Redditors support it?	9
Pop culture references—works from film and literature that deal with mind uploading	9
Other	2
Work/economy/philanthropy—how would mind uploading change these?	1
Loved ones/family—effect that mind uploading would have on them?	< 1

Many commenters denied that this was an issue, and explained instead that "The short answer is that a copy of you with sufficient fidelity *is* you, or else you aren't the same person as you were yesterday. That version of you had entirely different brain chemistry, a day's fewer memories, different electrons, different neurochemicals, we change *all the time*. Sure, a copy of you isn't exactly you as you are at this minute, but neither will you be in fifteen minutes."

Others argued that the self was fundamentally a misapprehension to begin with. As one Redditor on this same thread explained,

The error is in the assumption that "me" is somehow one discrete individual entity. It does feel like that yes. But that's an illusion. MRI shows that brain activity just moves from one place of the brain to another. Some parts of the brain work at one time then in the next moment, completely different parts are active, while the ones active before are completely dead. It feels continuous and as one whole. But it appears it's not. So it's an illusion. This way it would be theoretically possible to create a transition of consciousness from biological brain to computer. The consciousness moves around our brain. It would just move a bit further.

Some contrarians did insist on the fidelity of the original person, however. As one such commentator mockingly questioned, "Why

would I care about the experiences my copy would have? I'll be dead."
Another skeptic put it more generously:

> I think it's fair to point out this informational immortality is predicated
> on a dead end for one version of the self, an experience the copy won't
> have—a moment of divergence and loss that will, I think, still be pain-
> ful (incoherent as the concept of "self" undoubtedly is). Further, the
> uploaded self *won't have a body* and—speaking for myself—I can't disen-
> tangle self from mind from bodily experience. It's all one.

These discussions also frequently dovetailed into debates over the feasi-
bility of different forms of mind uploading: Will it ever even be possible
to copy one's brain into a computer, and to transfer that brain into some
sort of cloned body? How would that work, when might it happen, and
in what particular capacities? This theme appeared in 17 percent of the
comments in my sample, though in reality this category may be a little underrepresented in my coding, because lots of the posts about the
ontological nature of mind uploading assumed that this was technically
possible, though they didn't explicitly debate that point.

For instance, another post on the r/singularity subreddit was entitled
"Why is everyone here so sure mind uploading is possible?" It read,

> I consider myself a transhumanist. I was brought into the fold though
> Kurzweil, although I have now come to reject many of his crazier ideas,
> like a lot of people here. What I don't understand is why so many people
> on this sub are certain that mind uploading is at all possible. The idea of
> meaningfully transferring your consciousness (ie more than just making
> a copy of your brain patterns) onto a computer is totally unsupported by
> our current understanding of brain science, and no one has even sug-
> gested a theoretical method of doing so.

Many commenters rose to the challenge of this provocation. One wrote,

> It's important to note that we are already working on the science of per-
> fectly preserving the synaptic connectivity of the entire human brain for
> long-term storage. I disagree with OP's claim that meaningfully transfer-
> ring your consciousness onto a computer is unsupported by our current

understanding of brain science; however, even accepting that flawed assumption, it is certainly possible that future technologies might enable a perfectly preserved brain to be restored to its original functioning biological state.

Another asserted, "The brain is a machine, it exists in the physical world and as a tangible object, can be replicated like any other . . . provided we have enough computing power. Remember that no matter how absurd it may seem, the evidence concludes that consciousness is simply the result of the operations of your 'brain patterns.'"

At times these debates delved explicitly into the ethics of mind uploading. In 9 percent of the comments in the sample, Redditors weighed in on the pros and cons of the procedure, and whether it was morally acceptable to upload one's mind into a computer or a new body and then kill one's original body. For example, one thread discussed the controversy around a story about the brain preservation company called Nectome in *MIT Technology Review*, entitled "A startup is pitching a mind-uploading service that is '100 percent fatal.'" This article gave the false impression that people were killing themselves to donate their brains to Nectome, and ended up creating a significant backlash against the company.[26] Some Redditors commenting on it were part of this backlash. "Wanting to live forever is the apotheosis of being scared of the unknown, being terrified of being forgotten and left to rot in irrelevancy," wrote one such commenter. That Redditor continued,

> It's also the product of outdated religious thinking, placing mankind as originally immortal, thrown down to earth from the garden of eden as a punishment. To want to die is to stare into the abyss and embrace it, in the same way that all of life does. Acceptance of true death is framing humanity as a piece of the puzzle, not the true meaning of the puzzle—that's the religious view on humanity's place.

Another Redditor approvingly cited a quote from the tech critic Michael Hendricks, stating in agreement, "I hope future people are appalled that in the 21st century, the richest and most comfortable people in history spent their money and resources trying to live forever on the backs of their descendants."

However, many more supported Nectome and mind uploading in general. Responding to the quote above, one user replied,

> I quite disagree. The notion that brain uploads equals "trying to live for-ever on the backs of their descendants" is ridiculous. There's no rational where one can realistically assume that an uploaded individual would be living on in a manner significantly different than when in a biological body. "Rent" would likely change to "virtual machine hosting," but his wording makes it sound like he expects this to be some kind of public utility, provided for by organic citizens.

"Wanting to live forever is the most ancient human pursuit. it's one of the primary reasons we still have so many people believing in all the ridiculous variations of an afterlife," wrote another supportive Redditor. Yet another exclaimed, "People that stand in the way of immortality tech deserve to wait at the back of the line when it's finally invented." Many others on these threads simply chimed in without much elaboration just to say they approved of mind uploading and would do it if they ever got the chance.

These conversations did not always tread on such serious philosophi-cal ground, however. Pop culture references abounded, as the only prec-edents for much of mind uploading theory come from science fiction and other similarly speculative works. In 9 percent of the sample, Red-ditors discussed films and novels like *The Prestige*, in which a magician perfects a teleportation trick by creating a copy of himself and killing the original each time. They similarly discussed Star Trek–style transport-ers, hypothesizing that such transporters might have worked by making precise copies of crew members in new locations while killing the origi-nals. Other science fiction tales like John Barnes's *A Million Open Doors* and Greg Egan's *Permutation City* made appearances as well. Redditors in these posts also discussed an ancient thought experiment called the "Ship of Theseus," in which a vessel is gradually replaced, piece by piece, until eventually none of the original pieces remain. The point of this thought experiment is to call into question the nature of identity and authenticity, and in this context, to line up nicely with one theoretical method of mind uploading in which the brain is replaced, neuron by neuron, with synthetic copies of those neurons.

But lots of seemingly important considerations were almost entirely left out of these discussions. Only 1 percent of the posts discussed the effects of mind uploading on things like work, the economy, or philanthropy—that is, what people would do for a living or how society would function if virtual immortality was fully realized. Philanthropy was included here because a small number of Redditors explained what they would do to better society if they became immortal in newly fashioned bodies or computers. For example, in a post about what people would do with their digital immortality, one Redditor commented, "If I am in a robot body, build houses in third world countries/dig up wells/Decontaminate water." Another wrote, "I know it sounds corny but I would become a public servant helping third world nations (I can't do that now because of disability)."

Yet posts like these were very few. The economic implications of mind uploading were also surprisingly under-discussed. There was one substantive conversation in the comments of one particular post that was kicked off by this critical comment: "More people? More resources, please. We're running out of space and resources. We need less people in poverty before we make more people. Will creating another 1 billion humans save us from poverty?" Another user followed up with support for this critique: "What do you think is the carbon foot-print of the hyper-rich of today? Now multiple that by many because compound-interest is a monster after 100 years. Rich people tend to be pretty wasteful of resources."

Still, these critical sentiments were often combatted with much more utopian views of the future. One Redditor lamented,

> It's so sad that we can't even image a world where there's no rat race. Why would you need to pay rent? Why can't we just imagine post-capitalism without having to imagine gulags and total cultural stagnation? I think it's naive to think in a 100 years, we won't have replaced capitalism with some AI that manages things on a level that we can't even begin to categorize under the binary of market/central-planning.

On a different thread, another commenter argued in favor of a mind uploading utopia because "competition comes from limited resources. I don't see any reason why the same rules would apply because we don't need food, water and shelter."

Most surprisingly, less than 1 percent of comments on these posts discussed the effects of mind uploading on the loved ones or family members left behind. As mentioned earlier, Reddit's demographic tends to skew young,[27] so perhaps this was due in part to the fact that many of these Redditors were not adults with spouses and children of their own. Still, no one in these threads brought up fairly fundamental concerns about what it would mean to one's parents or friends, let alone one's spouses or children, to achieve techno-immortality. No one mentioned what this might do to one's existing relationships, or to the whole idea of family, childhood, romantic love, or intergenerational memory. At the same time, mind uploading is indeed championed and funded by many adults with spouses and children. So while these results speak partly to the demographics of Reddit users, they also say something about mind uploading as a concept, the enthusiasms it generates, and the issues and problems it overlooks.

Another subset of Internet users, my survey respondents, felt somewhat differently about the prospects of mind uploading. I asked them, "If the cost of doing so was not an issue, would you want to preserve your brain before you died by having your memories and personality uploaded into a computer, and then, after you died, into a new synthetic body?" Only 23 percent wanted to do so, while 50 percent would not, and 27 percent said they would need more information to decide. When I asked them whether they thought that such mind uploading technology would ever be available, 20 percent replied, "yes, in my lifetime," 59 percent said, "yes, but in the distant future," and 21 percent thought that it would never be possible. So while there was actually very broad agreement among my survey respondents that mind uploading would eventually be a reality, there was far less enthusiasm for actually having one's own mind preserved and uploaded in this manner.

Still, I wondered whether those in the transhumanist community who were actively working on issues related to mind uploading had different ideas about its social or cultural ramifications than the Redditors or my survey respondents. To that end I interviewed Bruce Duncan, the managing director of the Terasem Foundation and its Lifenaut project; Eric Klien, the president and founder of the Lifeboat Foundation; Robert McIntyre, the co-founder and CEO of Nectome; and Randal Koene, the chair of Carboncopies Foundation.

The Terasem Foundation is an organization created by entrepreneur, transgender activist, and transhumanist Martine Rothblatt. Rothblatt created Sirius XM Radio, among other tech ventures, and founded Terasem in 2004. Bruce Duncan has been with the organization since then. Terasem created the Lifenaut project mentioned earlier in the chapter. Lifenaut is just one part of Rothblatt's lifelong goal of stewarding society toward a transhuman future where intelligence and the brain are fully digital. As she put it in her 2014 book, *Virtually Human*, many "scientists, innovators, doctors, programmers and dreamers know that human consciousness is not limited to brains made of cerebral neurons. IT is rapidly closing in on creating humanlike consciousness because of what we know about how the brain works."[28]

The Lifeboat Foundation was founded by Klien in 2005, as a kind of think tank devoted to "encouraging scientific advancements while helping humanity survive existential risks and possible misuse of increasingly powerful technologies, including genetic engineering, nanotechnology, and robotics/AI, as we move towards the Singularity."[29] In this way the organization is somewhat skeptical about scientific advances, or at least cognizant of the inherent risks and potential unintended consequences of transhumanist technological developments, but it also accepts as almost a given that we are headed toward Ray Kurzweil's notion of a Singularity. Kurzweil himself sits on many of the foundation's "advisory boards," as do Martine Rothblatt and many other transhumanist luminaries. One of the Lifeboat Foundation programs, called "Personality-Preserver," covers concepts like mind uploading and cryopreservation.

Nectome is a company "dedicated to advancing the science of memory,"[30] especially by pioneering new techniques in brain preservation. It was founded by Robert McIntyre after he and a colleague won the Brain Preservation Foundation's $80,000 "Large Mammal Brain Preservation Prize" for preserving a pig's brain using glutaraldehyde. The goal of such preservation is to keep the entire brain, especially the trillions of synaptic connections known as the connectome, intact while avoiding some of the damage that may come from the more traditional cryogenic freezing techniques.

Carboncopies Foundation was created by neuroscientist Randal Koene as a way to "identify, facilitate, and conduct the research that will deliver whole brain emulation."[31] Whole brain emulation is essentially another way of saying mind uploading, though the way Carboncopies defines it—"a neuroprosthetic system that is able to serve the same function as the brain, and that can safely back-up its state and receive incremental upgrades to its physical design and implementation"—suggests even further capabilities beyond simply duplicating one's existing brain, which Koene discussed with me.

Bruce Duncan was the first mind uploading proponent with whom I spoke, and in his organization's "MindFile" concept we see the connecting lines between postmortem messaging and these more future-oriented, speculative forms of communicating from beyond the grave. After all, at present his organization is not really doing much more than offering people the chance to collect digital data that they already have, and to thoughtfully catalog it. As he explained, "Some people use it as, like, a legacy space to preserve and upload information that can be preserved, even for their own use while they're alive, and I think some people have shared with me that they see it as, at the very least it'll be a rich repository of information about them curated by them." Duncan explained that in addition to journals or photos or videos, people could also scrape their social media feeds and upload that data into the Mind-File, and add a variety of other forms of digital archival data in order "to capture in a qualitative way the phenomena of personal expression of their own unique idiosyncratic personality traits, mannerisms, behaviors, values, attitudes, and beliefs."

At their core, the data in a MindFile are not that different from the sort of things people might upload to a postmortem messaging site, although the goal is not to communicate with others in the near future but to preserve a robust representation of one's self until the distant future when its technological reconstitution becomes possible. Indeed, the option of "Spacecasting" this data out into the cosmos, and the addition of genetic material in a connected BioFile certainly speak to the fact that the Lifenaut project aims far beyond the more prosaic uses of postmortem messaging. Messaging services are rooted in a desire to maintain a connection with one's living family and friends after death, while mind uploading stems from a desire to transcend death itself, and in a manner that would leave behind any friends or family who had not also decided to preserve themselves in that fashion.

My interviews with mind uploading proponents confirmed some of the findings in my earlier review of Reddit threads about the subject. The focus on technological know-how and futuristic possibility was always greater than the focus on the concrete social changes that would occur if these technologies became realities. When I asked Eric Klien of Lifeboat Foundation what life would be like with mind uploading, his answers were vague:

> Well, it's going to be dramatically different, because, like, if the average person doesn't have to work, you know, well, what would their life be like? ... It will be a completely different society. And then, of course, if AIs are friendly but take over, well again, it's still a different society. People could end up being only pets. So whatever is going on, our society won't look remotely similar to how it looks now, a hundred years from now. People don't realize how much technology is about to advance.

Klien has himself been a member of Alcor, the cryogenic freezing company, since 1989, and when we spoke he informed me that he was preparing to cryogenically freeze his dog, Peanut. But when I asked him what he would do with his new life in the future, assuming he was successfully unfrozen, reanimated, or uploaded into some new form, he hedged a bit. Eventually he told me, "Well, it depends on what the world is like, but probably play a lot more games than I do now," meaning video games. He explained, "I bet people will spend a lot of time playing games like that . . . like in a virtual reality."

I asked roughly the same question to Robert McIntyre of Nectome— whether he planned to be preserved before he died and what he would do when he was eventually brought back to life and uploaded into a new body or computer. He replied that he does expect to eventually have himself preserved,

> but I think that the feeling behind it would be one of, like, much more confidence in it. And I hope that I'll look back on my life and think that, you know, I was able to help some people experience that too. And then if I did ever come back, I think what I would be intensely interested in doing is being one of the professionals who helps to rehabilitate and

reintegrate people and take care of them as they're coming back into society to help ease that transition process. . . . But I think the joy of expe-
riencing someone's feelings, that would be very profound, of like, they
didn't think they would live to this time, now they are. You know that
would be truly a wonderful thing to do.

This is a lovely sentiment, but it doesn't say much about what social
life will be like on a day-to-day basis, and one common refrain in these
interviews was that imagining these kinds of concrete details about life
with mind uploading was exceedingly difficult. For McIntyre, the sheer
fact of mortality "basically makes the whole world psychically wounded
to a severe degree. Because when you're a kid you learn that you're going
to die. And then you have to adopt some level of insanity to cope with
that. . . . That has grave consequences for the world, terribly grave consequences. If you got rid of that, if you lifted that psychic burden, it's
hard to imagine."

Randal Koene of Carboncopies initially found it hard to describe
what life with whole brain emulation would look like, but as we continued our conversation he suggested that it was likely to usher in a new
sort of "Cambrian explosion," where

instead of a bunch of new creatures what you end up with is a bunch of
new types of mind. People will decide that they want to extend themselves in one way or another. Some people want to always have the sensa-
tion of existing like a swarm of micro robots or something, so that they're
in many places at once, or maybe they want to merge with others and be
the Borg, hive minds, you know. That is a direction to go into. I can't even
really contemplate all the possibilities that are there . . . even just basic
stuff, like, it could be that some people are mostly going to end up being
aware, and living in the current time perception that we're in, and others
might choose to be living in a sort of awareness that is a microsecond
scale. . . . That would be really weird, but you can think about it.

These transhumanist ideas are, if nothing else, impressive feats of imagination. They are also, of course, profoundly unsettling to our notions
of selfhood and personal autonomy. It isn't particularly clear in the
explanations of the mind uploading enthusiasts I spoke with *why* people

would want to live in a hive mind or on a microsecond scale, or what sorts of problems that kind of whole brain emulation solves for individuals, besides the obvious problem of death. The assumption behind all of it, of course, is that death is indeed a problem that requires solving in the first place.

According to Robert McIntyre, for instance, death is inherently unjust. As he explained to me,

Death is bad because in general, coercion is the opposite of justice. You know, it's hard to say what does a just society look like, but I can tell you what an unjust society looks like—it's one with a lot of coercion, right? And in general, if you want to make more justice, getting rid of coercion tends to increase justice. But you know, coercion can come from other people lording it over you, giving you difficulties, but it also comes from nature and, you know, whether it comes from nature or it comes from other people, I'd say it's still an injustice. So, you know, someone dying of smallpox, or someone being crippled by disease—there's no person that crippled them, but it's still an injustice.

I told McIntyre I was unsure whether I agreed with his definition of coercion, and with the notion that death on its own was necessarily unjust, since everyone has to face death and since coercion implied, to me anyway, that humans are the ones doing the coercing—gravity isn't unjustly coercing you not to float, for instance. McIntyre was unconvinced, in any case, but with a view of death like his, I could understand why he would devote himself to achieving technologically induced immortality.

Still, the lengths necessary to preserve a brain, reanimate it decades or centuries later, emulate the whole thing in a computer and upload its contents into a new body or other new "substrate"—these seemed to imply that mind uploading would be tremendously costly. After all, simply having one's body cryogenically preserved by Alcor costs $200,000, plus a $660 annual membership fee until you die, and that is just to be preserved.[32] I wondered whether mind uploading might end up recreating or exacerbating many of our current inequalities, as suggested in some of the Reddit debates I read, so I asked my interviewees about this. Bruce Duncan reminded me that "a cell phone used to be, like, a really expensive item and really as big as a brick, twenty to thirty years ago. Now they're almost giving them away for free because they're really just a platform for commerce. So I think it depends." While acknowledging that it might not play out this way "in more autocratic and more totalitarian societies," he felt that "in democracies, if we start to value something as being so important and germane and critical to daily life," then it could be accomplished in an egalitarian manner. When I pointed out that iPhones are cheap precisely because they are manufactured in autocratic and totalitarian societies by workers with few or no rights and very low wages, then given to consumers in democratic societies who rarely complain about any of this, Duncan blanched. He told me that this was also "a matter of social policy" and that the Terasem Foundation could only be a small part of the larger conversation that needed to be led by concerned citizens.

For Eric Klien the matter was much simpler, because in the future, "automated technology will build most things, so you know you won't have to pay much. . . . Robots work for very cheap and so once you have robots building robots, suddenly the whole thing is very inexpensive. Instead of using slave labor, you're using robots." I asked Randal Koene whether it was possible to prevent whole brain emulation from being simply a tool for the rich to extend their lives while the poor and working-class died as usual, and he attempted to reassure me: "You can make whole brain emulation as cheap as you want it to be, you can make it available to everyone, if you make it a right and you just say that we afford that for everyone." He pointed to the falling costs associated with integrated circuits and computer data storage, and suggested that there was a natural tendency for technologies to get "cheaper and cheaper and better and better." Indeed, "it's mostly a question of economics and regulation and how you build those social systems and economic systems. If you want to you can make it very, very cheap and affordable for everyone, you just have to set it up that way."

Remarks like these seemed to conflate technological progress with social progress. They evinced a faith that well-worn tech axioms like Moore's Law have always and will continue to benefit society almost automatically. But even Gordon Moore's 1965 prediction that the number of transistors per integrated circuit chip would double every two years, which remained extremely accurate for decades, is on the verge of becoming outdated.[33] Moreover, despite some of the earliest libertarian visions of the Internet as a place free from government regulation, it is worth remembering that the Internet emerged out of US military research,[34] and has proven, time and again, to be subject to governmental regulation and control.[35] Big tech firms are also constantly receiving billions of dollars in subsidies from US cities and states,[36] while also spending exorbitant sums on lobbying those same entities in order to ensure that their unfair or monopolistic business practices are allowed to continue.[37] In sum, there is nothing natural or inevitable about technological progress or the ways it does or does not benefit particular segments of society. And given the wildly inequitable way that even obviously essential goods like food, housing, and healthcare are distributed in the United States and around the world, the eventual equitable distribution of mind uploading technology should not be taken for granted. Yet my interview subjects held firm to their faith in that inevitability with an almost religious zeal, and the imagery to boot.

Consider, for example, Bruce Duncan's claim that down the line, mind uploading might enable us to "travel on a beam of laser light, in the form of a digital avatar that's conscious and can communicate." These new forms of uploaded consciousness will be able to "go visit the stars that are hundreds of light years away, or explore the cosmos . . . to see the cosmos with our consciousness. . . . Or maybe meet ourselves as part of a cosmic pan-psychic consciousness." These struck me as clearly religious aspirations—transcending the body, living forever, unbound by space and time, merging with a universal consciousness. And indeed, Terasem has never shied away from the religious nature of its appeals for technological immortality.[38] But even other, more firmly secular interviewees made similar sorts of claims about the future.

Robert McIntyre, who told me very plainly that the idea of an "immaterial soul" never appealed to him because he simply did not think it was true, spoke nonetheless in terms similar to Duncan's when thinking through the possibilities of human consciousness detached from its physical form. "If you acknowledge that you're basically an information construct," he told me, "then you're really free to do a lot of things that you can't otherwise do. One example is you can actually travel at the speed of light. You want to go to Mars, you can beam information over and you'll get there at light speed. If you're stuck attached to matter, you'll never be able to do it." Eric Klien also mentioned the idea of travelling to "Alpha Centauri" as a beam of pure information, although he clarified that such travel would still be expensive because of the immense energy costs. Randal Koene too made the case that "anyone who's interested in space travel, probably is interested in whole brain emulation. Because if we think of just fitness for the environment, yeah, our bodies are great here, our bodies are crap in space." So brain preservation, emulation, and uploading might have us hurtling through the stars and seeing distant galaxies, but interestingly, these technologies might also discourage humans from having children, at least in the traditional ways. McIntyre told me that "you probably don't have kids, as we understand them, in this future because you can copy a mind." He wondered, "Why on earth would you create a helpless citizen, that is, by their very nature, coerced in everything they do if you didn't have to? If you want humanity to survive and not go extinct, we have to have kids, but I would argue a much more just way of creating more humans would be to take an already adult human mind and merge it with another adult human mind." Koene described a similar scenario:

> If we have the ability to tinker directly with the brain and, therefore, just, you know, turn up certain drive knobs and turn them down as we wish, right—that can certainly change our desire to, say, go ahead and procreate with someone, or even the ability, because the biology that we have then or technology we have may not be the kind where you do that so easily. It might require doing strange things like coming up with how to merge two brains into a new brain or something or whatever. . . . Yeah, so I don't know, I can't tell whether or not people will want to have children as much as they do now, or if they're going to want to have them for curiosity's sake, or because of some other reason at some point.

The future that mind uploading offers is, in many ways, a world without any of the conventions of self, family, or cultural memory that we have come to think of as fundamental elements of human society. The old ways in which society reproduced itself, culturally and biologically, may not survive it. It is striking to hear that mind uploading will, as McIntyre put it, create a new era of history. We won't be in oral history anymore, we'll be in living history. Living history, meaning that humanity has a living memory of events in question that you can go and actually talk to someone who lived through it and has the complete rich context that can only really exist inside the human mind. Basically the difference between living memory and written memory.

Or to hear Koene calmly explain that "once you're in the machine, let's say, or in the robotic body, you could easily make three, four, or five copies" of yourself. This makes sense in an information-centric transhumanist vision of the future, because as Bruce Duncan explained, mind uploading technology might be "redefining what it means to be alive. . . . You're still alive, maybe, as long as your information continues to be organized and accessible." Here we see a toggling between metaphorical and practical meanings of *alive*, because of course we have always been alive in our writing and in pictures and in the recollections of our family and friends—this was the traditional meaning of keeping someone's memory alive. But these things were generally seen as artifacts and memorials to departed souls and selves, not the substance of the individuals themselves. When one switches to viewing everything and everyone as simply "information," as many transhumanists do, this is what can be accomplished—for better or for worse.[39]

Since these technologies are still largely theoretical, any discussion of the affordances of mind uploading must necessarily steer back toward the way these are imagined rather than concretely utilized.[40] True, some services like Lifenaut encourage similar sorts of reflection and reflexivity as the terminally ill blogs or digital suicide notes in the previous chapters, since they specifically ask users to upload content that creates the right kind of presentation of self, and to imagine that self extending into the future, being recreated hundreds or thousands of years later. The affordances of other mind uploading technologies that are less fully realized would seem to have even more to do with the kind of future they enable their adherents to envision. It is a future in which the early utopian visions of the Internet have actually been realized: humans are no longer tied to the limits of physical distance or embodiment, old markers of personal identity have fallen by the wayside, and death itself is obsolete. But accepting many of these premises would seem to demand that users also accept a very disenchanted view of the self.

The Disenchantment of the Self and the Reenchantment of Technology

In his extraordinary book on transhumanism, *On Not Dying*, Abou Farman has pointed out that Max Weber's notion of disenchantment was always connected to modern, secular death anxiety. He noted that Weber's famous 1927 essay "Science as Vocation," which introduced the notion of disenchantment, explicitly discussed the fear of death. Summarizing Weber, Farman wrote,

> In premodern life, as in art, each life is its own fulfilment. In "civilized" life, each life is surpassed. Why? Because . . . the isolated, finite individual with no recourse to an afterlife or a cosmology stands in an infinite stream of progress which, he is aware, will surpass him, making his particular life appear insignificant or meaningless.[41]

To Farman, "this Weberian breach between personal horizons and cosmic ones" was a particularly novel element of modern life.[42] Not simply afraid of dying with no afterlife, modern people are made anxious by the certainty of progress, of life moving on without them, such that they and their contributions are rendered meaningless and ultimately unworthy of remembrance. This, Farman claimed, was the source of Weberian disenchantment—not simply the loss of premodern "magic" but the emptiness of a world anchored on rational notions of progress that inevitably rendered every individual legacy obsolete.

In the final analysis, postmortem messaging cannot really provide more than a temporary solution to this modern, existential problem. After all, the author of a postmortem message—the father on the beach in the SafeBeyond video, for instance—still knows that one day he will be forgotten. What SafeBeyond and services like it offer is simply a salve on that death anxiety, a chance to dip one's toe into transcendence. Such messages are a form of self-help: the value to oneself of knowing that one's loved ones will still be able to hear from you seems much greater

THE QUEST FOR VIRTUAL IMMORTALITY | 185

or more certain than the value to one's family and friends, which is much more debatable. The father in our opening vignette cannot actually know whether or whom his daughter will marry, and whether a potentially gut-wrenching message from her deceased dad would even be welcome on such a momentous day. Such things may fare better in one's imagination than in reality—his message might end up rendering him a party crasher in his own unlived future.

But mind uploading is a more radical solution to the modern denial of death. It reenchants science itself. Mind uploading generates such faith in technological progress that it assumes its own fantastical, magical quality— any imaginable form of existence is possible and seemingly inevitable, from hive minds to beams of sentient laser light bouncing around the stars. Of course, this reenchantment of science is coupled with the concurrent rationalization and disenchantment of the self. The self is simply information, and the sense that you and I are unique individuals with some kind of ineffable essence is purely an accident of the brain's peculiar evolution.

Sobering though that thought may be for those with more traditionally humanistic worldviews, such an informatic, computational vision of mind, self, and existence may not be as incontrovertible as its boosters believe. For one thing, it is worth remembering that AI research has a long history of overpromising and under-delivering, on everything from driverless cars to healthcare decision making.[43] This has been true on the neuroscientific end of things as well: one project that received a billion-euro grant in 2009 was supposed to have fully mapped the human brain by 2019, but could not.[44] This is partly because the human brain and human intelligence are so complicated, but even beyond that, the view of how the brain works that underlies these projects may be based more on metaphor than science.

Research psychologist Robert Epstein has persuasively argued that the brain does not actually function like a computer, and that this assumption—which currently undergirds a good deal of neuroscience and the concept of mind uploading in particular—is simply another in a long line of technological metaphors through which we have sought to make sense of the brain. From hydraulics to mechanical gears to electricity—new, cutting-edge technologies have always been used to explain the inner workings of the mind.[45]

Such metaphors are not, of course, adequate representations, and so Epstein noted that

> we are *not* born with: *information, data, rules, software, knowledge, lexicons, representations, algorithms, programs, models, memories, images, processors, subroutines, encoders, decoders, symbols, or buffers*—design elements that allow digital computers to behave somewhat intelligently. Not only are we not *born* with such things, we also don't *develop* them—ever.[46]

Memories are not actually stored in or retrieved by the brain in the ways that data are stored in and retrieved by a computer. Instead, it is better to think of the brain as being *changed* by experiences, in all sorts of deeply contextualized and unique ways. "Because neither 'memory banks' nor 'representations' of stimuli exist in the brain," he writes, "and because all that is required for us to function in the world is for the brain to change in an orderly way as a result of our experiences, *there is no reason to believe that any two of us are changed the same way by the same experience*."[47]

This model of the mind and brain, which cognitive psychologist Anthony Chemero has called "radical embodied cognitive science," posits that "cognition is to be described in terms of agent-environment dynamics, not in terms of computation and representation."[48] Interestingly, this vision of embodied cognition is heavily influenced by James Gibson's work,[49] which is also where the term "affordances" was coined—inspiring the many subsequent theorists who would eventually apply the term to media technologies and online platforms. The larger point, in any case, is that the brain is not in fact a computer, operating on the same highly portable protocols that a computer does, but is rather deeply enmeshed in its particular biological and social context. From this perspective, the assumptions of mind uploading that depend on these computational metaphors ought to be greeted with skepticism. The disenchanted, mechanistic view of the self and transcendence on offer in mind uploading is not on as firm philosophical or empirical footing as its many devotees might suggest.

At the same time that it largely renders selfhood and personal identity meaningless, however, mind uploading and the larger transhumanist movement reenchant the very notion of science into something approaching religion. Indeed, a 2012 article entitled "Transhumanism as a Secularist Faith" by Hava Tirosh-Samuelson made this case:

> Contemporary transhumanism theorizes about the human species in ultimate terms: it seeks transcendence by means of technology; it has authoritative doctrines, texts, and leaders, as well as normative beliefs and values; it articulates an eschatological vision that gives historical coherence and a narrative of directionality to trajectories of technological change; and it offers an ethical vision in which technological innovation is *the* central human achievement and thereby becomes the medium for achieving authenticity, liberty, and justice. . . . By all measures, then, transhumanism functions as a religion, albeit a secularized one.[50]

Put another way, "transhumanism is the most respectable and influential social movement today that specifically advocates replacement of traditional religions with a science-based alternative that could achieve all the traditional supernatural goals."[51] In sum, although they remain a long way from recreating a brain inside a computer, transhumanists have already recreated religion inside science. If nothing else, this is a clever way to salve the death anxiety of a subset of our most secular, tech-savvy citizens.

Conclusion

Postmortem messaging and mind uploading form two points on a kind of spectrum, extending toward the heavens. Though they both seek to extend one's reach beyond death, accessing the postmortem messaging sites that I studied was generally inexpensive, and often free. The sites themselves were maintained largely as hobbies, by people whose motivation stemmed from earthly, affective attachments to children, spouses, parents, and other loved ones, and the same desire for mnemonic freedom articulated in earlier chapters of this book. Postmortem messaging leveraged the phenomenon of absent presence, in a very calculated manner, to make it seem as if a departed loved one truly was still communicating. Though it felt, as I interviewed the postmortem messaging site creators, that I was recording the final days of a dying industry, it was hard not to root for them. It was hard not to understand the value of the services they were offering, and to see that despite some of the outlandish press they received, these services fulfilled some of the same, modest needs detailed throughout the rest of this book for confronting grief and the fear of death on a very human scale.

Mind uploading seems to exist further along that spectrum, further from everyday, earthly concerns or attachments. And though I also deeply enjoyed and appreciated my conversations with transhumanists about mind uploading, and was enlightened by reading the many Reddit comments I collected, I found it harder to root for this vision of the future to take hold. For instance, although inequality of access seemed to me to be an inherent and very serious issue with what they were proposing, the mind uploading enthusiasts largely ignored or brushed it off as in fact a rather easy problem to overcome. Yet I am not alone in these concerns. Writing about the dangers of a future filled with transhumanist digital enhancements, Alexander Thomas exclaimed that "rejecting an advanced technological orthodoxy could potentially render someone socially and economically moribund (perhaps evolutionarily so), while everyone with access is effectively forced to participate to keep up."[52] In other words, rather than simply feeling freed from the limits of their biological bodies, many people might feel coerced to digitally enhance themselves in uncomfortable ways, simply to remain economically competitive. Moreover, there is an undeniable whiff of eugenics around the transhumanist ideal of purposefully evolving a new and superior species of human being,[53] although certainly none of my interviewees spoke about mind uploading in such terms.

At the very least, mind uploading, whole brain emulation, and the various creative new types of human consciousness that they prophesize would seem to rely on a thoroughly disenchanted or devalued view of our existing conceptions of self, identity, and interpersonal connection. These technologies would undoubtedly represent tremendous feats of scientific achievement if ever fully realized. But what is a self without the threat of its own finitude? Why devote oneself to a place, a career, a spouse, a family, or to building any kind of coherent life if we can exist forever, and be whatever? Why make the most of our moments with those we love and care about if those moments never have to end, if we can always come back to them at some point in an endless future? A life spent bouncing around the cosmos as a beam of laser light, or as one of a dozen copies of an emulated brain in a cryonic freezer, is not really a life at all in the ways that we currently understand the term. In the end, it doesn't really seem to provide the things that make existence worth preserving or extending in the first place.

Conclusion

COVID-19, Collective Memory, and the Limits of Digital Transcendence

"I love you with all my heart. I love you so much. Take care of your mother. I love you." These were the last words of a thirty-five-year-old father of seven as he lay dying in a hospital bed from the COVID-19 virus in February 2021. On his stomach, his face covered by a ventilator mask, he recorded this message and sent it from a digital device that he had used to stay connected to his family throughout his illness.[1] Given the highly contagious and highly lethal nature of the virus, scenarios like this were all too common, and videos like this one often spread quickly on social media. One forty-three-year-old mother commented on the seriousness of the novel coronavirus in a video clip posted to Facebook before her death: "It's not a joke. I don't know what more or how much more I could express." She continued, "Never in my life did I ever think that I would be fighting for my breath, something that we take for granted every day when we wake up. . . . Please do not put your families at risk. . . . Put your masks on. Don't go out if you don't have to."[2]

Messages like these were also sometimes circulated to the press by family members as a public service, to help broadcast the dangers of COVID-19 to portions of the population who downplayed the risks, or to reinforce the importance of preventative measures like mask wearing and, later, vaccination. There were other reasons as well. One twenty-eight-year-old Mexican father's final video was shared with a California-based news outlet by his family living in the United States. In the video the man, who had worked as a nurse and had been helping others fight COVID-19, told his loved ones that he believed he would survive, but that he hoped that "no matter what happens, and the prognosis that God has reserved for me, you always remember me for who I was and who I am." His family took the video and the story to the press because the man's illness and death, coupled with the death of his sister and the illnesses of several other family members from COVID-19, had left the family $50,000 in debt. They were seeking donations to a GoFundMe page.[3]

Beyond raising money from crowdfunding sites—itself typically a losing proposition[4]—one wonders what role these sorts of digital videos will play over time in the lives of surviving family members and friends. How many people have died in a similar manner during this pandemic, with loved ones watching online? And what does it mean to those doing the recording, digitally documenting their own demise during a global pandemic that has physically isolated them from those they hold dear? As of this writing, we are still mired in the grip of this devastating pandemic. But even though we don't know how, when, or whether the COVID-19 pandemic will really end, the ideas discussed throughout this book can help us understand the ways that we have thus far experienced this moment of mass death, and the role of digital media in those experiences.

As such, these concluding pages will highlight the tensions and unresolved issues surrounding death and the digital self during COVID-19: how the Internet allows for deep interpersonal connections amidst mass death, but also provides fertile ground for highly polarized debates about the meaning of such death; how the notion of one's personal or cultural legacy can be made or unmade in online spaces; and how digital reenchantments may at once provide the possibilities for creative, populist efforts at extending the self beyond the limits of the mortal human body, while also papering over the more exploitative or unequal elements of life and death online.

As of this writing, COVID-19 has killed over a million people in the United States and 6.32 million people worldwide. There have been at least 86 million cases in the United States and 539 million cases globally,[5] and there is reason to think that all of these numbers are undercounts of the actual totals.[6] It is reasonable to assume, then, that a massive number of people have had the kind of technologically mediated experience, described above, of the death of a loved one due to COVID-19. What effect will that have on cultural attitudes toward death and digital media? For that matter, what effects are digital media having on attitudes toward death from this novel coronavirus?

The modern, highly medicalized experience of dying has often been a lonely and alienating one,[7] of course, and the pandemic has increased these feelings exponentially by making it frequently impossible for the dying to have any visitors at all.[8] "The historical image of a good death where one can exercise final control to die at home accompanied by friends or family continues in contemporary times," as does the related fear of dying alone or in a hospital intensive care unit without loved ones present.[9] Yet the conditions of the novel coronavirus have made such good deaths impossible for so many. In such a context, digital communication technologies have proven vital for the ill, the dying, and their loved ones who often can communicate with one another only through digital devices.

In the early days of the pandemic, Americans seemed united—at least as much as they can be during this hyper-polarized era—in an effort to "flatten the curve." This meant doing what needed to be done to avoid infection and maintain capacity in hospitals and other medical facilities. Despite initial missteps in public health messaging,[10] the response to COVID-19 in the spring of 2020 did indeed involve a successful public effort to mask up, work from home if possible, and switch to remote schooling in many locations.[11] During this period, the experience of staying connected to ill or simply isolated loved ones from great distances served as a reminder of the myriad ways that digital technologies can bring people together. Since the inception of social networking sites, such sentiments have often been treated as little more than marketing clichés, but in this case they rang true. Undoubtedly during the course of the pandemic, many Americans found themselves emotionally invested in digital media as never before. The Internet helped keep many of us safe from severe illness or death as we Zoomed into classrooms, work meetings, hangouts with friends, dinners with parents and grandparents, and a variety of other social interactions. Few would suggest that these digital interactions were superior to face-to-face contact, but surveys showed that a majority of Americans were glad to have these digitally mediated options.[12]

This moment of seeming unity quickly and predictably unraveled, however, and a larger political backlash against masks and vaccines soon came to dominate public discourse. Certainly the massive amount of conspiracy theorizing around the pandemic,[13] coupled with the wide amount of anti-mask and anti-vaccine sentiment,[14] and the way these things have fallen into place along heavily politically partisan lines,[15] can be blamed in part on the ways that social media platforms like Facebook and YouTube surface content and connect people.[16] These things also speak to the kind of tribalism that Ernest Becker claimed was a result of "immortality projects" gone awry. The impossibility of one's individual survival can always be offset by identifying with a larger group, but the survival of one's own group is often predicated on the destruction of threatening others.[17] This response to the threat of COVID-19 was evident in early efforts by the Trump administration and other Republicans to label it "the China virus" or to blame illegal immigrants for hastening its spread.[18]

Indeed, the intensity of anti-mask and anti-vax sentiment suggested to some commentators that the American right wing seemed to be dying just to spite the left.[19] After all, many far-right Republicans were suddenly staunchly opposed to basic lifesaving measures that would have secured the safety of many members of their own group.[20] But buoyed by Fox News and social media echo chambers, anti-vaccine and anti-mask Republicans had come to see themselves as bastions of individual liberty holding back against the tyranny of the majority.[21]

That sort of right-wing political stance generated its own digital backlash in places like the r/HermanCainAward subreddit. This Reddit page, named after the onetime Republican presidential candidate who died of COVID-19 shortly after attending a Trump rally unmasked, was a crowdsourced collection of "between two and 16 screenshots of a social media profile . . . belonging to someone who died after aggressively rejecting precautions that could have protected them and others."[22] The goal of this collection appeared to be simply a postmortem public shaming of the defiantly anti-vaccine, anti-mask, or COVID-19 conspiracy theorists, coupled with the catharsis and fleeting in-group bonding that came with it. This digital backlash was mimicked, to a certain extent, in President Biden's own remarks beginning in the summer of 2021 that, given the widespread availability of vaccines in the United States, we had entered into a "pandemic of the unvaccinated."[23]

However, subsequent information about the prominence of breakthrough infections, especially with the rise of the Delta and Omicron variants, and the delayed approval of the vaccine for younger people, demonstrated the flaw in such political framing.[24] In fact, variables like race, household income, and insurance status have been almost just as strong predictors of vaccination status as one's political affiliation, although the racial gap has begun to close in the United States. This should remind us that issues of access and equity are just as important as political identity when it comes to vaccination.[25] Moreover, these sorts of political conflicts hide the greater inequalities at the root of vaccine uptake in the United States; and of course globally there is an even greater disparity in the number of vaccines available to the citizens of rich and poor countries.[26]

In any case, as of this writing, COVID-19 has continued in a pattern of waves and lulls as new variants emerge and become dominant, with each successive wave rendering the original generation of vaccines less effective at preventing infection, transmission, and even hospitalization and death.[27] The herd immunity that some epidemiologists and many pundits and politicians assured us would develop out of all this has not come to pass[28]—we now know that people can get infected multiple times and that each infection raises the likelihood of one of the panoply of long-term side effects known as "long COVID."[29] Despite all this, elite pundits and politicians on both the left and right eventually pushed public opinion in the United States toward a kind of consensus against masks and for the importance of in-person work and school,[30] while other potential public health investments to improve the ventilation of schools and workplaces have largely not been made.

Given all of that, it is hard to know what to make of the "denial of death" hypothesis and its various iterations discussed throughout this book. Are people denying death by refusing to get vaccinated or wear masks in public spaces? Or are they accepting it? Given the now bipartisan push to get back to normal and remove mask mandates, or to look the other way as vaccine efficacy wanes, all in the face of over a million US deaths, can it be said that American society has sequestered such deaths? Or has it come to terms with them and embraced them? In some ways, the US response to COVID-19 shows that these are the wrong questions. A better set of questions would revolve around whose deaths matter and whose don't. Whose experiences with this deadly virus get pushed to the forefront of mass media—both traditional and digital—and whose are forgotten? Will the lives of those who died from

COVID-19 matter; will they be part of any broader effort to make the planet safer and healthier? And what role are digital platforms and online technologies likely to play in all of this? The early answers to these questions are not particularly inspiring.

For instance, the deaths of so many Americans and so many more worldwide seem to call for a memorial, some means to commemorate this monumental loss. But in some ways, the scale of loss is almost too great—prevailing memorial aesthetics that incorporate the names of the dead, for instance,[31] simply can't accommodate a tragedy with this many victims. To commemorate the first 100,000 American COVID-19 victims, the *New York Times* listed the names and brief biographical information for 1,000 victims on the paper's entire front page and three inside pages of its May 24, 2020, issue. It also produced an interactive web page called "An Incalculable Loss" that represented these names in chronological order in a manner that demonstrated the growing number of deaths over time. An art installation by Suzanne Brennan Firstenberg called *In America: Remember* similarly took up the challenge by planting 660,000 small white flags on the national mall in Washington, DC, between September 17 and October 3, 2021. Each flag represented an American victim of the COVID-19 virus at that point in time.

Another attempt at memorializing the victims in their individuality has been Faces of COVID. Alex Goldstein started the Twitter account @FacesofCOVID in March 2020. Using news reports, obituaries, and submissions from readers, this account with over 152,000 followers has posted biographical sketches of more than 6,000 COVID-19 victims. Though this is a proverbial drop in the bucket, its creator viewed it as a small way to help with the normal mourning rituals that were often thrown into chaos by COVID-related restrictions on public gatherings. As Goldstein put it, "It's a place where [family members] can share their loved one's story and see people from all over the country and all over the world saying, 'Your loved one meant something, and even if I didn't know them, we are all less because they're not here anymore, and we all share in your sadness.'"[32]

Some of the tweets at Faces of COVID shared simple memories of the character of those lost, like "Carole had such beauty and grace, and an infectious personality, including wit, charm, and a phenomenal sense of humor." Or "I never heard a bad thing said about Bill ever. He befriended everyone." Sometimes the account retweeted responses from loved ones of the deceased. One such tweet read, "The story of my partner . . . was one of your earliest posts back in April/May 2020. I have always been grateful for the comfort it gave me. I read all your posts every day to honor those who have been lost." Still others wrote in to use their loved ones' deaths as cautionary tales. One such tweet read, "My dad was anti-vax and anti-mask, he paid for that with his life."

What the Faces of COVID Twitter account, the temporary *In America: Remember* memorial, and the r/HermanCainAward subreddit all grappled with was the question of legacy. These memorial efforts asked us to ponder the meaning of these deaths, collectively and individually. If we established that meaning, they tested whether we could cement it in the physical landscape or in a digital space in a way that would do justice to the enormity of what had been lost. Of course, there are plenty of reasons to be skeptical about the possibility of ever settling on a permanent narrative about COVID-19, due to the atomizing nature of pandemic-era social distancing, the profoundly polarizing national context in which it has been received, and the fact that—as of this writing, at least—the pandemic shows no signs of stopping. As sociologist Christina Simko put it, "Meaningful commemoration—commemoration with the power to ameliorate grief, foster solidarity, and restore trust in the social—requires capacities for ritualization and narrativization that are strikingly absent in the era of COVID-19."[33]

It is worth noting, however, that the commemorative efforts described in the paragraph above have not been directed by the dying themselves. Although we have seen in previous chapters how the Internet can afford new possibilities for self-construction and self-commemoration to the dying and dead, a quick and deadly illness like COVID-19 tends to rob people of those chances. Undoubtedly many of the victims of COVID-19 have left behind the same sorts of digital data and social networking pages as those who have died for other reasons in the twenty-first century—a scattered, de facto representation of who they were, to be sure. But the inability to purposefully craft one's own legacy is a way in which the scandal of death gets compounded, as we have seen in the book's prior discussion of viral videos of Black men and women killed by police. To suddenly lose one's life is terrible, but to lose control of what that life meant, to be defined by the manner in which you died instead of the way that you lived, is an added form of degradation for the self and suffering for one's family and loved ones.

Indeed, the suffering brought forth by COVID-19 and the digital means by which such suffering has been combatted have not been distributed equally. Not everyone had the technical access or know-how to be able to use the Internet to connect with family members across the country or world. In the United States, twenty-one million households—6 percent of the population—still don't have high-speed Internet access.[34] This kind of digital divide was even more pronounced in the workplace—higher-paid, white-collar workers were much more likely to be able to shift to fully remote, online labor, while blue-collar and service workers were much more likely to have to remain in-person and risk exposure to the virus.[35] Especially because neither the Trump nor Biden administrations issued permanent OSHA guidelines mandating masking, air filtration, or social distancing protocols in the workplace,[36] the poor and working-class have been more likely to be infected and to die from COVID-19.[37] These facts speak to a truism in the social scientific research on disasters—the consequences of a natural disaster like this global pandemic are distributed not naturally but socially, along existing fault lines of race, class, gender, able-bodiedness, and other markers of vulnerability.

In the face of an unprecedented global pandemic, then, we have seen the sorts of things that digital technologies afford, for good and ill. Affordance theory accounts for a technology's features and its outcomes—what it could possibly provide to users as well as the differences in perception and dexterity among those users, and the cultural or institutional legitimacy socially assigned to those various possibilities. These factors go a long way toward determining how technologies actually get used and what they mean to those who use them.[38] Throughout this book we have seen examples of Internet users exerting agency to refashion a sense of self and secure its commemoration after death. We have witnessed new forms of collective memory that combine pushback against police brutality with a kind of subjunctive form of individual commemoration. But of course these actions were always constrained by the technological limitations of various digital platforms, the social norms about who should use them, and the unequal distribution of access to and knowledge about them. This dialectical tension between users and technologies, or between agency and structure, can itself generate new structures over time or make new uses for technologies appear as possibilities. This is the case with cutting-edge, speculative technologies-in-formation like mind uploading, but even as this new technology is imagined and pursued, as this book has shown, the possibilities of new exclusions and inequalities come into focus as well.

The reenchanting nature of the Internet often makes such things difficult to apprehend, however. Throughout the book, we have seen how digital technologies have helped reenchant the very project of selfhood, and that this has resulted in a variety of possibilities for transforming the digital self into the digital soul. These reenchantments include, in chapter 1, the fact that mourning friends and family often view the social networking profiles of the dead as still, in some way, "alive." All communication media generate a sense of absent presence, but as discussed in chapter 2, new and seemingly cutting-edge communication technologies tend to reignite the haunting or uncanny aspects of such absent presence. Chapter 3 demonstrated another kind of reenchantment as terminally ill individuals used blogging to share their suffering with others and, in the process, transform themselves. In chapter 4, the authors of digital suicide notes used the presumption of digital permanence to commemorate themselves, and cement their legacies, by generating a kind of mnemonic freedom. In chapter 5, Black people transformed their own anxieties about police brutality and state racism into a form of subjunctive collective memory. In chapter 6 this sort of reenchantment took shape as people used postmortem messaging to extend their social interactions with loved ones beyond the grave, or to imagine mind uploading as a way to never die at all—or at least be resurrected in the distant future. Each of these examples showcased a new sense of self, with new contours and possibilities for connection and transcendence, made possible in the first place because so much of social life has migrated onto the Internet.

One key theme emerging out of all of these developments has been a kind of populism where everyday people's selves, legacies, and souls can get enshrined as part of collective memory in ways that would have been reserved for only the powerful or heroic in eras past. At the same time, the public reaction to, and usage of, all of the technologies and platforms described in this book has been mixed. Norms around death and dying online are not settled. Postmortem messaging services never really achieved the popularity that early press coverage suggested, and we don't know whether mind uploading will ever be possible or, if it is, whether it would ever be desirable for most people. After all, there are obviously very many Internet users who have chosen not to blog about their illnesses, many recent suicides who have left paper notes or no notes at all, and indeed, the fact that the "right to be forgotten" has been enshrined in law in the European Union and some Latin American countries[39] suggests that many people are hoping *not* to live on, online, when they die. And chapter 1 showed that although much news coverage of digital death and dying was framed in positive or supportive terms, many articles also engaged in forms of "grief policing" regarding the healthfulness or propriety of various communal digital death practices.[40]

Nonetheless, unless we all suddenly begin to stop connecting to the Internet, the issues around digital death and dying raised throughout the book are likely to remain with us. Platforms and technologies may change, but the ubiquity of digital social life assures us that the dead will still circulate throughout our social networks in ways both purposeful and accidental. After all, one study estimated that the dead may outnumber the living on Facebook by the end of the twenty-first century.[41] The authors of that study made that estimate in order to argue for the need to ensure that all of our social networking data gets archived and curated, rather than simply lost to the ages. But whether or not such efforts at widespread social media archiving ever get off the ground, it is clear that digital life and digital death will remain intertwined for a long time to come.

The digital reenchantment of the self enables such entanglements, as this book has shown, but what to make of the concept of reenchantment itself? For scholars like George Ritzer, the idea of reenchantment contains a critical bent, pointing to the many ways that modern capitalist enterprises use simulation and spectacle to distract from their fundamentally exploitative business models.[42] But others have suggested that Max Weber's work always allowed for the dialectical possibility of futures in which magic and charisma did not simply paper over rationalization, but actually provided real alternatives to it.[43] As demonstrated throughout this book, the notion of a digital soul has largely been an ad hoc, grassroots development—a by-product of the self's reenchantment that initially came about as people made use of digital affordances in unexpected ways. But that sort of populist character is certainly under threat from the small handful of companies currently monopolizing the Internet, who may simply choose to change policies pertaining to something like the social networking profiles of the dead at a moment's notice. Reenchantment helps obscure this very reality. Yet as the book has also shown, there remain kernels of real humanity beneath these magical ones and zeros, which hint at a future where our digital selves are treated with reverence and dignity in life and in death.

There is, after all, a persistent way of thinking and talking about the online, digital fragments of our selves that we create, share, and curate. It imbues them with a certain kind of value, a sense that the self and its digital components are more than just the sum of their parts. Such a worldview allows for the concept of a digital soul to flourish. We have seen that this digital soul transcends death—either in the very limited sense that a Facebook profile keeps one "alive" to one's relatives and friends, or in the more particular sense that a digital suicide note can cement one's legacy, or in the imagined notion of a future in which we might literally be kept alive by transferring our consciousness into computers. These varied visions of the digital soul provide a salve to the death anxiety that some consider an inherent feature of human existence, and others attribute to living in a more secular, rational, death-denying world. In either case, it may suffice to say that modern societies are searching for new cultural scripts to make sense of death and dying,[44] and that the varieties of digital death practices described throughout this book are the tentative results of such searching.

As such practices show, grief over the deaths of others often intermingles with the fear of one's own death. But as Zygmunt Bauman once wrote, "The death of others does not affect the continuity of my perception. . . . It is my death that cannot be narrated, that is to remain unspeakable. I am not able to experience it, and once I go through it, I shall not be around to tell the story."[45] Though the varieties of online platforms and digital technologies discussed throughout this book do not literally conquer death, they bring us closer and closer to this unspeakable narrative precipice. They capture the final thoughts and memories of the departed on their social networking pages, suddenly frozen in time at the moment of death. They narrate the course of a terminal illness, in intimate and often punishing detail, until the moment when their authors are rendered unable to write any longer. And they bring us a view into the suicidal mind. Step even closer toward that abyss, and they invite us to imagine our own deaths at the hands of racist police. Further still, and we can keep emailing, texting, and sending videos to those we loved for years after we have actually died—a process that requires imagining our loved ones in a world without us. Move even closer to the edge, and we come to believe that biological death will soon be rendered obsolete by minds uploaded into sophisticated computers. But step back from this chasm, and the fundamental ineffability of death remains. The technologies of digital death may soothe personal anxieties around death in an individualistic age; they may provide new ways to help those who will mourn one's loss; they may be able to affirm one's sense of self and connections to others when one is gone. But death remains in some essential ways unknowable.

The digital soul and its digital afterlife are largely imaginary, after all. They rest on perceptions of the Internet's permanence and the safety of our digital data that are debatable at best, and foolhardy at worst. Websites still get deleted, links rot, and data degrade, much the same way that our physical bodies do. People move on too, as we saw in the comments on AkumaPRIME's suicide note, or on the various blogs of terminally ill authors. Eventually the only ones who visit the social networking profiles or personal websites of the dead are likely to be spammers and bots—tumbleweeds momentarily bumping up against gravestones in a cemetery.

But just because digital permanence is a product of our collective imagination does not mean that it is not meaningful, nor does it mean that its consequences are not real. Reality is socially constructed, as most sociologists will tell you. This means that vitally important social concepts often do not have an identifiable biological or physical location. For example, mind uploading aficionados on Reddit were sometimes flummoxed by the concept of "the self" because it wasn't found in a particular region of the brain, and must therefore have been an illusion. But the self is very real; it is an act of agency occurring across the life course, in the face of a variety of social and technological limitations. Constructing a narrative about who we are, how we want to be thought of by others, and how we ought to be remembered when we're gone is a fundamental act of humanity. To the extent that death can be considered unjust, it stems from the irony that it leaves us unable to control the end- ing to that narrative. As we have seen, the Internet offers us vital aid in that regard.

Of course, as we have also seen, that aid is itself highly unequally distributed. Though in developed countries like the United States, ac- cess to the Internet has risen to very high levels, access itself doesn't always equal the ability to produce meaningful content.[46] Additionally, the various online spaces and platforms where people confront death and dying are subject to a variety of norms about who ought to be there and how these spaces ought to be used. Sometimes this can play out to a marginalized group's advantage, as when blogging became viewed as a kind of feminized practice, which is one of the reasons for the predominance of women blogging about terminal illness in my sample. But often the stark realities of life offline are, perhaps un- surprisingly, the same online—one only needs to think about the viral circulation of videos in which Black people are murdered by police to understand this point. Collective pushback against digital inequalities like these—racism, state violence, and the mass-mediated stereotypes that enable both—must necessarily be creative and tentative, as with the hashtags discussed in chapter 5.

Yet if the online parts of our selves are recast, when we die, as souls in a literal digital afterlife, then clearly this afterlife will reflect the kinds of social problems that bedeviled us while alive. In a way, this isn't so different from the kinds of afterlife beliefs of some hunter-gatherers, in which the physical state of one's remains dictated the progress—or lack thereof—of one's soul through the afterlife.[47] It is also similar to the medieval-era practice of selling "indulgences" that allowed sinning, wealthy Christians to pay their way into heaven.[48] The material and the spiritual, the physical and metaphysical—these have always been dia- lectically entwined. And their entanglements have meant that humans often confront the fear of death through attempts to achieve a kind of symbolic immortality via the permanence of their artistic creations.[49] Today, the Internet affords a vision of personal immortality because, in some ways, it is literally true—those online parts of yourself will remain when you're gone, at least for a time. But of course, the online spaces in which our digital souls will reside bear little resemblance to the peace and perfection of many traditional theological visions of the afterlife.

With that insight in place, the solution to inequality in the digital afterlife is also clear, and it starts on the ground, not in the heavens. Creating an equitable and just society will go a long way toward creating an equitable and just digital afterlife as well. This may be an obvious point, but it is worth reaffirming that our digital souls and their imagined posterity stem from digital selves that are mired in relations of inequality, racism, sexism, homophobia, and transphobia, among others. This is not just a rattling off of the standard laundry list of social justice causes—these intersecting identity points have directly influenced many of the cases in this book. Leelah Alcorn's digital suicide note was a response to her parents' transphobia. The hashtag #IfIDieInPoliceCustody was a response to the death of Sandra Bland. One digital suicide note in my sample detailed the lifetime effects of horrific child abuse. Even the legal battles described in chapter 1, in which the parents of a deceased child had to fight with Facebook to get postmortem access to his page, speak to the perils of digital monopoly capitalism and the need for better data portability laws.[50]

Keeping these examples in mind, we should also be skeptical of narratives of inherent progress that assume that all technology will eventually be cheaply and equitably distributed. The book has taken a skeptical stance toward the technologies behind mind uploading, for instance, but even if mind uploading were to eventually work exactly as imagined by its most devoted proponents, would it ever be made available to most of the people in the world? In a time of skyrocketing inequality, two and a half years into a pandemic that has killed millions across the globe, with the threat of catastrophic climate change bearing down on all of us, many of the world's richest people are focused on building up space tourism as a kind of massive vanity project.[51] Unless our global elites undergo a rapid mindset shift in the fifty years or so that some of its proponents believe it will take mind uploading to really work, the idea that anyone besides the most rich and powerful will ever get to live forever in this manner remains highly dubious.

At the same time, programmers, computer scientists, and hobbyists continue to experiment with new means of keeping the dead alive, like chatbots powered by artificial intelligence. Tech journalist James

Vlahos spent three months recording over ninety-thousand words' worth of interviews with his terminally ill father, then used those words to construct a "Dadbot" who could converse over text with his surviving family members.[52] Joshua Barbeau created a chatbot simulation of his girlfriend who had died eight years prior by feeding all her texts and Facebook messages into an AI called Project December.[53] Eugenia Kyuda, the founder of an AI start-up called Luka, performed a similar feat of engineering after the death of her best friend Roman.[54] Such experiments are meant to salve the grief of surviving loved ones, of course. As one journalist explained when describing Barbeau's interactions with his resurrected AI girlfriend, Jessica, "He wondered: By speaking to Jessica as if she were alive again, could he engineer a moment of catharsis that had eluded him for eight years? Could this trick actually heal his grief?"[55] But such projects also raise issues of consent—in these three examples, only Vlahos's father had actually agreed to be a part of the project. In the other two, the deceased had no control over the fact of their resurrection or how they would be represented by the AI. Today anyone can download the Roman chatbot and exchange text messages with it, but would the real Roman have been okay with this?

Still, it is hard to fault grieving tech sophisticates for doing what comes naturally to them—looking for a technological solution to a universal problem of human existence. The situation becomes perhaps more dubious when it is steered by one of the largest companies on the planet, as is the case with the recent revelation that Amazon's Alexa will soon be able to speak in a manner that mimics any voice after hearing it for less than a minute—including the voices of the dead.[56] Rohit Prasad, a senior vice president at Amazon, said the idea was to "make the memories last" since "so many of us have lost someone we love" in the pandemic.[57] The hypothetical example proposed by Amazon was that of a child who would be able to listen to his deceased grandmother read a new book to him at bedtime. But this is once again a highly individualistic solution to a pandemic that has left many thousands of children missing their grandparents—indeed, over 250,000 American kids have lost a primary or secondary caregiver to COVID-19 as of this writing.[58]

Perhaps most troublingly, such efforts move us further away from the forms of agency and selfhood imbued in other digital death-related media discussed throughout this book. Grafting a deceased grandmother's voice onto Alexa is a far cry from that grandmother actually choosing to record and preserve a postmortem message of herself reading a story for her future grandchildren. The latter is bound up with one's sense of self; it leaves behind a meaningful personal legacy and, just maybe, generates the kind of ineffable quality that I have referred to as a digital soul. The former, however, is simply a means of reenchanting Amazon's home surveillance device[59] and generating new, nostalgia-laden content. But if nothing else, death is about running out of new content. Certainly it is impossible to know whether Amazon's plans here will come to fruition, but like Facebook's near-dominance of death-related norms and practices on social media, the market power alone of a company like Amazon should leave us wary when it wades into such waters, lest we lose what remains of the populist, democratizing element of the digital soul.

The Internet allows us to curate, imagine, invent, reinvent, and circulate a sense of who we are to an audience that is at once intimate and vast, which may feel private when only a few are looking but can turn broadly public at a moment's notice. It allows us to discover ourselves, connect with others, and learn about a seemingly infinite number of things in split seconds. In these ways and more, it is a tool of reenchantment. And when someone we love dies, there are more ways than ever to maintain that sense of enchantment, either because the deceased has purposefully left behind text, images, videos, or other forms of online communication for us to see, or because we continue to interact with what has been haphazardly left behind, or sometimes even because algorithms surface such postmortem content for us. In these ways the digital self becomes a digital soul, a testament to who one was in life that, in at least some small way, transcends one's corporeal death.

But in reenchanting the self this way, we also risk losing sight of the cold, rational calculus behind all of life online today. The minerals scratched out of the dirt that become our circuits and phones. The governments surveilling and profiling us. The untold billions of dollars' worth of data that our digital selves collectively generate for the platforms that sell it all to advertisers. The hundreds of millions of kilowatt hours of electricity powering the data processing centers that store our digital lives, all while the planet continues to warm at an unsustainable pace. Combine all of that with the various forms of harassment and hate found all across the Internet, and the utopian dreams of early Internet pioneers seem to have turned into nightmares. What is clear is that, although our digital selves may at times feel transcendent, they cannot be free until the world they occupy is radically transformed. Until then, the digital soul will inhabit a kind of purgatory—close enough to envision the digital afterlife as it could be, but perpetually reenacting the trials of life here on earth.

ACKNOWLEDGMENTS

In 2002 I worked as a research assistant for Richard Harvey Brown at the University of Maryland. I helped him finish two book projects as he suffered from terminal cancer. He once told me that he thought dying was one of the last remaining taboos—his own openness about his illness had seemed to him to make people more uncomfortable than any other possible topic of conversation. After he passed away in October 2003, I was asked to create a website that would contain his biographical information and some of his unpublished works. I learned a lot from Richard about being a scholar and about what it meant to confront one's own mortality, many years before I would actually make them the subjects of my academic inquiry.

Other mentors at Maryland who deserve my continued thanks include Bill Falk, Lory Dance, and especially George Ritzer, whose own work on Weber and disenchantment informed my analysis throughout this book. My mentors at the CUNY Graduate Center, where I later received my PhD—Stuart Ewen, John Torpey, and Sharon Zukin—also deserve much of the credit for shaping the academic I am today, and I would not be here without their guidance.

During the long time that I spent researching this book, my students at Princeton University, Hamilton College, and Smith College provided me with thought-provoking discussions whenever I brought readings about death, dying, and media technology into the classroom. Beyond that, I would especially like to thank the two students who served briefly as my research assistants: Ian Rothenberg at Hamilton College helped code blogs of the terminally ill for chapter 3, and Maxine Gunther-Segal at Smith College helped code newspaper articles for chapter 1. Also at Smith, Camille Butera designed a special studies course with me on the ethics of digital research methods that helped clarify my thinking on that subject.

Many colleagues have provided thoughtful commentary on these chapters while they were being written and rewritten. Dan Chambliss,

Stephen Ellingson, Matt Grace, Jamie Kucinskas, and Yvonne Zylan gave comments on an early draft of chapter 3 at Hamilton College. Catherine Waite Phelan and the late Tom Phelan were also very encouraging of my work while I was at Hamilton. My colleagues at Smith College's Kahn Liberal Arts Institute in 2019–2020 also provided helpful feedback; these were Kevin Rozario, James Lowenthal, Ambreen Hai, Lane Hall-Witt, Mehammed Mack, Josh Miller, Andrea Rossi-Reder, Ninette Rothmueller, Katy Schneider, and Camille Washington-Ottombre. Smith students involved with Kahn that semester were Amanda Jiang, Patience Kayira, Emma Kelley, Mieko Kuramoto, and the aforementioned Maxine Gunther-Segal. Members of the Five College Crossroads in the Study of the Americas (CISA) Program gave insightful commentary when I presented the book to them as a work-in-progress as well, and for that I thank Ray Rennard, Cameron Awkward-Rich, Alexis Callender, Meredith Coleman-Tobias, Sony Coranez Bolton, Adam Dahl, Fumi Okiji, and Corine Tachtiris. At Smith College, Liz Pryor also helped me strategize about this book and its audience. My wonderful colleagues in the Sociology Department at Smith have always been very supportive of my work, so thank you to Payal Banerjee, Ginetta Candelario, Leslie King, Nancy Whittier, Tina Wildhagen, and Rick Fantasia—with a special thanks to Rick, who also gave me feedback on two chapter drafts.

Chapter 5 of this book is based on a journal article called "Race, Racism, and Mnemonic Freedom in the Digital Afterlife" that I published in the journal *Information, Communication & Society*. I would like to thank the anonymous peer reviewers of that article, as well as the generous peer reviewers of this book, whose thoughtful feedback improved the book tremendously. I am also grateful to all the people who have provided an audience for my work and occasionally asked questions as I presented papers at a variety of conferences over the years. I would especially like to thank Ilene Kalish and Yasemin Torfilli at New York University Press for their enthusiastic support and assistance.

In addition to all the textual data collected from online spaces that went into the book, I interviewed twelve people as part of my research, and I greatly appreciate the time they took to talk to me and the insights I gained from those conversations. Those interviewees were Peter Barrett, Bruce Duncan, Tamar Goudsmit, Tim Hewson, Eric Klien, Randal

Koene, Robert McIntyre, Nicola Piccinini, John Thornton, Marius Ursache, Aristotelis Zournas, and Moran Zur.

My wife, Jenna, and my children, Margot and Simon, have been the sources of joy that helped me stay happy while thinking, reading, and writing about some very sad subjects. Along with the rest of my family and friends, they have been constant reminders of all that is good and worthwhile about our time among the living. At the same time, spending so much of my time thinking about death and dying has kept my late grandparents on my mind. Though they all passed away long ago, I feel the need to acknowledge them as well, since in some way they felt present as I wrote this book.

Finally, I must acknowledge that this book could not exist without the many deceased individuals whose words were collected, analyzed, and often quoted in it. Though their words were not written with that outcome in mind, I thank these authors for the things they taught me not just about death and dying, but about life as well. I hope that I have learned the lessons that they would have wanted to teach me, and that I have done justice to their stories when sharing them with others.

NOTES

INTRODUCTION

1 See Barnett (2011); Bonior (2011).
2 See Brubaker, Hayes, and Dourish (2013); Irwin (2015); Church (2013).
3 DeGroot (2012); DeGroot (2014); Kern, Forman, and Gil-Egui (2013); Bouc, Han, and Pennington (2016).
4 Marwick and Ellison (2012); Bennett and Huberman (2015); Martin (2016).
5 Jamison-Powell et al. (2016).
6 For an exception, see Kneese (2018); Kneese (2019).
7 D. Gross (2013).
8 Parry (2014).
9 Mannix (2014).
10 Quoted in Elliott (2014).
11 Keller (2014).
12 Farhi (2014); McKenna (2014).
13 Jolly (2016).
14 Carroll (2013).
15 O'Connell (2017, p. 6).
16 Bernstein (2019); Farman (2020).
17 Farman (2020, p. 240).
18 See Rheingold (1993); Barlow (1996).
19 See Kendall (1998).
20 See, for instance, Turkle (2012); Turkle (2015).
21 Hampton, Livio, and Sessions Goulet (2010); Rainie and Wellman (2012).
22 Bassett (2015).
23 Cann (2014, p. 113).
24 Steinhart (2007, p. 262).
25 See Briggs and Thomas (2014).
26 Stokes (2012, p. 370).
27 Stokes (2012, p. 369).
28 Stokes (2012); see also Stokes (2021).
29 Mead (1934, pp. 139–140).
30 Cooley (1922, p. 88).
31 Peters (1999, p. 186).
32 Mead (1934).
33 Goffman (1959).

34 Spence (1984); Wiley (2016).

35 Weber (1958, p. 117).

36 Weber (1958, p. 131).

37 Greenstein (2015); Goldsmith and Wu (2006).

38 Parikka (2015).

39 Zuboff (2019).

40 Weber (2011).

41 See Jenkins (2000).

42 Bloomfield, Latham, and Vurdubakis (2010, p. 416).

43 Davis (2020, p. 6).

44 Emirbayer and Mische (1998, p. 962).

45 See Campbell (2009).

46 Hitlin and Elder (2007).

47 SurveyMonkey (n.d.).

48 Bentley, Daskalova, and White (2017); Kimball (2019); Loomis and Paterson (2018).

49 Hauser and Schwarz (2016); Cassese et al. (2013).

50 The survey slightly overrepresented the Asian, Indian, or Pacific Islander and White or Caucasian categories, and slightly underrepresented Black or African American and Hispanic, Latino, or Latin/x categories, by between five and ten points for each category relative to the 2019 US census (United States Census Bureau, n.d.). In terms of total household income, 25 percent of the sample made less than $40,100; 49 percent made between $40,100 and $120,400; and 18 percent made more than $120,400. In all, the demographics of the survey respondents were comparable to overall US demographics.

51 Recuber (2016b, p. 49).

52 Herring (2004, p. 66).

53 Boellstorff (2008, p. 62).

54 Lane (2019); boyd (2014).

55 Cupit (2012, p. 207).

56 See Jerolmack and Khan (2014).

57 Duneier (1999, p. 338).

58 See Clough (1998).

59 National Commission for the Protection of Human Subjects of Biomedical and Behavioral Research (1979).

60 See Fiesler and Proferes (2018).

61 Shklovski and Vertesi (2013, p. 2172).

62 See Markham and Buchanan (2012); Antunes and Dhoest (2019).

63 Whiting and Pritchard (2018).

64 Jerolmack and Murphy (2017).

65 See Lubet (2017).

66 See Lincoln and Guba (1985).

67 Denzin and Lincoln (1998).

68 Lifton and Olson (2004, p. 32).
69 Lifton and Olson (2004, p. 35).
70 See Joralemon (2016); Walter (2020).
71 Bauman (1992, p. 55).
72 Stokes (2021).
73 Georges (2003).
74 Zussman (2012).
75 Ali (2017); Farman (2020).

CHAPTER 1. NEWS COVERAGE OF DIGITAL DEATH AND
THE BIRTH OF THE DIGITAL SOUL
 1 Quoted in Baker (2014).
 2 Altman (2014).
 3 Altman (2014).
 4 Madhukar and Rajaram (2016).
 5 Madhukar and Rajaram (2016).
 6 See Wambach (1986).
 7 See Fairclough (1989); van Dijk (1995); Manzoor, Saeed, and Hameed Panhwar (2019).
 8 I used the Nexis Uni database to search for news articles with the terms "terminal or grief or mourning" and "Facebook or Twitter or Myspace or blog" and "death or dying." The resulting list was quite extensive, but I read through the first 1,500 hits—many of which were duplicates or not actually relevant—and ended up whittling my sample down to 228 unique articles that were centrally about some aspect of online death and dying.
 9 Patterson (2007).
10 Quoted in Heher (2007).
11 Iyer (2016).
12 Johnston and Nappi (2012).
13 M. Harris (2008).
14 Koul (2015).
15 Pietras (2007).
16 Patterson (2007).
17 Rankin (2010).
18 Robitaille (2017).
19 Larson (2014).
20 Quoted in Roseman (2011).
21 Esbenshade (2010).
22 S. Miller (2016).
23 Facebook (n.d.).
24 Heher (2007).
25 Zimmerman (2007).

26 See Kneese (2019).
27 Facebook (n.d.).
28 Bartlett (2014).
29 De Groote (2013).
30 De Groote (2013).
31 Gallaga (2012).
32 McQuade (2013).
33 Kleeman (2014).
34 Balkissoon (2009).
35 Klass, Silverman, and Nickman (1996, p. xvii).
36 Becker (1973).
37 Giddens (1991, p. 161).
38 Ariès (1974, pp. 11–12).
39 Ariès (1981, pp. 562–563).
40 Ariès (1981, p. 605).
41 See, for example, Ariès (1974, 1981); Becker (1973); Bauman (1992); Giddens (1991); Gorer (1965).
42 Dumont and Foss (1972).
43 Walter (1991); Walter (2020).
44 Joralemon (2016).
45 See Bauman (1992).
46 Howe (1992, p. 249).
47 See Wiley (2016) on these debates.
48 Giddens (1991, p. 74).
49 Giddens (1991, p. 75).
50 Giddens (1991, pp. 76–80).
51 Mellor and Shilling (1993, p. 427).
52 Mellor and Shilling (1993, p. 427).
53 Buckley (2013).
54 Buckley (2013).
55 Mullaly (2015).
56 Lasch (1979).
57 Walker (2011).
58 Floridi (2013, p. 211).
59 Turkle (1996, p. 163).
60 Turkle (1999, p. 646).
61 Goffman (1959).
62 Barlow (1996).
63 See White (2009).
64 Robinson (2007).
65 Szulc (2019).
66 Quoted in Kirkpatrick (2010, p. 199).

67 Langham (2015); van Dijck (2012).

68 Goffman (1959, p. 113).

69 Marwick and boyd (2010).

70 See Kidshealth (2018); Lee-Won et al. (2014).

71 Robinson (2007, pp. 107–108).

72 Wiley (2016).

73 Polkinghorne (1988, p. 150).

74 See Cassano (2008).

75 Whyte (1956).

76 See Binkley (2007).

77 Shevory (1995).

78 See Cassidy (2002); Willim (2014).

79 Jenkins (2000, p. 29).

80 Kravets (2017).

81 See Sherlock (2013) for a discussion in these terms of digital "resurrections" of deceased celebrities.

82 Stokes (2015); Stokes (2020).

83 Stokes (2015, p. 244).

84 Kasket (2014).

85 Hamilton (2018).

86 Lewis (1973); Martin and Barrresi (2006).

87 Ariès (1981, p. 603).

88 Ariès (1981, p. 606).

89 Martin and Barresi (2006, p. 297).

90 Wiley (2016, p. 38).

91 Martin and Barresi (2000, p. 1).

92 Martin and Barresi (2000, p. 1).

93 Weber (1978).

94 See, for instance, Gane (2002).

95 Ritzer (1999); Kravets (2017).

96 Sherlock (2013, p. 164).

97 Snyder (2007).

98 Ryan Benjamin (2009).

99 Z. Harris (2013).

100 E. Jacobs (2018).

101 Mosco (2016, p. 3).

102 Peters (2015, p. 332).

103 Ruin (2018, p. 201).

104 This was a fundamental insight of some of the world's earliest sociologists—trailblazing scholars like Harriet Martineau, Ida B. Wells, and W. E. B Du Bois, whose work is not always associated with the study of death and dying, though it should be. See Puri (2021).

CHAPTER 2. ABSENT PRESENCE, DEATH, AND THE HISTORY OF COMMUNICATION TECHNOLOGIES

1 See V. Kim (2020).
2 V. Kim (2020, para. 2).
3 Solomon, Greenberg, and Pyszczynski (2016, p. 6).
4 Solomon, Greenberg, and Pyszczynski (2016, p. 7).
5 Kellehear (2007, p. 15).
6 Stiner (2017).
7 See Pettitt (2010).
8 J. Gibson (1977, pp. 67–68).
9 Norman (1988, p. 9).
10 Davis and Chouinard (2016, p. 246).
11 Davis (2020).
12 See Evans, Pearce, Vitak, and Treem (2017).
13 Johnston and Strayer (2001).
14 Kolodny and Edelman (2018); de Boer (2017), Ackermann, Hage, and Ziegler (2014); Johansson (2014).
15 Conkey (1987).
16 Wreschner (1980, p. 631).
17 Tarlach (2018).
18 See Turner (1967).
19 Watts (2009).
20 Tarlach (2018); Watts (2009).
21 Tarlach (2018).
22 Rifkin (2015, p. 10).
23 See Hovers et al. (2003); Rifkin (2015); Watts (2009); Wreschner (1980).
24 Watts (2009).
25 Hovers et al. (2003).
26 Stone (1976); Breuil (1979).
27 Lewis-Williams (2002, p. 80).
28 Though elaborate burials occur throughout the archaeological record, some have argued that special burials for important or heroic individuals did not become a regular feature of social life until the Bronze Age, around 3100 BCE (see Graeber and Wengrow 2021; Helwig 2012).
29 Petru (2018, p. 9).
30 Sedikides and Skowronski (2003); Mithen (1996).
31 Pfeiffer (1982).
32 Pfeiffer (1982, p. 100).
33 See Graeber and Wengrow (2021).
34 See Melcher and Wade (2006).
35 Sahlins (2022).
36 Hertz (1960, p. 34).

37 Ruin (2018, p. 104).
38 Fields (1996, p. 197).
39 Durkheim (1995, p. 271).
40 Gamble (2014, p. 157).
41 Gamble (2014, p. 149).
42 Graeber and Wengrow (2021).
43 Giddens (1995).
44 Ong (1988, p. 77).
45 McLuhan (1962, p. 57).
46 Ariès (1981, p. 18).
47 Ariès (1981, p. 197).
48 Kellehear (2007, p. 155).
49 Friedman (2009).
50 Clanchy (2013).
51 See, for instance, Man (2002).
52 Latour (2005); see also Bille (2013).
53 Bille (2013).
54 Thomas and Thomas (1928).
55 Arnold et al. (2018, p. 18).
56 Nyord (2013).
57 Bourdon (2019).
58 Barbagli (2015).
59 See Fincham et al. (2011).
60 Steadman, Palmer, and Tilly (1996).
61 Winkelman and Baker (2016, p. 259).
62 Plato (2005, p. 62).
63 Ong (1988, p. 80).
64 Peters (1999, p. 36).
65 Peters (1999, p. 37).
66 Peters (1999, p. 139).
67 Peters (1999, p. 149).
68 Gergen (2002, p. 231).
69 Harvey (1990).
70 Peters (1999, p. 138).
71 Kocamaz et al. (2003); Buerger (1989).
72 Kaplan (2003).
73 Kaplan (2003, p. 19).
74 W. Benjamin (1999, p. 510).
75 See Sontag (2003).
76 Ruby (1995).
77 Schillace (2015, p. 117).
78 Arnold et al. (2018, p. 18).
79 Meinwald (1990).

80 Barthes (1980, p. 27).
81 Lutz (2015, p. 126).
82 Davis (2020, p. 89).
83 Davis (2020, p. 11).
84 Standage (2013).
85 Quoted in Standage (2013, p. 40).
86 Bauman and Raud (2015, p. 2).
87 Brown (1990); Swart (1962); Meer (2011).
88 Meer (2011, p. 3).
89 Ariès (1981, p. 216).
90 Peters (1999, pp. 94–95).
91 Arnold et al. (2018, p. 22).
92 Lamont (2004).
93 See Peters (1999); Arnold et al. (2018); Squier (2003).
94 See Coon (2002).
95 Graves (2007, p. 336).
96 See Giddens (1991); Harvey (1990).
97 See Barrow (2016).
98 Schillace (2015).
99 Schillace (2015, p. 111).
100 Samuel (2013, p. ix).
101 Jalland (2010, p. 5).
102 Jalland (2010, p. 2).
103 Gorer (1965).
104 Blauner (1968, p. 522).
105 Ariès (1974, pp. 99–100).
106 Samuel (2013, p. xi).
107 Becker (1973).
108 See, for instance, Barnouw (1978).
109 See Clarke Dillman (2014); M. Gibson (2007).
110 See Recuber (2016a).
111 Killilea (1981, p. 185).
112 Kellehear (2007, p. 57).
113 See Gorski and Altinordu (2008); Stark (1999); Chaves (1994).
114 Gorski and Altinordu (2008, p. 62).
115 Dugdale (2017, p. 23).
116 Walter (1993, p. 127).
117 Kolata (2019).
118 Macrotrends (n.d.).
119 Didion (2004).
120 Joralemon (2016, p. 25).
121 Kübler-Ross (1969, p. 9).
122 See Feldman (2017).

123 Klass, Silverman, and Nickman (1996).
124 Kolata (2019).
125 Kelly (2017); see also Doughty (2014); Schillace (2015).
126 Cummins (2020).
127 See Uriu et al. (2019); D. Miller (2017).
128 Walter (2017, p. 19).
129 Ruin (2018, p. 42).
130 See Peoples, Duda, and Marlow (2016).
131 Peters (1999); Hall (1980).
132 Lepore (2015, para. 4).
133 Bowers, Stanton, and Zittrain (2021).
134 Veix (2018).
135 Kleinman (2019).
136 Madrigal (2013).
137 Nagy and Neff (2015, p. 1).

CHAPTER 3. SUFFERING, THE SELF, AND NARRATIVE
FREEDOM IN BLOGS OF THE TERMINALLY ILL

1 Erickson (2013, p. 8); see also Kiernan (2006).
2 Pew Research Center (2013).
3 Barclay (2013).
4 M. Chen (2015); Das (2017); Schor and Attwood-Charles (2017).
5 Charmaz (1980, p. 164).
6 Zussman (2012, p. 808).
7 Rettberg (2013, pp. 8–10).
8 See Rettberg (2013, pp. 115–116).
9 Ekdale et al. (2010).
10 McGaughey (2010).
11 Morrison (2011); Pettigrew, Archer, and Harrigan (2015).
12 G. Chen (2013).
13 Powell (2010).
14 L. Lopez (2009); Webb and Lee (2011).
15 Morrison (2011, p. 37).
16 Davis (2020, p. 101).
17 Davis (2020, p. 101).
18 Blower (2016, p. 100).
19 Van Cleaf (2020, p. 38).
20 Van Cleaf (2020, p. 50).
21 I selected these twenty blogs based on a combination of Google searching and following the links from the blogs that my initial Google searches turned up. I used
   Google searches because I wanted to confirm the real-life identities of the bloggers I studied; I wanted to not only find these blogs but also find news stories that
   would confirm that in fact these authors had passed away, and not simply stopped

blogging. I also did this on the assumption that blogs of terminally ill authors could be significantly different from those of simply chronically ill authors, or those blogging about the terminal illnesses of their spouses or children, and different even from those hosted on platforms like Posthope or CaringBridge. CaringBridge, for example, is a free website that helps people with serious illnesses keep family and friends updated about their "health journeys." The site boasts 300,000 daily users and has been active for twenty-five years as of 2021 (Caring-Bridge 2021), so it is definitely a venue where end-of-life blogging frequently happens. I did not study CaringBridge blogs for two related reasons, however. First, CaringBridge allows users to set their blogs to private, and many do, thus marking them as off-limits to researchers. Secondly, even those who haven't set their blogs to private may have an expectation of privacy by virtue of using that platform, whereas the blogs that I studied were more clearly directed at the public. Though this may raise the issue of "selecting on the dependent variable," I don't think it affects the claims I'm making about the things blogs can afford, and it seems an important ethical move regardless.

22 Several of the blogs I initially selected during this process were offline by the time I went to analyze them, necessitating new selections, and undoubtedly there have been other blogs that were taken down after their authors died, which I was thus unable to see in my initial search results. Nonetheless, the blogs in my sample represent the twenty most prominent blogs from terminally ill authors in the search results that remained publicly accessible during the period of my initial research—from November 2016 to July 2017.

23 I did not code any posts written by anyone other than the author herself, since these blogs occasionally featured guest posts from family or loved ones, and I did not code any posts that contained only images or only links to other websites. Four of the blogs contained fewer than fifty total posts, while the majority of the blogs contained many more than fifty posts. But by stopping at that number, I avoided oversampling the most prolific bloggers and was able to focus on the period closest to the authors' deaths.

24 Stage (2017, p. 131).

25 Kneese (2017).

26 See Stage (2014).

27 Perkins (1992); Perkins (1995).

28 See Scarry (1985).

29 Marwick and Ellison (2012).

30 McEwen and Scheaffer (2013); Kern, Forman, and Gil-Egui (2013); Lingel (2013).

31 D. Miller (2017).

32 Bingley et al. (2006).

33 Kneese (2017, p. 182).

34 Stage (2014).

35 Rousseau (1781/1953, p. 17).

36 Gutman (1988, p. 100).

37 Ogrodnick (1999, p. 4).
38 Gutman (1988, p. 108).
39 See Wexler (1976).
40 Saccarelli (2009, n. 6).
41 Ogrodnick (1999, p. 188).
42 Hutton (1988, p. 123).
43 Mead (1934); Cooley (1922).
44 Foucault (1988, p. 18).
45 Foucault (1988, pp. 19–20).
46 Foucault (1988, p. 49).
47 Siles (2012, p. 412).
48 Siles (2012, p. 413).
49 Bakardjieva and Gaden (2012).
50 Schneider (2012, pp. 416–417).
51 Bosch (2011).
52 Rocamora (2011).
53 Belk (1988, p. 160).
54 Belk (2013, p. 483).
55 Haraway (2016).
56 See Bettany (2018).
57 Zussman (2012, p. 808).
58 Zussman (2012, p. 809).
59 Perkins (1992); Perkins (1995).
60 Perkins (1995, p. 3).
61 Quoted in J. Johnson (2014).
62 Hick (1968, p. 290).
63 Hick (1968, pp. 370–372).
64 Hasker (1988, p. 3).
65 Berlant (2011).
66 Warraich (2017, p. 44).
67 Warraich (2017, p. 45).
68 See Charmaz (2002).
69 Steiner (1971, p. 89).
70 See Brook, O'Brien, and Taylor (2018).
71 See Schradie (2011).

CHAPTER 4. SELF-DESTRUCTION AS SELF-COMMEMORATION
IN DIGITAL SUICIDE NOTES

 1 D. Gross (2013).
 2 Helling (2015, para. 1).
 3 Sandler (2009).
 4 Barnett (2011, para. 7).
 5 Bonior (2011, para. 3).

6 Golbeck (2015); Barnett (2011).

7 Hess (2015).

8 See, for instance, Shneidman and Farberow (1957); Leenaars (1988); Lester (2008a).

9 Baumeister (1990).

10 Chandler (1994); see also Lester (2013).

11 The first set of notes comes from the collection of Edwin Shneidman and Norman Farberow (1957), which launched the field of suicidology and inspired numerous other suicide note studies.

12 The second set comes from Antoon Leenaars (1988), who like Shneidman and Farberow culled his sample from the Los Angeles County coroner's office. Both collections have already provided the data for many subsequent studies, for example, Jones and Bennell (2007) and Edelman and Renshaw (1982).

13 I collected the paper suicide notes from 2002–2017 using publicly available news stories and, in a handful of cases, with the help of a coroner from a small midwestern county.

14 I collected the notes from 2004–2015 in online spaces such as Facebook, Twitter, MySpace, and others.

15 Zussman (2012).

16 Moore and Williamson (2003).

17 Neimeyer and Chapman (1981).

18 See Tomasi (2000).

19 Goldney, Schioldann, and Dunn (2008); Brancaccio, Engstrom, and Lederer (2013); Giddens (1965).

20 Giddens (1965, p. 5).

21 B. Johnson (1965).

22 Barbagli (2015).

23 B. Johnson (1965); Pope (1976); Gibbs and Martin (1964).

24 Wray, Colen, and Pescosolido (2011).

25 Centers for Disease Control and Prevention (2008).

26 See Hampton and Wellman (2018).

27 Luxton, June, and Fairall (2012, p. 198).

28 Hinduja and Patchin (2010).

29 Westerlund (2012).

30 Abrutyn and Mueller (2014a).

31 See Romer, Jamieson, and Jamieson (2006).

32 Daine et al. (2013); Baker and Fortune (2008); Harris, McLean, and Sheffield (2009).

33 Mori et al. (2012).

34 See Hasinoff and Bivens (2021).

35 Leenaars (2010).

36 See Tuckman, Kleiner, and Lavell (1959); Shneidman (1980).

37 J. Jacobs (1967, p. 61).

38 J. Jacobs (1967, p. 61).
39 J. Jacobs (1967, p. 67).
40 Wray, Colen, and Pescosolido (2011, p. 522).
41 See Canetto (1997); Zayas and Pilat (2008).
42 Abrutyn and Mueller (2014b, p. 345).
43 See Cash et al. (2013); Huang, Goh, and Liew (2007).
44 Synnott et al. (2017). Those researchers looked to see whether the author of a purported suicide note had posted anything else to their pseudonymous account on
the Suicide Project after the date they posted the note. If the author did not post
anything else, it was assumed that the note was legitimate and its author had actually committed suicide. In the late stages of finishing this book I did come across
a second academic paper analyzing suicide notes from that website, Grayson et al.
(2020), which used the same assumptions about the notes it selected.
45 To find these texts, I Google-searched for phrases like "online suicide note," "suicide note blog," and derivations of the phrase "suicide note on Facebook" using
the names of all the popular social networking sites. I also searched for cases of
suicide on MyDeathSpace, a site that archives the social networking sites of the
dead.
46 I also excluded the notes of any murder-suicides from the list, since these did not
appear to be included in the Shneidman and Farberow (1957) or Leenaars (1988)
portions of the sample.
47 It is also possible these suicides left paper notes as well, to which I did not have
access. In the news articles I used to confirm the veracity of all ninety-two initial
cases, however, I found only one that mentioned additional paper notes, which I
did not include in my sample.
48 See Shneidman and Faberow (1957); Tuckman, Kleiner, and Lavell (1959); J. Jacobs
(1967); Leenaars (1988).
49 Pestian, Matykiewicz, and Linn-Gust (2012).
50 Tuckman, Kleiner, and Lavell (1959) used 165 suicide notes. J. Jacobs's (1967) study
analyzed 112 notes. Sanger and Veach (2008) looked at 186 notes written by 138
individuals. Other content analyses of suicide notes have used smaller samples
than those: 77 notes were examined in one study of Belarusian suicides (Lasy and
Navadvorskaya 2012), 72 notes comprised the sample in a study of female Finnish
suicides (Utriainen and Honkasalo 1996), and several other studies have used
40-note samples (see Zhang and Lester 2008; Bhatia, Verma, and Murty 2006;
Black and Lester 2002).
51 See Jäger and Maier (2009); Ruiz (2009).
52 Centers for Disease Control and Prevention (2008).
53 Goldman (2010).
54 Shneidman and Farberow (1957).
55 Leenaars (1988).
56 See Lester (2008b).
57 Fincham et al. (2011); Samraj and Gawron (2015).

58 See, for example, Rogers et al. (2007).

59 See Illouz (2008).

60 Weaver and Munro (2010, p. 100).

61 MacDonald and Murphy (1990).

62 Minois (1999).

63 Leenaars (1988, p. 39).

64 Fine (1996).

65 See Hogan (2010).

66 van Dijck (2013, p. 199).

67 See Sudak, Maxim, and Carpenter (2008).

68 Timmermans (2006, p. 101).

69 Timmermans (2006).

70 Jan Assmann (1995) distinguished between collective memory, which he claimed was rooted in the everyday, and cultural memory, which was exemplified by texts and monuments that aimed to unify populations over longer time spans. I adopt Assmann's framing here but use "collective memory" elsewhere in the book. For a more detailed discussion on the various terms for these forms of "social memory," see Olick and Robbins (1998).

71 J. Assmann (2012, pp. 45–46).

72 J. Assmann (2012, p. 46).

73 See Yang and Lester (2011); Fincham et al. (2011).

74 Cohen (1965, p. 13).

75 Becker (1973); Giddens (1991); Solomon, Greenberg, and Pyszczynski (2016).

76 Shneidman (1980, p. 5).

77 Stannard (1977, p. 11).

78 Martineau (1838, p. 97).

79 Stannard (1977, p. 194).

80 Shneidman (1980, p. 56).

81 Smythe (1844, p. 529).

82 Baumeister (1990, p. 90).

83 A. Assmann (2012, p. 23).

CHAPTER 5. RACE, RACISM, AND MNEMONIC FREEDOM IN THE DIGITAL AFTERLIFE

1 See also Arnold et al. (2018); Lagerkvist (2019).

2 See Wertheim (1999).

3 Wright (2014); Savin-Baden (2019).

4 Wertheim (1999, pp. 18–19).

5 Noble (2018).

6 Ruha Benjamin (2019, p. 123).

7 Barlow (1996, para. 7).

8 Barlow (1996, para. 6).

9 Kendall (1998); Nakamura (2002).
10 See, for instance, Daniels (2009); Nakamura and Chow-White (2013); Noble and Tynes (2016).
11 G. Kim (2016); McLean and Maalsen (2019).
12 Anderson et al. (2019).
13 Schradie (2011).
14 Brock (2012); Brock (2020).
15 Sharma (2013).
16 Freelon, McIlwain, and Clark (2016, p. 9).
17 Freelon, McIlwain, and Clark (2016, p. 9).
18 Benjamin (2019); boyd (2014); Daniels (2009); Noble (2018); Schradie (2019).
19 See M. Sullivan (2014).
20 N. Gross (2017, p. 417).
21 Cassell (2014, para. 1).
22 BBC Trending (2014).
23 N. Gross (2017).
24 N. Gross (2017, p. 428).
25 Bonilla and Rosa (2015, p. 8).
26 Prupis (2015).
27 Silverstein (2016).
28 Carey-Mahoney (2015).
29 N. Gross (2017, p. 431).
30 Davis (2020).
31 Sweeney and Brock (2014, para. 16).
32 Rathnayake and Suthers (2018).
33 See Hill (2018); Brock (2012).
34 I focused on tweets from the earliest days of each of the hashtags. However, I also wanted to understand which tweets had the farthest reach, so I sometimes made use of the "top tweets" function in Twitter's search feature. According to Twitter, top tweets are determined "based on the popularity of a Tweet (e.g., when a lot of people are interacting with or sharing via Retweets and replies), the keywords it contains, and many other factors" (Twitter n.d.).
35 I stopped coding during the third day of top tweets when it became clear that no new themes were emerging, nor were patterns in the substantive themes changing, and instead the hashtag was increasingly populated with retweets and other forms of signal boosting. This left me with 338 tweets in the sample.
36 Since my initial collection of 338 tweets contained only 58 with the original paired-image format, I sought out an additional 44 image-based tweets for this portion of my analysis.
37 Almukhtar et al. (2018).
38 Almukhtar et al. (2018, para. 1).
39 Almukhtar et al. (2018, para. 5).

40 Although it pained me to do so, I watched all the embedded videos, and made basic notes about the source of the video, how long the victim was on-screen, and whether the actual death was shown on camera.

41 Also, in one case—Eric Garner's—the full, iconic viral video of his death was not included, so I sought it out on YouTube. Similarly, I sought out Sandra Bland's self-recorded cell phone video of her arrest, which was also not included in the *Times*' collection, although it did feature the dashboard camera footage of that incident.

42 See Baudry (1986); Metz (1992); Mulvey (1992).

43 Diawara (1993).

44 Malkowski (2017, p. 203).

45 Malkowski (2017, p. 203).

46 N. Gross (2017, p. 425).

47 N. Gross (2017, p. 428).

48 Poniewozik (2014, para. 5).

49 See, for instance, Matias et al. (2015).

50 Bruns and Highfield (2015).

51 Graham and Smith (2016, p. 446).

52 Gunn (2015).

53 Bonilla and Rosa (2015, p. 9).

54 G. Lopez (2015, paras. 5–6).

55 Carney (2016, p. 184).

56 Jackson and Welles (2015).

57 Hill (2018).

58 N. Gross (2017).

59 Du Bois (1997, p. 38).

60 Brock (2020, p. 172).

61 Zelizer (2010, p. 14).

62 Zussman (2012, p. 809).

63 Dean (2016, para. 28).

64 See Olick (1999) on the distinction between collected and collective memory.

65 Bauman (1992).

66 Becker (1973); Giddens (1991).

67 Bauman (1992, p. 4).

68 Bauman (1992, pp. 125–126).

69 Bauman (1992, p. 125).

70 Recuber (2015).

71 Sharpe (2016, p. 116).

72 Sharpe (2016, p. 15).

73 Dean (2016, para. 23).

74 Plummer (2019, p. 90).

75 Micheli, Lutz, and Büchi (2018).

CHAPTER 6. THE REENCHANTMENT OF TECHNOLOGY AND THE
QUEST FOR VIRTUAL IMMORTALITY

1 Lifenaut, home page, www.lifenaut.com

2 LaPonsie (2015).

3 Kleeman (2014).

4 P. Sullivan (2015).

5 Billingham (2016).

6 Cunningham (2020).

7 The interview with the founder of SafeBeyond took place via Skype in March 2017, while the rest of these interviews took place over Zoom between October 28 and December 11, 2020.

8 Reddit bills itself as the "front page of the Internet," and its rules and structures are meant to encourage free and open debate, though its user base skews male and tech-oriented (Sattleberg 2021). To get a good sense of the discourse surrounding mind uploading on Reddit, I planned to read the first hundred comments for the top ten Reddit posts about mind uploading, for a total of one thousand posts. I searched Reddit for "mind uploading" and sorted the resulting posts based on the most comments. I chose the first ten of those Reddit posts that were centrally about mind uploading—seven of the first seventeen results were not primarily concerned with mind uploading, so I did not include them. Within each post, I sorted the comments by "Top" and read the first hundred comments. One of the posts had only seventy-seven comments, pulling my total number under a thousand.

9 The interviews with these mind uploading figures took place on Zoom between October 26, 2020, and February 3, 2021. My interviews with postmortem messaging founders and mind uploading figures were semi-structured, and lasted between a half hour and two hours.

10 Kneese (2019).

11 See Joralemon (2016); Walter (2020).

12 Vita-More (2019, p. 49).

13 Bostrom (2005, p. 4).

14 Bostrom (2005, pp. 4–6).

15 Ettinger (1972, p. 7).

16 Kurzweil (2005, p. 4).

17 Kurzweil (2005, p. 7).

18 Kurzweil (2005, p. 7).

19 Farman (2020, p. 114).

20 Farman (2020, pp. 115–116).

21 Tirosh-Samuelson (2012).

22 Bernstein (2019, pp. 52–53).

23 O'Connell (2017, p. 74).

24 Kurzweil (2005); Bostrom (2005); Vita-More (2019).
25 Farman (2020); Levin (2021); O'Connell (2017).
26 See Begley (2019); Regalado (2018).
27 Sattleberg (2021).
28 Rothblatt (2014, p. 4).
29 Lifeboat Foundation, mission statement, https://lifeboat.com/ex/about
30 See Nectome's home page, https://nectome.com/
31 Carboncopies Foundation, mission statement, https://carboncopies.org/mission/
32 See Alcor, Membership Benefits, www.alcor.org/membership/
33 Theis and Wong (2017); Sterling (2020).
34 Tarnoff (2016).
35 Goldsmith and Wu (2006).
36 Rushe (2018).
37 See Chung (2021).
38 Bainbridge (2017).
39 See Farman (2020).
40 See Nagy and Neff (2015).
41 Farman (2020, p. 139).
42 Farman (2020, p. 157).
43 See Funk and Smith (2021).
44 Yong (2019).
45 Epstein (2016).
46 Epstein (2016, para. 6).
47 Epstein (2016, para. 47).
48 Chemero (2009, p. x).
49 J. Gibson (1966); J. Gibson (1977); J. Gibson (1979).
50 Tirosh-Samuelson (2012, p. 728); see also Shoffstall (2021) on the blurring of science and religion within transhumanism, specifically around cryonics.
51 Bainbridge (2017, p. 209).
52 Thomas (2017, para. 12).
53 See Koch (2010).

CONCLUSION

1 Rice (2021).
2 Holohan (2020).
3 ABC News30 (2020).
4 Kenworthy (2021).
5 Ritchie et al. (2022).
6 *Economist* (2021); Schreiber (2022).
7 See Moller (2018); Schwarz and Benson (2018); Erickson (2013); Gawande (2014).
8 Hernández-Fernández and Meneses-Falcón (2021).
9 Nelson-Becker and Victor (2020, p. 2).
10 See Roubein and Beard (2022).

11 Courtemanche et al. (2020).
12 McClain et al. (2021); Collins (2021).
13 Uscinski et al. (2020).
14 Gilbert (2021).
15 Galston (2021).
16 De Vynck and Lerman (2021).
17 Becker (1973).
18 Rogers, Jakes, and Swanson (2021); De Loera-Brust (2020).
19 Frum (2021).
20 Scott (2021).
21 Graham (2021).
22 Loofbourow (2021, para. 2).
23 Z. Miller (2021).
24 Kampf (2021); Mervosh (2021).
25 Hamel et al. (2021); Bosman et al. (2021); Ndugga et al. (2021).
26 Irfan (2021).
27 Hachmann et al. (2022).
28 Morens, Folkers, and Fauci (2022); Sridhar (2022).
29 Al-Aly, Bowe, and Xie (2022).
30 Kapur (2022); Kenen (2022).
31 See Savage (2006).
32 Quoted in Dominguez (2021).
33 Simko (2021, p. 111).
34 Broom (2020).
35 Early and Hernandez (2021); Ellison (2020); Wolfe, Harknett, and Schneider (2021).
36 Kimball (2021).
37 Adhikari et al. (2020).
38 Davis (2020).
39 Van Calster, Gonzalez Arreaza, and Apers (2018).
40 Garber (2016).
41 Öhman and Watson (2019).
42 Ritzer (1999).
43 Adam (2009); Lee (2010).
44 Joralemon (2016).
45 Bauman (1992, p. 3).
46 See Schradie (2011).
47 See Hertz (1960).
48 Ekelund, Hébert, and Tollison (1992).
49 Lifton and Olson (2004).
50 See Liss (2021); López Blanco (2015).
51 Reimann (2021).
52 Vlahos (2017).

53 Fangone (2021).
54 Newton (2016).
55 Fangone (2021, para. 98).
56 SkyNews (2022).
57 Quoted in SkyNews (2022, para. 4).
58 Imperial College London (2022).
59 See Clauser (2019) on some of the ways Alexa surveils households.

REFERENCES

ABC News30. (2020, November 12). The cruelty of COVID-19: Nurse sends Valley family reassuring video message hours before losing his life. https://abc30.com

Abrutyn, Seth, & Anna S. Mueller. (2014a). Are suicidal behaviors contagious in adolescence? Using longitudinal data to examine suicide suggestion. *American Sociological Review*, 79(2), 211–227.

Abrutyn, Seth, & Anna S. Mueller. (2014b). The socioemotional foundations of suicide: A microsociological view of Durkheim's *Suicide*. *Sociological Theory*, 32(4), 327–351.

Ackermann, Hermann, Steffen Hage, & Wolfram Ziegler. (2014). Brain mechanisms of acoustic communication in humans and nonhuman primates: An evolutionary perspective. *Behavioral and Brain Sciences*, 37(6), 529–546.

Adam, Barbara. (2009). Cultural future matters: An exploration in the spirit of Max Weber's methodological writings. *Time & Society*, 18(1), 7–25.

Adhikari, Samrachana, Nicholas P. Pantaleo, Justin M. Feldman, Olugbenga Ogedegbe, Lorna Thorpe, & Andrea B. Troxel. (2020, July 28). Assessment of community-level disparities in coronavirus disease 2019 (COVID-19) infections and deaths in large US metropolitan areas. *JAMA Network Open*. https://jamanetwork.com

Al-Aly, Ziyad, Benjamin Bowe, & Yan Xie. (2022). Outcomes of SARS-CoV-2 reinfection. *Nature Portfolio*. Article preprint.

Ali, Syed Mustafa. (2017). Transhumanism and/as whiteness. Paper presented at the IS4SI 2017 Summit *Digitalisation for a Sustainable Society*. Gothenburg, Sweden.

Almukhtar, Sarah, Mercy Benzaquen, Damien Cave, Sahil Chinoy, Kenan Davis, K. Josh, K. K. Rebecca Lai, J. C. Lee, R. Oliver, H. Park, & D. C. Royal. (2018, April 19). Black lives upended by policing: The raw videos sparking outrage. *New York Times*. www.nytimes.com

Altman, Anna. (2014, October 22). Retweet if you're grieving. *New York Times*.

Anderson, Monica, Andrew Perrin, Jing Jing Jiang, & Madhumitha Kumar. (2019, April 22). 10% of Americans don't use the Internet. Who are they? *Pew Research Center*. www.pewresearch.org

Antunes, Débora, & Alexander Dhoest. (2019). We are people and so are they: Shared intimacies and the ethics of digital ethnography in autism communities. *Research Ethics*, 15(2), 1–17.

Ariès, Philippe. (1974). *Western attitudes toward death: From the Middle Ages to the present* (Patricia M. Ranum, Trans.). Baltimore, MD: Johns Hopkins University Press.

Ariès, Philippe. (1981). *The hour of our death* (Helen Weaver, Trans.). New York: Oxford University Press.

Arnold, Michael, Martin Gibbs, Tamara Kohn, James Meese, & Bjorn Nansen. (2018). *Death and digital media*. New York: Routledge.

Assmann, Aleida. (2012). *Cultural memory and Western civilization: Arts of memory*. New York: Cambridge University Press.

Assmann, Jan. (1995). Collective memory and cultural identity (John Czaplicka, Trans.). *New German Critique*, 65, 125–133.

Assmann, Jan. (2012). *Cultural memory and early civilization: Writing, remembrance, and political imagination*. New York: Cambridge University Press.

Bainbridge, William Sims. (2017). *Dynamic secularization: Information technology and the tension between religion and science*. Cham, Switzerland: Springer.

Bakardjieva, Maria, & Georgia Gaden. (2012). Web 2.0 technologies of the self. *Philosophy and Technology*, 25(3), 399–413.

Baker, Darren, & Sarah Fortune. (2008). Understanding self-harm and suicide websites. *Crisis*, 29(3), 118–122.

Baker, Mark. (2014, June 8). Amid the to and fro of the onc . . . *Examiner*.

Balkissoon, Denise. (2009, October 31). Online mourning evolves; Facebook's decision to maintain profiles of the deceased makes macabre sense. *Toronto Star*.

Barbagli, Marzio. (2015). *Farewell to the world: A history of suicide* (Lucinda Byatt, Trans.). Malden, MA: Polity.

Barclay, Eliza. (2013, March 28). Why more patients should blog about illness and death. *NPR*. www.npr.org

Barlow, John Perry. (1996, February 8). A declaration of the independence of cyberspace. *Electronic Frontier Foundation*. www.eff.org

Barnett, Emma. (2011, December 13). Facebook offers counseling to suicidal users. *Telegraph*. www.telegraph.co.uk

Barnouw, Erik. (1978). *The sponsor: Notes on a modern potentate*. New York: Oxford University Press.

Barrow, Logie. (2016). *Independent spirits: Spiritualism and English plebians, 1850–1910*. New York: Routledge.

Barthes, Roland. (1980). *Camera lucida: Reflections on photography* (Richard Howard, Trans.). New York: Hill and Wang.

Bartlett, Jamie. (2014, April 9). Peaches Geldof, "Twitter grief," and the strange, poignant phenomenon of dying online. *Telegraph UK*.

Bassett, Debra. (2015). Who wants to live forever? Living, dying and grieving in our digital society. *Social Sciences*, 4(4), 1127–1139.

Baudry, Jean-Louis. (1986). The apparatus: Metapsychological approaches to the impression of reality in cinema. In P. Rosen (Ed.), *Narrative, apparatus, ideology* (pp. 299–318). New York: Columbia University Press.

Bauman, Zygmunt. (1992). *Mortality, immortality and other life strategies*. Stanford, CA: Stanford University Press.

Bauman, Zygmunt, & Rein Raud. (2015). *Practices of selfhood*. Malden, MA: Polity.

Baumeister, Roy F. (1990.) Suicide as escape from self. *Psychological Review*, 97, 90–113.

BBC Trending. (2014, August 11). #BBC Trending: The two faces of Michael Brown. *BBC*. www.bbc.com

Becker, Ernest. (1973). *The denial of death*. New York: Free Press.

Begley, Sharon. (2019, January 30). After ghoulish allegations, a brain-preservation company seeks redemption. *STAT News*. www.statnews.com

Belk, Russell W. (1988). Possessions and the extended self. *Journal of Consumer Research*, 15, 139–168.

Belk, Russell W. (2013). Extended self in a digital world. *Journal of Consumer Research*, 40, 477–500.

Benjamin, Ruha. (2019). *Race after technology: Abolitionist tools for the new Jim Code*. Medford, MA: Polity.

Benjamin, Ryan. (2009, January 16). Column: Leaving expressions of grief on a Facebook wall. *Daily Pennsylvanian*.

Benjamin, Walter. (1999). *Selected writings*, volume 2: *1927–1934* (Rodney Livingstone, Trans.). Cambridge, MA: Harvard University Press.

Bennett, Jeffrey, & Jenny Huberman. (2015). From monuments to megapixels: Death, memory, and symbolic immortality in the contemporary United States. *Anthropological Theory*, 15(3), 338–357.

Bentley, Frank R., Nediyana Daskalova, & Brooke White. (2017). Comparing the reliability of Amazon Mechanical Turk and Survey Monkey to traditional market research surveys. *CHI EA '17: Proceedings of the 2017 CHI Conference Extended Abstracts on Human Factors in Computing Systems*, pp. 1092–1099.

Berlant, Lauren. (2011). *Cruel optimism*. Durham, NC: Duke University Press.

Bernstein, Anya. (2019). *The future of immortality: Remaking life and death in contemporary Russia*. Princeton, NJ: Princeton University Press.

Bettany, Shona. (2018). Chapter 21: Subject/object relations and consumer culture. In Olga Kravets, Pauline Maclaran, Steven Miles, & Alladi Venkatesh (Eds.), *The SAGE Handbook of Consumer Culture* (pp. 365–383). Los Angeles: Sage.

Bhatia, Manjeet S., Satish K. Verma, & O. P. Murty. (2006). Suicide notes: Psychological and clinical profile. *International Journal of Psychiatry in Medicine*, 36(2), 163–170.

Bille, Mikkel. (2013). Dealing with dead saints. In Dorthe Refslund Christensen & Rane Willerslev (Eds.), *Taming time, timing death: Social technologies and ritual* (pp. 137–156). Burlington, VT: Ashgate.

Billingham, Peter. (2016). 8 digital legacy apps that can make you immortal. *Death Goes Digital*. www.deathgoesdigital.com

Bingley, Amanda F., Elizabeth McDermott, C. Thomas, Sheila Payne, Jayne E. Seymour, & D. Clark. (2006). Making sense of dying: A review of narratives written since 1950 by people facing death from cancer and other diseases. *Palliative Medicine*, 20, 183–195.

Binkley, Sam. (2007). *Getting loose: Lifestyle consumption in the 1970s*. Durham, NC: Duke University Press.

Black, Stephen T., & David Lester. (2002). The content of suicide notes: Does it vary by method of suicide, sex, or age? *Omega: Journal of Death and Dying*, 46(3), 241–249.

Blauner, Robert. (1968). Death, grief, and mourning, by Geoffrey Gorer [Book Review]. *Psychoanalytic Review*, 55(3), 521–522.

Bloomfield, Brian P., Yvonne Latham, & Theo Vurdubakis. (2010). Bodies, technologies, and action possibilities: When is an affordance? *Sociology*, 44(3), 415–433.

Blower, Lisa. (2016). It's "because I am a woman": Realizing identity to reconstruct identity for the female auto*blog*raphical inquiry. *Convergence: The International Journal of Research into New Media Technologies*, 22(1), 88–101.

Boellstorff, Tom. (2008). *Coming of age in Second Life: An anthropologist explores the virtually human*. Princeton, NJ: Princeton University Press.

Bonilla, Yarimar, & Jonathan Rosa. (2015). #Ferguson: Digital protest, hashtag ethnography, and the racial politics of social media in the United States. *American Ethnologist*, 42(1), 4–17.

Bonior, Andrea. (2011, April 30). The suicidal Facebook status: Social networking as a new opportunity for prevention. *Psychology Today*. www.psychologytoday.com

Bosch, Tanja. (2011). Young women and "technologies of the self": Social networking and sexualities. *Agenda: Empowering Women for Gender Equity*, 25(4), 75–86.

Bosman, Julie, Jan Hoffman, Margot Sanger-Katz, & Tim Arango. (2021, July 31). Who are the unvaccinated in America? There's no one answer. *New York Times*. www.nytimes.com

Bostrom, Nick. (2005). A history of transhumanist thought. *Journal of Evolution and Technology*, 14(1), 1–25.

Bouc, Amanda, Soo-Hye Han, & Natalie Pennington. (2016). "Why are they commenting on his page?": Using Facebook profile pages to continue connections with the deceased. *Computers in Human Behavior*, 62, 635–643.

Bourdon, Jerome. (2019). The Internet of letters: Comparing epistolary and digital audiences. *Participations: Journal of Audience and Reception Studies*, 16(2), 350–373.

Bowers, John, Clare Stanton, & Jonathan Zittrain. (2021, May 21). What the ephemerality of the web means for your hyperlinks. *Columbia Journalism Review*. www.cjr.org

boyd, danah. (2014). *It's complicated: The social lives of networked teens*. New Haven, CT: Yale University Press.

Brancaccio, Maria T., Eric J. Engstrom, & David Lederer. (2013). The politics of suicide: Historical perspectives on suicidology before Durkheim: An introduction. *Journal of Social History*, 46(3), 607–619.

Breuil, Henry. (1979). *400 centuries of cave art*. New York: Hacker Art Books.

Briggs, Pam, & Lisa Thomas. (2014). The social value of digital ghosts. In Christopher M. Moreman & A. David Lewis (Eds.), *Digital death: Mortality and beyond in the online age* (pp. 125–142). Santa Barbara, CA: Praeger.

Brock, André, Jr. (2012). From the blackhand side: Twitter as a cultural conversation. *Journal of Broadcasting and Electronic Media*, 56(4), 529–549.

Brock, André, Jr. (2020). *Distributed blackness: African American cybercultures*. New York: New York University Press.

Brook, Orian, David O'Brien, & Mark Taylor. (2018). *Panic! Social class, taste, and inequalities in the creative industries*. Arts and Humanities Research Council. www.nsead.org

Broom, Douglas. (2020, April 22). Coronavirus has exposed the digital divide like never before. *World Economic Forum*. www.weforum.org

Brown, Gillian. (1990). *Domestic individualism: Imagining self in nineteenth-century America*. Berkeley: University of California Press.

Brubaker, Jed R., Gillian R. Hayes, & Paul Dourish. (2013). Beyond the grave: Facebook as a site for the expansion of death and mourning. *Information Society*, 29(3), 152–163.

Bruns, Axel, & Tim Highfield. (2015). Is Habermas on Twitter? Social media and the public sphere. In Axel Bruns, Gunn Enli, Eli Skogerbo, Anders O. Larsson, & Christian Christensen (Eds.), *The Routledge companion to social media and politics* (pp. 56–73). New York: Routledge.

Buckley, Kim. (2013, March 8). Post-death social media messages help grief. *Daily Nebraskan*.

Buerger, Janet E. (1989). *French daguerreotypes*. Chicago: University of Chicago Press.

Campbell, Colin. (2009). Distinguishing the power of agency from agentic power: A note on Weber and the "Black Box" of personal agency. *Sociological Theory*, 27(4), 407–418.

Canetto, Silvia Sara. (1997). Meanings of gender and suicidal behavior during adolescence. *Suicide and Life-Threatening Behavior*, 27(4), 339–351.

Cann, Candi K. (2014). *Virtual afterlives: Grieving the dead in the twenty-first century*. Lexington: University Press of Kentucky.

Carey-Mahoney, Ryan. (2015, July 22). Sandra Bland death triggers #IfIDieInPoliceCustody trend. *USA Today*. www.usatoday.com

CaringBridge. (2021). About Us. www.caringbridge.org

Carney, Nikita. (2016). All lives matter, but so does race: Black Lives Matter and the evolving role of social media. *Humanity & Society*, 40(2), 180–199.

Carroll, Paul. (2013, April 23). Tweeting from beyond the grave—Why sometimes it's good not to talk. *Huffington Post*. www.huffingtonpost.co.uk

Cash, Scottye J., Michael Thelwall, Sydney N. Peck, Jared Z. Ferrell, & Jeffrey A. Bridge. (2013). Adolescent suicide statements on MySpace. *Cyberpsychology, Behavior, and Social Networking*, 16(3), 166–174.

Cassano, Graham. (2008). The acquisitive machine: Max Weber, Thorsten Veblen, and the culture of consumptive individualism. In David Chalcraft, Fanon Howell, Marisa Lopez Menendez, and Hector Vera (Eds.), *Max Weber matters: Interweaving past and present* (pp. 177–190). New York: Routledge.

Cassell, Paul. (2014, November 26). Officer Wilson had a powerful case for self-defense under Missouri law. *Washington Post*. www.washingtonpost.com

Cassese, Erin C., Leonie Huddy, Todd K. Hartman, Lilliana Mason, & Christopher R. Weber. (2013). Socially mediated Internet surveys: Recruiting participants for online experiments. *PS: Political Science & Politics*, 46(4), 775–784.

Cassidy, John. (2002). *Dot.con: How America lost its mind and its money in the Internet era.* New York: Harper Collins.

Centers for Disease Control and Prevention. (2008). Promoting individual, family, and community connectedness to prevent suicidal behavior. www.cdc.gov

Chandler, Michael. (1994). Adolescent suicide and the loss of personal continuity. In Dante Cicchetti & Sheree L. Toth (Eds.), *Disorders and dysfunctions of the self* (pp. 371–390). Rochester, NY: University of Rochester Press.

Charmaz, Kathy. (1980). *The social reality of death.* Reading, MA: Addison-Wesley.

Charmaz, Kathy. (2002). Stories and silences: Disclosures and self in chronic illness. *Qualitative Inquiry,* 8(3), 302–328.

Chaves, Mark. (1994). Secularization as declining church authority. *Social Forces,* 72, 749–774.

Chemero, Anthony. (2009). *Radical embodied cognitive science.* Cambridge, MA: MIT Press.

Chen, Gina Masullo. (2013). Don't call me that: A techno-feminist critique of the term *mommy blogger. Mass Communication & Society,* 16(4), 510–532.

Chen, Michelle. (2015, September 14). This is how bad the sharing economy is for workers. *Nation.* www.thenation.com

Chung, Jane. (2021, March 24). Big tech, big cash: Washington's new power players. *Public Citizen.* www.citizen.org

Church, Scott. (2013). Digital gravescapes: Digital memorializing on Facebook. *Information Society,* 29(3), 184–189.

Clanchy, Michael T. (2013). *From memory to written record: England, 1066–1307* (3rd ed.). Malden, MA: Wiley-Blackwell.

Clarke Dillman, Joanne. (2014). *Women and death in film, television, and news: Dead but not gone.* New York: Palgrave Macmillan.

Clauser, Grant. (2019, August 8). Amazon's Alexa never stops listening to you. Should you worry? *New York Times Wirecutter.* www.nytimes.com

Clough, Patricia Ticineto. (1998). The end(s) of ethnography: Now and then. *Qualitative Inquiry,* 4(1), 3–14.

Cohen, Albert K. (1965). The sociology of the deviant act: Anomie theory and beyond. *American Sociological Review,* 30(1), 5–14.

Collins, Terry. (2021, November 11). Work remote after COVID? Nearly 50% of US workers would take a pay cut for it, survey says. *USA Today.* www.usatoday.com

Conkey, Margaret. (1987). New approaches in the search for meaning? A review of research in "Paleolithic Art." *Journal of Field Archaeology,* 14(4), 413–430.

Cooley, Charles Horton. (1922). *Human nature and the social order* (rev. ed.). New York: Charles Scribner's Sons.

Coon, Deborah J. (2002). Testing the limits of sense and science: American experimental psychologists combat spiritualism, 1880–1920. In W. E. Pickren & D. A. Dewsbury (Eds.), *Evolving perspectives on the history of psychology* (pp. 121–139). Washington, DC: American Psychological Association.

Courtemanche, Charles, Joseph Garuccio, Anh Le, Joshua Pinkston, & Aaron Yelow-itz. (2020). Strong social distancing measures in the United States reduced the COVID-19 growth rate. *Health Affairs*, 39(7), 1237–1246.

Cummins, Eleanor. (2020, January 22). Why millennials are the "Death Positive" generation. *Vox*. www.vox.com

Cunningham, Joel. (2020, August 14). Make sure that new app you're tweeting about is real. *Life Hacker*. https://lifehacker.com

Cupit, Illene Noppe. (2012). Research in thanatechnology. In Carla Sofka, Illene Noppe Cupit, & Kathleen Gilbert (Eds.), *Dying, death, and grief in an online universe* (pp. 198–216). New York: Springer.

Daine, Kate, Keith Hawton, Vinod Singaravelu, Anne Stewart, Sue Simkin, & Paul Montgomery. (2013). The power of the web: A systematic review of studies of the influence of the Internet on self-harm and suicide in young people. *PLoS ONE*, 8(10), 1–6.

Daniels, Jessie. (2009). *Cyber-racism: White supremacy online and the new attack on civil rights*. New York: Rowman and Littlefield.

Das, Satyajit. (2017, February 12). The sharing economy creates a Dickensian world for workers—It masks a dark problem in the labour market. *Independent*. www.independent.co.uk

Davis, Jenny L. (2020). *How artifacts afford: The power and politics of everyday things*. Cambridge, MA: MIT Press.

Davis, Jenny L., & James B. Chouinard. (2016). Theorizing affordances: From request to refuse. *Bulletin of Science, Technology & Society*, 36(4), 241–248.

de Boer, Bart. (2017). Evolution of speech and evolution of language. *Psychonomic Bulletin & Review*, 24, 158–162.

De Groote, Michael. (2013, September 17). Digital death: Preparing for your afterlife on the cloud. *Deseret Morning News*.

De Loera-Brust, Antonio. (2020, July 14). As the US exports coronavirus, Trump is blaming Mexicans. *Foreign Policy*. https://foreignpolicy.com

De Vynck, Gerritt, & Rachel Lerman. (2021, July 22). Facebook and YouTube spent a year fighting COVID misinformation. It's still spreading. *Washington Post*. www.washingtonpost.com

Dean, Aria. (2016, July 25). Poor meme, rich meme. *Real Life*. https://reallifemag.com

DeGroot, Jocelyn M. (2012). Maintaining relational continuity with the deceased on Facebook. *Omega: Journal of Death and Dying*, 65(3), 195–212.

DeGroot, Jocelyn M. (2014). "For whom the bell tolls": Emotional rubbernecking in Facebook memorial groups. *Death Studies*, 38(2), 79–84.

Denzin, Norman K., & Yvonne S. Lincoln. (1998). Introduction: Entering the field of qualitative research. In Norman K. Denzin & Yvonne S. Lincoln (Eds.), *The landscape of qualitative research: Theories and issues* (pp. 1–34). Thousand Oaks, CA: Sage.

Diawara, Manthia. (1993). Black spectatorship: Problems of identification and re-sistance. In M. Diawara (Ed.), *Black American cinema* (pp. 211–220). New York: Routledge.

Didion, Joan. (2004). *The year of magical thinking*. New York: Vintage.

Dominguez, Tori. (2021, June 15). This Twitter account is honoring COVID victims, with 5,000 obituaries and counting. *NPR*. www.npr.org

Doughty, Caitlin. (2014). *Smoke gets in your eyes and other lessons from the crematory*. New York: Norton.

Du Bois, W. E. B. (1997). *The souls of black folk*. David W. Blight and Robert Gooding-Williams (Eds.). Boston: Bedford Books.

Dugdale, Lydia S. (2017). Desecularizing death. *Christian Bioethics*, 23(1), 22–37.

Dumont, Richard G., & Dennis C. Foss. (1972). *The American view of death: Acceptance or denial?* Cambridge, MA: Schenkman.

Duneier, Mitchell. (1999). *Sidewalk*. New York: Farrar, Strauss, and Giroux.

Durkheim, Emile. (1951). *Suicide: A study in sociology* (J. A. Spaulding & G. Simpson, Trans). New York: Free Press.

Durkheim, Emile. (1995). *The elementary forms of religious life* (Karen E. Fields, Trans.). New York: Free Press.

Early, Jody, & Alyssa Hernandez. (2021). Digital disenfranchisement and COVID-19: Broadband Internet access as a social determinant of health. *Health Promotion Practice*, 22(5), 605–610.

Economist. (2021, November 22). Tracking COVID-19 excess deaths across countries. www.economist.com

Edelman, Ann M., & Steven L. Renshaw. (1982). Genuine versus simulated suicide notes: An issue revisited through discourse analysis. *Suicide and Life-Threatening Behavior*, 12(2), 103–113.

Ekdale, Brian, Kang Namkoong, Timothy K. F. Fung, & David D. Perlmutter. (2010). Why blog? (then and now): Exploring the motivations for blogging by popular American political bloggers. *New Media & Society*, 12(2), 217–234.

Ekelund, Robert B., Jr., Robert F. Hébert, & Robert D. Tollison. (1992). The economics of sin and redemption: Purgatory as a market-pull innovation? *Journal of Economic Behavior and Organization*, 19, 1–15.

Elliott, Chris. (2014, January 16). Why an article on Lisa Bonchek Adams was removed from the *Guardian* site. *Guardian*. www.theguardian.com

Ellison, Jake. (2020, June 23). 75% of US workers can't work exclusively from home, face greater risks during pandemic. *UW News*. www.washington.edu

Emirbayer, Mustafa, & Anne Mische. (1998). What is agency? *American Journal of Sociology*, 103(4), 962–1023.

Epstein, Robert. (2016, May 18). The empty brain. *Aeon*. https://aeon.co

Erickson, Karla A. (2013). *How we die now: Americans aging and dying in the twenty-first century*. Philadelphia, PA: Temple University Press.

Esbenshade, Claudia W. (2010, October 31). Grieving online social networking sites help family/friends memorialize deceased loved ones. *Sunday News*.

Ettinger, R. C. W. (1962). *The prospect of immortality*. London: Sidgwick and Jackson.

Ettinger, R. C. W. (1972). *Man into Superman: The startling potential of human evolution . . . and how to be a part of it*. New York: Avon Books.

Evans, Sandra K., Katy E. Pearce, Jessica Vitak, & Jeffrey W. Treem. (2017). Explicating affordances: A conceptual framework for understanding affordances in communication research. *Journal of Computer-Mediated Communication, 22*(1), 35–52.

Facebook. (n.d.). Memorialized accounts. www.facebook.com

Fairclough, Norman. (1989). *Language and power*. London: Longman.

Fangone, Jason. (2021, July 23). The Jessica simulation: Love and loss in the age of A.I. *San Francisco Chronicle*. www.sfchronicle.com

Farhi, Paul. (2014, January 13). Former NYT editor Bill Keller and his wife under fire for commentary on cancer patient. *Washington Post*. www.washingtonpost.com

Farman, Abou. (2020). *On not dying: Secular immortality and the age of technoscience*. Minneapolis: University of Minnesota Press.

Feldman, David B. (2017, July 7). Why the five stages of grief are wrong. *Psychology Today* www.psychologytoday.com

Fields, Karen E. (1996). Durkheim and the idea of soul. *Theory & Society, 25*(2), 193–203.

Fiesler, Casey, & Nicholas Proferes. (2018). "Participant" perceptions of Twitter research ethics. *Social Media & Society, 4*(1), 1–14.

Fincham, Ben, Susanne Langer, Jonathan Scourfield, & Michael Shiner. (2011). *Understanding suicide: A sociological autopsy*. London: Palgrave Macmillan.

Fine, Gary Alan. (1996). Reputational entrepreneurs and the memory of incompetence: Melting supporters, partisan warriors, and images of President Harding. *American Journal of Sociology, 101*(5), 1159–1193.

Floridi, Luciano. (2013). *The ethics of information*. Oxford, UK: Oxford University Press.

Foucault, Michel. (1988). Technologies of the self. In L. H. Martin, H. Gutman, & P. H. Hutton (Eds.), *Technologies of the self: A seminar with Michel Foucault* (pp. 16–49). Amherst: University of Massachusetts Press.

Freelon, Deen, Charlton D. McIlwain, & Meredith D. Clark. (2016, February 29). *Beyond the hashtags: #Ferguson, #Blacklivesmatter, and the online struggle for offline justice*. Center for Media and Social Impact. https://cmsimpact.org

Friedman, Lawrence M. (2009). *Dead hands: A social history of wills, trusts, and inheritance law*. Stanford, CA: Stanford University Press.

Frum, David. (2021, July 23). Vaccinated America has had enough. *Atlantic*. www.theatlantic.com

Funk, Jeffrey, & Gary Smith. (2021, May 4). Why AI moonshots miss. *Slate*. https://slate.com

Gallaga, Omar L. (2012, December 10). Expressing grief online becomes more common. *Austin-American Statesman*.

Galston, William A. (2021, October 21). For COVID-19 vaccinations, party affiliation matters more than race and ethnicity. *Brookings Institute*. www.brookings.edu

Gamble, Clive. (2014). The after-life. In William Brown & Andrew Fabian (Eds.), *Life* (pp. 147–165). Cambridge, UK: Cambridge University Press.

Gane, Nicholas. (2002). *Max Weber and postmodernity: Rationalization versus re-enchantment*. New York: Palgrave.

Garber, Megan. (2016, January 20). Enter the grief police. *Atlantic*. www.theatlantic .com

Gawande, Atul. (2014). *Being mortal: Illness, medicine, and what matters in the end.* London: Profile Books.

Georges, Thomas M. (2003). *Digital soul: Intelligent machines and human values.* Boulder, CO: Westview Press.

Gergen, Kenneth J. (2002). The challenge of absent presence. In James E. Katz & Mark Aakhus (Eds.), *Perpetual contact: Mobile communication, private talk, public performance* (pp. 227–241). Cambridge, UK: Cambridge University Press.

Gibbs, Jack P., & Walter T. Martin. (1964). *Status integration and suicide.* Eugene, OR: University of Oregon Press.

Gibson, James J. (1966). *The senses considered as perceptual systems.* London: Allen and Unwin.

Gibson, James J. (1977). The theory of affordances. In Robert Shaw & John Bransford (Eds.), *Perceiving, acting and knowing: Toward an ecological perspective* (pp. 67–82). Hillsdale, NJ: Lawrence Erlbaum Associates.

Gibson, James J. (1979). *The ecological approach to visual perception.* Boston: Houghton Mifflin.

Gibson, Margaret. (2007). Death and mourning in technologically mediated culture. *Health Sociology Review,* 16(5), 415–424.

Giddens, Anthony. (1965). The suicide problem in French sociology. *British Journal of Sociology,* 16(1), 3–18.

Giddens, Anthony. (1991). *Modernity and self-identity: Self and society in the late modern age.* Stanford, CA: Stanford University Press.

Giddens, Anthony. (1995). *A contemporary critique of historical materialism* (2nd ed.). New York: Palgrave Macmillan.

Gilbert, Ben. (2021, June 7). Less than half of Americans who don't plan to get vaccinated have worn a mask recently, according to a new survey. *Business Insider.* www.businessinsider.com

Goffman, Erving. (1959). *The presentation of self in everyday life.* New York: Anchor Books.

Golbeck, Jennifer. (2015, March 6). Facebook introduces suicide prevention support. *Psychology Today.* www.psychologytoday.com

Goldman, Abigail. (2010, April 6). 2B or not 2B? The age of the Twitter suicide note is upon us. *Las Vegas Sun.* www.lasvegasweekly.com

Goldney, Robert D., Johan A. Schioldann, & Kirsten I. Dunn. (2008). Suicide research before Durkheim. *Health and History,* 10(2), 73–93.

Goldsmith, Jack, & Tim Wu. (2006). *Who controls the Internet? Illusions of a borderless world.* New York: Oxford University Press.

Gorer, Geoffrey. (1965). *Death, grief and mourning.* New York: Doubleday.

Gorski, Philip S., and Ateş Altinordu. (2008). After secularization? *Annual Review of Sociology,* 34, 55–85.

Graeber, David, & David Wengrow. (2021). *The dawn of everything: A new history of humanity*. New York: Farrar, Strauss, and Giroux.

Graham, David A. (2021, August 22). The noisy minority. *Atlantic*. www.theatlantic.com

Graham, Roderick, & Shawn Smith. (2016). The content of our #Characters: Black Twitter as counterpublic. *Sociology of Race and Ethnicity*, 2(4), 433–449.

Graves, Lucas. (2007). The affordances of blogging: A case study in cultural and technological effects. *Journal of Communication Inquiry*, 31(4), 331–346.

Grayson, Stacey, Calli Tzani-Pepelasi, Ntaniella-Roumpini Pylarinou, Maria Ioannou, & Vasiliki Artinopoulou. (2020). Examining the narrative roles in suicide notes. *Journal of Investigative Psychology and Offender Profiling*, 17(2), 142–159.

Greenstein, Shane. (2015). *How the Internet became commercial: Innovation, privatization, and the birth of a new network*. Princeton, NJ: Princeton University Press.

Gross, Doug. (2013, August 23). The sportswriter who blogged his own suicide. *CNN*. www.cnn.com

Gross, Nora. (2017). #IfTheyGunnedMeDown: The double consciousness of Black youth in response to oppressive media. *Souls: A Critical Journal of Black Politics, Culture, and Society*, 19(4), 416–437.

Gunn, Caitlin. (2015). Hashtagging from the margins: Women of color engaged in feminist consciousness-raising on Twitter. In K. Edwards Tassie & S. Brown Givens (Eds.), *Women of color and social media multitasking: Blogs, timelines, feeds, and community* (pp. 21–34). Lanham, MD: Lexington Books.

Gutman, Huck. (1998). Rousseau's *Confessions*: A technology of the self. In L. H. Martin, H. Gutman, and P. H. Hutton (Eds.), *Technologies of the self: A seminar with Michel Foucault* (pp. 99–120). Amherst: University of Massachusetts Press.

Hachmann, Nicole P., Jessica Miller, Ai-ris Y. Collier, John D. Ventura, Jingyou Yu, Marjorie Rowe, Esther A. Bondzie, Olivia Powers, Nehalee Surve, Kevin Hall, & Dan H. Barouch. (2022). Correspondence: Neutralization escape by SARS-CoV-2 Omicron subvariants BA.2.12.1, BA.4, and BA.5. *New England Journal of Medicine*. https://www.nejm.org/doi/full/10.1056/NEJMc2206576

Hall, Stuart. (1980). Encoding/decoding. In Stuart Hall, Dorothy Hobson, Andrew Lowe, & Paul Willis (Eds.), *Culture, media, language: Working papers in cultural studies, 1972–79* (pp. 117–127). London: Hutchinson.

Hamel, Liz, Lunna Lopes, Grace Sparks, Ashley Kirzinger, Audrey Kearney, Mellisha Stokes, & Mollyann Brodie. (2021, October 28). KFF COVID-19 vaccine monitor: October 2021. *Kaiser Family Foundation*. www.kff.org

Hamilton, Isobel Asher. (2018, June 20). Facebook ordered to explain why it deleted the profile of a dead man after a mysterious request. *Business Insider*.

Hampton, Keith N., Oren Livio, & Lauren Sessions Goulet. (2010). The social life of wireless urban spaces: Internet use, social networks, and the public realm. *Journal of Communication*, 60(4), 701–722.

Hampton, Keith N., & Barry Wellman. (2018). Lost and saved . . . again: The moral panic about the loss of community takes hold of social media. *Contemporary Sociology*, 47(6), 643–651.

Haraway, Donna J. (2016). A cyborg manifesto. In *Manifestly Haraway*. Minneapolis: University of Minnesota Press.

Harris, Keith M., John P. McLean, & Jeanie K. Sheffield. (2009). Examining suicide-risk individuals who go online for suicide-related purposes. *Archives of Suicide Research*, 13(3), 264–76.

Harris, Misty. (2008, January 15). Mourning rituals shift to Internet; Tragedy brings up our own experiences with grief: Friends grieve loss of seven basketball players through Facebook group. *Alberni Valley Times*.

Harris, Zack. (2013, May 13). The new afterlife. *Huffington Post*.

Harvey, David. (1990). *The condition of postmodernity: An enquiry into the origins of cultural change*. Cambridge, MA: Blackwell.

Hasinoff, Amy, & Rena Bivens. (2021). Feature analysis: A method for analyzing the role of ideology in app design. *Journal of Digital Social Research*, 3(2), 89–113.

Hasker, William. (1988). Suffering, soul-making, and salvation. *International Philosophical Quarterly*, 28(1), 3–19.

Hauser, David J., & Norbert Schwarz. (2016). Attentive Turkers: MTurk participants perform better on online attention checks than do subject pool participants. *Behavior Research Methods*, 48, 400–407.

Heher, Ashley. (2007, February 16). Grieving in an Internet age: Personal spaces on popular sites have become as important in death as they were in life. *Vancouver Sun*.

Helling, Steve. (2015, January 2). Suicide of transgender teen Leelah Alcorn sparks emotional debate. *People*. www.people.com

Helwig, Barbara. (2012). An age of heroes? Some thoughts on early Bronze Age funerary customs in northern Mesopotamia. In Peter Pfälzner, Herbert Niehr, Ernst Pernicka, & Anne Wissing (Eds.), *(Re-)constructing funerary rituals in the ancient Near East* (pp. 47–58). Wiesbaden: Harrassowitz.

Hernández-Fernández, Carlos, & Carmen Meneses-Falcón. (2021). Nobody should die alone: Loneliness and a dignified death during the COVID-19 pandemic. *Omega: Journal of Death and Dying*. Article preprint.

Herring, Susan C. (2004). Online communication: Through the lens of discourse. In M. Consalvo, N. Baym, J. Hunsinger, K. B. Jensen, J. Logie, M. Murero, & L. R. Shade (Eds.), *Internet research annual*, volume 1 (pp. 65–76). New York: Peter Lang.

Hertz, Robert. (1960). *Death and the right hand* (Rodney & Claudia Needham, Trans.). Aberdeen, UK: Cohen and West.

Hess, Amanda. (2015, March 3). "Please don't downvote anyone who's asked for help:" How Reddit is changing suicide intervention. *Slate*. www.slate.com

Hick, John. (1968). *Evil and the God of love*. Great Britain: William Collins and Sons.

Hill, Marc Lamont. (2018). "Thank you, Black Twitter": State violence, digital counterpublics, and pedagogies of resistance. *Urban Education*, 53(2), 286–302.

Hinduja, Sameer, & Justin W. Patchin. (2010). Bullying, cyberbullying, and suicide. *Archives of Suicide Research*, 14(3), 206–221.

Hitlin, Steven, & Glen H. Elder. (2007). Time, self, and the curiously abstract concept of agency. *Sociological Theory*, 25(2), 170–191.

Hogan, Bernie. (2010). The presentation of self in the age of social media: Distinguishing performances and exhibitions online. *Bulletin of Science, Technology & Society*, 30(6), 377–386.

Holohan, Meghan. (2020, August 18). "Put your masks on": Mom warns others about COVID-19 before dying. *Today*. www.today.com

Hovers, Erella, Shimon Ilani, Ofer Bar-Yosef, & Bernard Vandermeersch. (2003). An early case of color symbolism: Ochre use by modern humans in Qafzeh Cave. *Current Anthropology*, 44(4), 491–522.

Howe, Irving. (1992). The self in literature. In George Levin (Ed.), *Constructions of the self* (pp. 249–268). New Brunswick, NJ: Rutgers University Press.

Huang, Yen-Pei, Tiong Goh, & Chern Li Liew. (2007). Hunting suicide notes in Web 2.0—Preliminary findings. *Proceedings of the Ninth IEEE International Symposium on Multimedia* (pp. 517–521).

Hutton, Patrick H. (1998). Foucault, Freud, and the technologies of the self. In L. H. Martin, H. Gutman, and P. H. Hutton (Eds.), *Technologies of the self: A seminar with Michel Foucault* (pp. 121–144). Amherst: University of Massachusetts Press.

Illouz, Eva. (2008). *Saving the modern soul: Therapy, emotions, and the culture of self-help*. Berkeley: University of California Press.

Imperial College London. (2022, July 11). COVID-19 orphanhood. https://imperialcollegelondon.github.io

Irfan, Umair. (2021, November 9). Why are rich countries still monopolizing COVID-19 vaccines? *Vox*. www.vox.com

Irwin, Melissa D. (2015). Mourning 2.0—Continuing bonds between the living and the dead on Facebook. *Omega: Journal of Death and Dying*, 72(2), 119–150.

Iyer, Maitrayee. (2016, August 26). Here's how social media redefines how people grieve. *BGR: Your Mobile Life*.

Jackson, Sarah J., & Brooke Foucault Welles. (2015). #Ferguson is everywhere: Initiators in emerging counterpublic networks. *Information, Communication & Society*, 19(3), 397–418.

Jacobs, Emma. (2018, March 3). How technology is changing the way we grieve. *Financial Times*.

Jacobs, Jerry. (1967). A phenomenological study of suicide notes. *Social Problems*, 15(1), 60–72.

Jäger, Siegfried, & Florentine Maier. (2009). Theoretical and methodological aspects of Foucauldian critical discourse analysis and dispositive analysis. In R. Wodak and M. Meyer (Eds.), *Methods of critical discourse analysis* (2nd ed.) (pp. 34–61). Los Angeles, CA: Sage.

Jalland, Pat. (2010). *Death in war and peace: Loss and grief in England, 1914–1970*. Oxford, UK: Oxford University Press.

Jamison-Powell, Sue, Pam Biggs, Shaun Lawson, Conor Linehan, Karen Windle, & Harriet Gross. (2016). "PS. I love you": Understanding the impact of posthumous digital messages. *Proceedings of the 2016 CHI Conference on Human Factors in Computing Systems*, Association for Computing Machinery (pp. 2920–2932).

Jenkins, Richard. (2000). Disenchantment, enchantment and re-enchantment: Max Weber at the millennium. *Max Weber Studies*, 1(1), 11–32.

Jerolmack, Colin, & Shamus Khan. (2014). Talk is cheap: Ethnography and the attitudinal fallacy. *Sociological Methods & Research*, 43(2), 178–209.

Jerolmack, Colin, & Alexandra K. Murphy. (2017). The ethical dilemmas and social scientific trade-offs of masking in ethnography. *Sociological Methods & Research*, 48(4), 801–827.

Johansson, Sverker. (2014). Neanderthals did speak, but FOXP2 doesn't prove it. *Behavioral and Brain Sciences*, 37(6), 558–559.

Johnson, Barclay D. (1965). Durkheim's one cause of suicide. *American Sociological Review*, 30(6), 875–886.

Johnson, Jeffrey C. (2014, July 25). The vale of soul-making. *Paris Review*. www.theparisreview.org

Johnston, Catherine, & Rebecca Nappi. (2012, January 24). LAST RESPECTS, 2.0: No protocol yet for digital-age condolences. *Spokesman-Review*.

Johnston, William A., & David L. Strayer. (2001). A dynamic, evolutionary perspective on attention capture. In Charley L. Folk & Bradley S. Gibson (Eds.), *Advances in psychology, 133. Attraction, distraction and action: Multiple perspectives on attentional capture* (pp. 375–397). New York: Elsevier.

Jolly, Bradley. (2016, July 2). "Sickening" social media apps—that make you live on after death rise in popularity. *Daily Star*. www.dailystar.co.uk

Jones, Natalie J., & Craig Bennell. (2007). The development and validation of statistical prediction rules for discriminating between genuine and simulated suicide notes. *Archives of Suicide Research*, 11(2), 219–233.

Joralemon, Donald. (2016). *Mortal dilemmas: The troubled landscape of death in America*. Walnut Creek, CA: Left Coast Press.

Kampf, Günter. (2021, November 9). COVID-19: Stigmatising the unvaccinated is not justified. *Lancet*, 398(10314), 1871. www.thelancet.com

Kaplan, Louis. (2003). Where the paranoid meets the paranormal: Speculations on spirit photography. *Art Journal*, 62(3), 18–27.

Kapur, Sahil. (2022, March 1). Democrats turn against mask mandates as COVID landscape and voter attitudes shift. *NBC News*. www.nbcnews.com

Kasket, Elaine. (2014, October 3). Social media sites provide another place to mourn loved ones. *Irish Independent*.

Kellehear, Allan. (2007). *A social history of dying*. New York: Cambridge University Press.

Keller, Bill. (2014, January 12). Heroic measures. *New York Times*. www.nytimes.com

Kelly, Kim. (2017, October 27). Welcome the reaper: Caitlin Doughty and the "death-positivity" movement. *Guardian*. www.theguardian.com

Kendall, Lori. (1998). Meaning and identity in "Cyberspace": The performance of gender, class, and race online. *Symbolic Interaction*, 21(2), 129–153.

Kenen, Joanne. (2022, January 27). The NYT's polarizing pandemic pundit. *Politico*. www.politico.com

Kenworthy, Nora. (2021). Like a grinding stone: How crowdfunding platforms create, perpetuate, and value health inequities. *Medical Anthropology Quarterly*, 35(3), 327–345.

Kern, Rebecca, Abbe E. Forman, and Gisela Gil-Egui. (2013). R.I.P.: Remain in perpetuity. Facebook memorial pages. *Telematics and Informatics*, 30(1), 2–10.

Kidshealth. (2018, April). Teaching kids to be smart about social media. https://kidshealth.org

Kiernan, Stephen P. (2006). *Last rights: Rescuing the end of life from the medical system*. New York: St. Martin's Griffin.

Killilea, Alfred G. (1981). Death consciousness and social consciousness: A critique of Ernest Becker and Jacques Choron on denying death. *OMEGA—Journal of Death and Dying*, 11(3), 185–200.

Kim, Grace MyHyun. (2016). Transcultural digital literacies: Cross-border connections and self-representations in an online forum. *Reading Research Quarterly*, 51(2), 199–219.

Kim, Violet. (2020, May 27). Virtual reality, real grief. *Slate*. https://slate.com/

Kimball, Spencer H. (2019). Survey data collection; online panel efficacy: A comparative study of Amazon MTurk and Research Now SSI/Survey Monkey/Opinion Access. *Journal of Business Diversity*, 19(2), 16–45.

Kimball, Spencer. (2021, October 29). Labor unions push White House to add worker protections to Biden COVID vaccine mandate. *CNBC*. www.cnbc.com

Kirkpatrick, David. (2010). *The Facebook effect: The inside story of the company that is connecting the world*. New York: Simon and Schuster.

Klass, Dennis, Phyllis R. Silverman, & Steven Nickman (Eds.). (1996). *Continuing bonds: New understandings of grief*. New York: Routledge.

Kleeman, Jenny. (2014, June 7). Web immortality: The social media sites that keep you alive in the digital world. *Guardian*. www.theguardian.com

Kleinman, Zoe. (2019, March 18). MySpace admits to losing 12 years' worth of music uploads. *BBC News*. www.bbc.com

Kneese, Tamara. (2017). Mediating mortality: Transtemporal illness blogs and digital care work. In Sebastian Penmellen Boret, Susan Orpett Long, & Sergei Kan (Eds.), *Death in the early 21st century: Authority, innovation, and mortuary rites* (pp. 179–216). Cham, Switzerland: Palgrave Macmillan.

Kneese, Tamara. (2018). Networked heirlooms: The affective and financial logics of digital estate planning. *Cultural Studies*, 33(2), 297–324.

Kneese, Tamara. (2019). Death, disrupted. *Continent*, 8(1–2), 70–75.

Kocamaz Mehmet K., Adnan Kaya, Eun-Young Elaine Kang, & Alexandre Francois. (2003, May). The virtual daguerreotype. *IMSC Technical Report, University of Southern California*.

Koch, Tom. (2010). Enhancing who? Enhancing what? Ethics, bioethics, and transhumanism. *Journal of Medicine and Philosophy*, 35, 685–699.

Kolata, Gina. (2019, December 11). More Americans are dying at home than in hospitals. *New York Times*. www.nytimes.com

Kolodny, Oren, and Shimon Edelman. (2018). The evolution of the capacity for language: The ecological context and adaptive value of a process of cognitive hijacking. *Philosophical Transactions of the Royal Society B*, 373(1473), 1–13.

Koul, Scaachi. (2015, January 6). Good grief: What social media gets wrong about grief and mourning. *Globe and Mail*.

Kravets, Olga. (2017). On technology, magic and changing the world. *Journal of Macromarketing*, 37(3), 331–333.

Kübler-Ross, Elisabeth. (1969). *On death and dying*. New York: Touchstone.

Kurzweil, Ray. (2005). *The Singularity is near: When humans transcend biology*. New York: Viking.

Lagerkvist, Amanda (Ed.). (2019). *Digital existence: Ontology, ethics and transcendence in digital culture*. New York: Routledge.

Lamont, Peter. (2004). Spiritualism and a mid-Victorian crisis of evidence. *Historical Journal*, 47(4), 897–920.

Lane, Jeffrey. (2019). *The digital street*. New York: Oxford University Press.

Langham, Mark. (2015, January 30). Facebook's real name policy set to return. *Social Media Today*. www.socialmediatoday.com

LaPonsie, Maryalene. (2015, October 29). Technology now lets you speak from beyond the grave. *Yahoo News*. https://news.yahoo.com

Larson, Selena. (2014, January 9). Dealing with death in a digital age. *ReadWriteWeb*.

Lasch, Christopher. (1979). *The culture of narcissism: American life in an age of diminishing expectations*. New York: Norton.

Lasy, E., & M. Navadvorskaya. (2012). The analysis of suicide notes. *European Psychiatry*, 27(1), 1.

Latour, Bruno. (2005). *Reassembling the social: An introduction to actor-network theory*. New York: Oxford University Press.

Lee, Raymond L. M. (2010). Weber, re-enchantment, and social futures. *Time & Society*, 19(2), 180–192.

Leenaars, Antoon. (1988). *Suicide notes: Predictive clues and patterns*. New York: Human Sciences Press.

Leenaars, Antoon A. (2010). Lives and deaths: Biographical notes on selections from the works of Edwin S. Shneidman. *Suicide and Life-Threatening Behavior*, 40(5), 476–491.

Lee-Won, Roselyn J., Minsun Shim, Yeon Kyoung Joo, & Sung Gwan Park. (2014). Who puts the best "face" forward on Facebook? Positive self-presentation in online social networking and the role of self-consciousness, actual-to-total friends ratio, and culture. *Computers in Human Behavior*, 39, 413–423.

Lepore, Jill. (2015, January 19). The cobweb. *New Yorker*. www.newyorker.com

Lester, David. (2008a). Differences between genuine and simulated suicide notes. *Psychological Reports*, 103(2), 527–528.

Lester, David. (2008b). Computer analysis of the content of suicide notes from men and women. *Psychological Reports*, 102(2), 575–576.

Lester, David. (2013). An essay on loss of self versus escape from self in suicide: Illustrative cases from diaries left by those who died by suicide. *Suicidology Online*, 4, 16–20.

Levin, Susan B. (2021). *Posthuman bliss? The failed promise of transhumanism*. New York: Oxford University Press.

Lewis, Hywel D. (1973). *The self and immortality*. New York: Macmillan.

Lewis-Williams, David. (2002). *The mind in the cave: Consciousness and the origins of art*. London: Thames and Hudson.

Lifton, Robert Jaym, and Eric Olson. (2004). Symbolic immortality. In Antonius C. G. M. Robben (Ed.), *Death, mourning, and burial: A cross-cultural reader* (pp. 32–39). Malden, MA: Wiley-Blackwell.

Lincoln, Yvonna S., & Egon G. Guba. (1985). *Naturalistic inquiry*. Newbury Park, CA: Sage.

Lingel, Jessa. (2013). The digital remains: Social media and practices of online grief. *Information Society: An International Journal*, 29(3), 190–195.

Liss, Daniel. (2021, August 19). Today's real story: The Facebook monopoly. *TechCrunch*. https://techcrunch.com

Loofbourow, Lili. (2021, September 21). The unbelievable grimness of HermanCainAward, the subreddit that catalogs anti-vaxxer COVID deaths. *Slate*. https://slate.com

Loomis, David K., & Shona Paterson. (2018). A comparison of data collection methods: Mail versus online surveys. *Journal of Leisure Research*, 49(2), 133–149.

Lopez, German. (2015, July 18). Sandra Bland's mysterious death inspired these tragic #IfIDieInPoliceCustody tweets. *Vox*. www.vox.com

Lopez, Lori Kido. (2009). The radical act of "mommy blogging": Redefining motherhood through the blogosphere. *New Media & Society*, 11(5), 729–747.

López Blanco, Carlos. (2015, August 8). Unshackling our digital life: Portability of digital life, openness, and freedom besides digital confidence. *Telefónica*. www.telefonica.com

Lubet, Steven. (2017). *Interrogating ethnography: Why evidence matters*. New York: Oxford University Press.

Lutz, Deborah. (2015). *Relics of death in Victorian literature and culture*. Cambridge, UK: Cambridge University Press.

Luxton, David D., Jennifer D. June, & Jonathan M. Fairall. (2012). Social media and suicide: A public health perspective. *American Journal of Public Health*, 102 (S2), 195–200.

MacDonald, Michael, & Terrence R. Murphy. (1990). *Sleepless souls: Suicide in early modern England*. Oxford, UK: Clarendon Press.

Macrotrends. (n.d.). US life expectancy 1950–2020. www.macrotrends.net

Madhukar, Jayanthi, & Sowmya Rajaram. (2016, March 21). Dead and clicking. *Bangalore Mirror*.

Madrigal, Alexis C. (2013, January 7). How much of the web is archived? Truth is, we don't really know. *Atlantic*. www.theatlantic.com

Malkowski, Jennifer. (2017). *Dying in full detail: Mortality and digital documentary*. Durham, NC: Duke University Press.

Man, John. (2002). *Gutenberg: How one man remade the world with words*. New York: John Wiley and Sons.

Mannix, Liam. (2014, December 30). Physician-assisted death campaigner Peter Short dies at 57. *Sydney Morning Herald*. www.smh.com.au

Manzoor, Hina, Sumera Saeed, & Abdul Hameed Panhwar. (2019). Use of discourse analysis in various disciplines. *International Journal of English Linguistics*, 9(3), 301–309.

Markham, Annette, & Elizabeth Buchanan. (2012). Ethical decision-making and Internet research: Recommendations from the AOIR ethics committee (Version 2.0). *Association of Internet Researchers*. www.aoir.org

Martin, Kristen. (2016, December 21). Memetic mori. *Real Life*. http://reallifemag .com

Martin, Raymond, & John Barresi. (2000). *The naturalization of the soul: Self and personal identity in the eighteenth century*. New York: Routledge.

Martin, Raymond, & John Barresi. (2006). *The rise and fall of soul and self: An intellectual history of personal identity*. New York: Columbia University Press.

Martineau, Harriet. (1838). *How to observe morals and manners*. London: Charles Knight.

Marwick, Alice E., & danah boyd. (2010). I tweet honestly, I tweet passionately: Twitter users, context collapse, and the imagined audience. *New Media & Society*, 13(1), 114–133.

Marwick, Alice E., & Nicole Ellison. (2012). "There isn't Wifi in heaven!" Negotiating visibility on Facebook memorial pages. *Journal of Broadcasting and Electronic Media*, 56(3), 378–400.

Matias, J., Amy Johnson, Whitney E. Boesel, Brian Keegan, Jaclyn Friedman, & Charlie DeTar. (2015, May 13). Reporting, reviewing, and responding to harassment on Twitter. https://ssrn.com

McCarthy, Caroline. (2018, June 12). Silicon Valley has a problem with conservatives. But not the political kind. *Vox*. www.vox.com

McClain, Colleen, Emily A. Vogels, Andrew Perrin, Stella Sechopoulos, & Lee Rainie. (2021, September 1). The Internet and the pandemic. *Pew Research Center*. www .pewresearch.org

McEwen, Rhonda N., & Kathleen Scheaffer. (2013). Virtual mourning and memory construction on Facebook. *Bulletin of Science, Technology & Society*, 33(3–4), 64–75.

McGaughey, Kerstin. (2010). Food in binary: Identity and interaction in two German food blogs. *Cultural Analysis*, 9, 69–99.

McKenna, Maryn. (2014). Former *New York Times* editor, wife publicly tag-team criticism of cancer survivor. Ugh. *Wired*. www.wired.com

McLean, J., & Maalsen, S. (2019). Disrupting sexism and sexualities online? Gender, activism and digital spaces. In C. J. Nash & A. Gorman-Murray (Eds.), *The geographies of digital sexuality* (pp. 183–202). New York: Palgrave Macmillan.

McLuhan, Marshall. (1962). *The Gutenberg galaxy: The making of typographic man.* Toronto: University of Toronto Press.

McQuade, Zan. (2013, October 29). Grappling with mortality in the Facebook era. *Daily Dot.*

Mead, George Herbert. (1934). *Mind, self, and society from the standpoint of a social behaviorist.* Edited and with an introduction by Charles W. Morris. Chicago: University of Chicago Press.

Meer, Zubin. (2011). Introduction: Individualism revisited. In Zubin Meer (Ed.), *Individualism: The cultural logic of modernity* (pp. 1–32). New York: Lexington Books.

Meinwald, Dan. (1990). Memento mori: Death in nineteenth century photography. *CMP Bulletin*, 9(4).

Melcher, David, & Nicholas J. Wade. (2006). Cave art interpretation II. *Perception*, 35, 719–722.

Mellor, Philip A., & Chris Shilling. (1993). Modernity, self-identity and the sequestration of death. *Sociology*, 27(3), 411–431.

Mervosh, Sarah. (2021, September 2). When vaccines aren't an option: Life for families with children under 12. *New York Times.* www.nytimes.com

Metz, Christian. (1992). Identification, mirror. In G. Mast, M. Cohen, & L. Braudy (Eds.), *Film theory and criticism: Introductory readings* (4th ed.). New York: Oxford University Press.

Micheli, Marina, Christopher Lutz, & Moritz Büchi. (2018). Digital footprints: An emerging dimension of digital inequality. *Journal of Information Communication and Ethics in Society*, 16(3), 242–251.

Miller, Daniel. (2017). *The comfort of people.* Malden, MA: Polity.

Miller, Stephen. (2016, July 6). The booming afterlife of the obituary. *Wealth Management.*

Miller, Zeke. (2021, July 17). Biden grappling with "pandemic of the unvaccinated." *Associated Press.* https://apnews.com

Minois, Georges. (1999). *History of suicide: Voluntary death in Western culture.* Baltimore, MD: Johns Hopkins University Press.

Mithen, Steven. (1996). *The prehistory of the mind: A search for the origins of art, religion and science.* London: Thames and Hudson.

Moller, David W. (2018). *On death without dignity: The human impact of technological dying.* Boca Raton, FL: CRC Press.

Moore, Calvin Conzelus, & John B. Williamson. (2003). The universal fear of death and the cultural response. In C. D. Bryant & D. L. Peck (Eds.), *Handbook of death and dying* (pp. 3–13). New York: Sage.

Morens, David M., Gregory K. Folkers, & Anthony S. Fauci. (2022). The concept of classical herd immunity may not apply to COVID-19. *Journal of Infectious Diseases*, 109.

Mori, Joji, Martin Gibbs, Michael Arnold, Bjorn Nansen, & Tamara Kohn. (2012). Design considerations for after death: Comparing the affordances of three online platforms. *Proceedings of the 24th Australian Computer-Human Interaction Conference* (pp. 395–404).

Morrison, Aimée. (2011). "Suffused by feeling and affect": The intimate public of personal mommy blogging. *Biography*, 34(1), 37–55.

Mosco, Vincent. (2016). *To the cloud: Big data in a turbulent world*. New York: Routledge.

Mullaly, Una. (2015, December 28). The desire to live forever is ultimate act of narcissism. *Irish Times*.

Mulvey, Laura. (1992). Visual pleasure and narrative cinema. In G. Mast, M. Cohen, & L. Braudy (Eds.), *Film theory and criticism: Introductory readings* (4th ed.). New York: Oxford University Press.

Nagy, Peter, & Gina Neff. (2015). Imagined affordance: Reconstructing a keyword for communication theory. *Social Media & Society*, 1(2), 1–9.

Nakamura, Lisa. (2002). *Cybertypes: Race, ethnicity, and identity on the Internet*. New York: Routledge.

Nakamura, Lisa, & Peter Chow-White (Eds.). (2013). *Race after the Internet*. New York: Routledge.

National Commission for the Protection of Human Subjects of Biomedical and Behavioral Research. (1979). *The Belmont report: Ethical principles and guidelines for the protection of human subjects of research*. www.hhs.gov

Ndugga, Nambi, Latoya Hill, Samantha Artiga, & Sweta Haldar. (2021). Latest data on COVID-19 vaccinations by race/ethnicity. *Kaiser Family Foundation*. www.kff.org

Neimeyer, Robert A., & Kenneth M. Chapman. (1981). Self/ideal discrepancy and fear of death: The test of an existential hypothesis. *OMEGA: Journal of Death and Dying*, 11(3), 233–240.

Nelson-Becker, Holly, & Christina Victor. (2020). Dying alone and lonely dying: Media discourse and pandemic conditions. *Journal of Aging Studies*, 55, 1–9.

Newton, Casey. (2016, October 7). Speak, memory. *Verge*. www.theverge.com

Noble, Safiya U. (2018). *Algorithms of oppression: How search engines reinforce racism*. New York: New York University Press.

Noble, Safiya U., & Brendesha M. Tynes (Eds.). (2016). *The intersectional Internet: Race, sex, class, and culture online*. New York: Peter Lang.

Norman, Donald A. (1988). *The design of everyday things*. New York: Currency.

Nyord, Rune. (2013). Memory and succession in the city of the dead: Temporality in the Egyptian mortuary cult. In Dorthe Refslund Christensen & Rane Willerslev (Eds.), *Taming time, timing death: Social technologies and ritual* (pp. 195–212). Burlington, VT: Ashgate.

O'Connell, Mark. (2017). *To be a machine: Adventures among cyborgs, utopians, hackers, and the futurists solving the modest problem of death*. London: Granta Publications.

Ogrodnick, Margaret. (1999). *Instinct and intimacy: Political philosophy and autobiography in Rousseau*. Toronto: University of Toronto Press.

Öhman, Carl J., & David Watson. (2019). Are the dead taking over Facebook? A Big Data approach to the future of death online. *Big Data & Society*, 6(1), 1–13.

Olick, Jeffrey. (1999). Collective memory: The two cultures. *Sociological Theory*, 17(3), 333–348.

Olick, Jeffrey, & Joyce Robbins. (1998). Social memory studies: From "collective memory" to the historical sociology of mnemonic practices. *Annual Review of Sociology*, 24, 105–140.

Ong, Walter J. (1988). *Orality and literacy: The technologizing of the word*. New York: Routledge.

Parikka, Jussi. (2015). *A geology of media*. Minneapolis, MN: University of Minnesota Press.

Parry, Lizzie. (2014, September 22). Mother, 36, who died of bowel cancer calls on others to "please, please grab life and enjoy it" in her heartbreaking final blog viewed by millions. *Daily Mail*. www.dailymail.co.uk

Patterson, Michael. (2007, April 22). For the MySpace generation, a new place to mourn. *Washington Post*.

Peoples, Hervey C., Pavel Duda, & Frank W. Marlowe. (2016). Hunter-gatherers and the origins of religion. *Human Nature*, 27, 261–282.

Perkins, Judith. (1992). The "self" as sufferer. *Harvard Theological Review*, 85(3), 245–277.

Perkins, Judith. (1995). *The suffering self: Pain and narrative representation in the early Christian era*. New York: Taylor and Francis.

Pestian, John P., Pawel Matykiewicz, & Michelle Linn-Gust. (2012). What's in a note: Construction of a suicide note corpus. *Biomedical Informatics Insights*, 5, 1–6.

Peters, John D. (1999). *Speaking into the air: A brief history of the idea of communication*. Chicago: University of Chicago Press.

Peters, John D. (2015). *The marvelous clouds: Towards a philosophy of elemental media*. Chicago: University of Chicago Press.

Petru, Simona. (2018). Identity and fear—burials in the Upper Palaeolithic. *Documenta Praehistorica*, 6–13.

Pettigrew, Simone, Catherine Archer, & Paul Harrigan. (2015). A thematic analysis of mothers' motivations for blogging. *Maternal Child Health Journal*, 20, 1025–1031.

Pettitt, Paul. (2010). *The Paleolithic origins of human burial*. London: Routledge.

Pew Research Center for the People and the Press. (2013, January 15). Health online 2013. www.pewinternet.org

Pfeiffer, John E. (1982). *The creative explosion: An inquiry into the origins of art and religion*. New York: Harper and Row.

Pietras, Jamie. (2007, July 31). The new American way of death. *Salon*. www.salon.com

Plato. (2005). *Phaedrus*. New York: Penguin Classics.

Plummer, Ken. (2019). *Narrative power: The struggle for human value*. Medford, MA: Polity.

Polkinghorne, Donald E. (1988). *Narrative knowing and the human sciences*. Albany, NY: State University of New York Press.

Poniewozik, James (2014, August 11). "#IfTheyGunnedMeDown and what hashtag activism does right." *Time*. https://time.com

Pope, Whitney. (1976). *Durkheim's Suicide*. Chicago: University of Chicago Press.

Powell, Rebecca. (2010). Good mothers, bad mothers and mommy bloggers: Rhetorical resistance and fluid subjectivities. *MP: An Online Feminist Journal*, 2(5), 37–50.

Prupis, Nadia. (2015, July 15). FBI joins investigation into "unfathomable" death of Sandra Bland. *Common Dreams*. www.commondreams.org

Puri, Jyoti. (2021). The forgotten lives of sociology of death: Remembering Du Bois, Martineau and Wells. *American Sociologist*, 52, 638–655.

Rainie, Lee, & Barry Wellman. (2012). *Networked: The new social operating system*. Cambridge, MA: MIT Press.

Rankin, Beth. (2010, August 15). Mourners turn to social networks to express grief, remember the dead. Web of sorrow. *Beaumont Express*.

Rathnayake, Chamil, & Daniel D. Suthers. (2018). Twitter issue response hashtags as affordances for momentary connectedness. *Social Media & Society*, 4(3), 1–14.

Recuber, Timothy. (2015). Occupy empathy? Online politics and micro-narratives of suffering. *New Media & Society*, 17(1), 62–77.

Recuber, Timothy. (2016a). *Consuming catastrophe: Mass culture in America's decade of disaster*. Philadelphia, PA: Temple University Press.

Recuber, Timothy. (2016b). Digital discourse analysis: Finding meaning in small online spaces. In Jessie Daniels, Karen Gregory, & Tressie McMillan Cottom (Eds.), *Digital sociologies* (pp. 47–60). Bristol, UK: Policy Press.

Regalado, Antonio. (2018, March 13). A startup is pitching a mind-uploading service that is "100 percent fatal." *MIT Technology Review*. www.technologyreview.com

Reimann, Nicholas. (2021, July 21). Leaving a planet in crisis: Here's why many say the billionaire space race is a terrible idea. *Forbes*. www.forbes.com

Rettberg, Jill Walker. (2013). *Blogging*. Malden, MA: Polity.

Rheingold, Howard. (1993). *The virtual community: Homesteading on the electronic frontier*. Cambridge, MA: MIT Press.

Rice, Nicholas. (2021, March 5). Texas father of 7 records goodbye video for his children shortly before dying of COVID-19. *People*. https://people.com

Rifkin, Riaan F. (2015). Ethnographic insight into the prehistoric significance of red ochre. *Digging Stick*, 32(2), 7–10.

Ritchie, Hannah, Edouard Mathieu, Lucas Rodés-Guirao, Cameron Appel, Charlie Giattino, Esteban Ortiz-Ospina, Joe Hasell, Bobbie MacDonald, Diana Beltekian, Saloni Dattani, & Max Roser. (2022, June 18). Coronavirus pandemic (COVID-19)—the data. Our World in Data. https://ourworldindata.org

Ritzer, George. (1999). *Enchanting a disenchanted world*. Thousand Oaks, CA: Sage.

Robinson, Laura. (2007). The cyberself: The self-ing project goes online, symbolic interaction on the digital age. *New Media & Society*, 9(1), 93–110.

Robitaille, Celeste. (2017, December 26). First person; Running into mom's social-media ghost; I'm forced to confront my grief every time I'm connected to WiFi—and it's helping me cope. *Globe and Mail*.

Rocamora, Agnès. (2011). Personal fashion blogs: Screens and mirrors in digital self-portraits. *Fashion Theory*, 15(4), 407–424.

Rogers, James R., Jamie L. Bromley, Christopher J. McNally, & David Lester. (2007). Content analysis of suicide notes as a test of the motivational component of the existential-constructivist model of suicide. *Journal of Counseling and Development*, 85, 182–188.

Rogers, Katie, Lara Jakes, & Ana Swanson. (2021, March 18). Trump defends using "Chinese virus" label, ignoring growing criticism. *New York Times*. www.nytimes.com

Romer, Daniel, Patrick E. Jamieson, & Kathleen H. Jamieson. (2006). Are news reports of suicide contagious? A stringent test in six cities. *Journal of Communication*, 56, 253–270.

Roseman, Ellen. (2011, November 26). Grieving mom fights Facebook. *Toronto Star*.

Rothblatt, Martine. (2014). *Virtually human: The promise and the peril of digital immortality*. New York: Picador St. Martin's Press.

Roubein, Rachel, & McKenzie Beard. (2022, June 21). Ventilation is crucial, but until recently it took a backseat to other COVID measures. *Washington Post*. www.washingtonpost.com

Rousseau, Jean-Jacques. (1781/1953). *The confessions of Jean-Jacques Rousseau* (J. M. Cohen, Trans.). New York: Penguin Classics.

Ruby, Jay. (1995). *Secure the shadow: Death and photography in America*. Cambridge, MA: MIT Press.

Ruin, Hans. (2018). *Being with the dead: Burial, ancestral politics, and the roots of historical consciousness*. Stanford, CA: Stanford University Press.

Ruiz, Jorge R. (2009). Sociological discourse analysis: Methods and logic. *Forum: Qualitative Social Research*, 10(2).

Rushe, Dominic. (2018, July 2). US cities and states give big tech $9.3bn in subsidies in five years. *Guardian*. www.theguardian.com

Saccarelli, Emanuele. (2009). The Machiavellian Rousseau: Gender and family relations in the *Discourse on the Origin of Inequality*. *Political Theory*, 37(4), 482–510.

Sahlins, Marshall. (2022). *The new science of the enchanted universe: An anthropology of most of humanity*. With the assistance of Frederick B. Henry Jr. Princeton, NJ: Princeton University Press.

Samraj, Betty, & Jean Mark Gawron. (2015). The suicide note as a genre: Implications for genre theory. *Journal of English for Academic Purposes*, 19, 88–101.

Samuel, Lawrence R. (2013). *Death, American style: A cultural history of dying in America*. Lanham, MD: Rowman and Littlefield.

Sandler, Elana Premack. (2009, April 6). Can social media help prevent suicide? *Psychology Today*. www.psychologytoday.com

Sanger, Sandra, & Patricia McCarthy Veach. (2008). The interpersonal nature of suicide: A qualitative investigation of suicide notes. *Archives of Suicide Research*, 12, 352–365.

Sattleberg, William. (2021, April 6). The demographics of Reddit: Who uses the site? *Alphr*. www.alphr.com

Savage, Kirk. (2006). Trauma, healing, and the therapeutic monument. In Daniel Sherman & Terry Nardin (Eds.), *Terror, culture, politics: Rethinking 9/11* (pp. 103–120). Bloomington: University of Indiana Press.

Savin-Baden, M. (2019). Postdigital afterlife? *Postdigital Science and Education*, 1, 303–306.

Scarry, Elaine. (1985). *The body in pain*. New York: Oxford University Press.

Schillace, Brandy. (2015). *Death's summer coat: What the history of death and dying can tell us about life and living*. New York: Pegasus Books.

Schneider, Barbara. (2012). Blogging homelessness: Technology of the self or practice of freedom? *Canadian Journal of Communication*, 37(3), 405–419.

Schor, Juliet B., & William Attwood-Charles. (2017). The "sharing" economy: Labor, inequality, and social connection on for-profit platforms. *Sociology Compass*, 11(8), 1–16.

Schradie, Jen. (2011). The digital production gap: The digital divide and Web 2.0 collide. *Poetics*, 39(2), 145–168.

Schradie, Jen. (2019). *The revolution that wasn't: How digital activism favors conservatives*. Cambridge, MA: Harvard University Press.

Schreiber, Melody. (2022, June 2). "We're playing with fire": US COVID cases may be 30 times higher than reported. *Guardian*. www.theguardian.com

Schwarz, Benyamin, & Jacqueline J. Benson. (2018). The "medicalized death": Dying in the hospital. *Journal of Housing for the Elderly*, 32(3–4), 379–430.

Scott, Dylan. (2021, October 1). Why people who don't trust vaccines are embracing unproven drugs. *Vox*. www.vox.com

Sedikides, Constantine, & John J. Skowronski. (2003). Evolution of the symbolic self: Issues and prospects. In M. R. Leary & J. P. Tangney (Eds.), *Handbook of self and identity* (pp. 594–609). New York: Guilford Press.

Sharma, Sanjay (2013). Black Twitter? Racial hashtags, networks, and contagion. *New Formations*, 78(2), 46–64.

Sharpe, Christina. (2016). *In the wake: On blackness and being*. Durham, NC: Duke University Press.

Sherlock, Alexandra. (2013). Larger than life: Digital resurrection and the re-enchantment of society. *Information Society*, 29, 164–176.

Shevory, Thomas C. (1995). Bleached resistance: The politics of grunge. *Popular Music & Society*, 19(2), 23–48.

Shklovski, Irina, & Janet Vertesi. (2013). "Un-Googling" publications: The ethics and problems of anonymization. *CHI '13 Extended Abstracts on Human Factors in Computing Systems* (pp. 2169–2178).

Shneidman, Edwin S. (1980). *Voices of death*. New York: Harper and Row.

Shneidman, Edwin S., & Norman L. Farberow (Eds.). (1957). *Clues to suicide*. New York: McGraw-Hill.

Shoffstall, Grant. (2021). Policing hybridity: Cryonic suspension at the "nexus" of religion and technoscience. *Nova Religio: The Journal of Alternative and Emergent Religions*, 25(2), 87–113.

Siles, Ignacio. (2012). Web technologies of the self: The arising of the "blogger" identity. *Journal of Computer-Mediated Communication*, 17, 408–421.

Silverstein, J. (2016, September 15). Sandra Bland family agrees to $1.9 million wrongful death settlement, lawyer says. *New York Daily News*. www.nydailynews.com

Simko, Christina. (2021). Mourning and memory in the age of COVID-19. *Sociologica*, 15(1), 109–124.

SkyNews. (2022, June 22). Amazon's Alexa will soon be able to read you stories in a loved one's voice—even if they're dead. https://news.sky.com

Smythe, G. A. F. P. S. (1844). The duty of self commemoration. *New Monthly Magazine and Humorist*, 70(280), 529–533.

Snyder, Steven. (2007, April 26). Living forever on a place at MySpace: Mourners find comfort in visiting online profiles of departed loved ones. *Newsday*.

Solomon, Sheldon, Jeff Greenberg, & Tom Pyszczynski. (2016). *The worm at the core: On the role of death in life*. New York: Penguin.

Sontag, Susan. (2003). *Regarding the pain of others*. New York: Picador.

Spence, Donald. (1984). *Narrative truth and historical truth: Meaning and interpretation in psychoanalysis*. New York: Norton.

Squier, Susan M. (2003). Wireless possibilities, posthuman possibilities: Brain radio, community radio, radio lazarus. In Susan M. Squier (Ed.), *Communities of the air: Radio century, radio culture* (pp. 275–299). Durham, NC: Duke University Press.

Sridhar, Devi. (2022, April 12). Herd immunity now seems impossible. Welcome to the age of COVID reinfection. *Guardian*. www.theguardian.com

Stage, Carsten. (2014). Online a-liveness: A "rhythmanalysis" of three illness blogs made by Rosie Kilburn, Jessica Joy Rees and Eva Markvoort. In Dorthe Refslund Christensen & Kjetil Sandvik (Eds.), *Mediating and remediating death* (pp. 199–216). New York: Routledge.

Stage, Carsten. (2017). *Networked cancer: Affect, narrative, and measurement*. New York: Palgrave Macmillan.

Standage, Tom. (2013). *The Victorian Internet: The remarkable story of the telegraph and the nineteenth century's on-line pioneers*. New York: Bloomsbury.

Stannard, David E. (1977). *The puritan way of death: A study in religion, culture, and social change*. New York: Oxford University Press.

Stark, Rodney. (1999). Secularization, R.I.P. *Sociology of Religion*, 60(3), 249–273.

Steadman, Lyle B., Craig T. Palmer, & Christopher F. Tilly. (1996). The universality of ancestor worship. *Ethnology*, 36(1), 63–76.

Steiner, George. (1971). *In Bluebeard's cave: Some notes towards the redefinition of culture*. New Haven, CT: Yale University Press.

Steinhart, Eric. (2007). Survival as a digital ghost. *Minds and Machines*, 17(3), 261–271.

Sterling, Bruce. (2020, March 10). Preparing for the end of Moore's Law. *Wired*. www.wired.com

Stiner, Mary C. (2017). Love and death in the Stone Age: What constitutes first evidence of mortuary treatment of the human body? *Biological Theory*, 12, 248–261.

Stokes, Patrick. (2012). Ghosts in the machine: Do the dead live on in Facebook? *Philosophy & Technology*, 25(3), 363–379.

Stokes, Patrick. (2015). Deletion as second death: The moral status of digital remains. *Ethics and Information Technology*, 17(4), 237–248.

Stokes, Patrick. (2021). *Digital souls: A philosophy of online death.* New York: Bloomsbury.

Stone, Merlin. (1976). *When God was a woman.* New York: Harvest/Harcourt Brace.

Sudak, Howard, Karen Maxim, & Maryellen Carpenter. (2008). Suicide and stigma: A review of the literature and personal reflections. *Academic Psychiatry*, 32, 136–142.

Sullivan, Margaret. (2014, August 25). An ill-chosen phrase, "no angel," brings a storm of protest. *New York Times.* https://publiceditor.blogs.nytimes.com

Sullivan, Paul. (2015, October 23). Digital messages for loved ones from beyond the grave. *New York Times.* www.nytimes.com

SurveyMonkey. (n.d.). How we find survey participants around the world. www.surveymonkey.com

Swart, Koenraad W. (1962). "Individualism" in mid-nineteenth century America (1826–1860). *Journal of the History of Ideas*, 23(1), 77–90.

Sweeney, Miriam E., & André Brock Jr. (2014). Critical informatics: New methods and practices. Paper presented at *77th ASIS&T Annual Meeting.*

Synnott, John, Maria Ioannou, Angela Coyne, & Siobhan Hemingway. (2017). A content analysis of online suicide notes: Attempted suicide versus attempt resulting in suicide. *Suicide and Life-Threatening Behavior*, 48(6), 767–778.

Szulc, Lukasz. (2019). Profiles, identities, data: Making abundant and anchored selves in a platform society. *Communication Theory*, 29, 257–276.

Tarlach, Gemma. (2018, March 15). What the ancient pigment ochre tells us about the human mind. *Discover.* www.discovermagazine.com

Tarnoff, Ben. (2016, July 15). How the Internet was invented. *Guardian.* www.theguardian.com

Theis, Thomas, & H-S. Philip Wong. (2017). The end of Moore's Law: A new beginning for information technology. *Computing in Science & Engineering*, 19(2), 41–50.

Thomas, Alexander. (2017, September 21). Transhumanism and inequality: Enhancing human life could bring dystopian consequences. *Genetic Literacy Project.* https://geneticliteracyproject.org

Thomas, William I., & Dorothy S. Thomas. (1928). *The child in America: Behavior problems and programs.* New York: Knopf.

Timmermans, Stefan. (2006). *Postmortem: How medical examiners explain suspicious deaths.* Chicago: University of Chicago Press.

Tirosh-Samuelson, Hava. (2012). Transhumanism as a secularist faith. *Zygon: Journal of Religion and Science*, 47(4), 710–734.

Tomasi, Luigi. (2000). Emile Durkheim's contribution to the sociological explanation of suicide. In W. S. F. Pickering & Geoffrey Walford (Eds.), *Durkheim's Suicide: A century of research and debate* (pp. 11–21). New York: Routledge.

Tuckman, Jacob, Robert J. Kleiner, & Martha Lavell. (1959). Emotional content of suicide notes. *American Journal of Psychiatry*, 116, 59–63.

Turkle, Sherry. (1996). Parallel lives: Working on identity in virtual space. In Deborah Grodin & Thomas R. Lindlof (Eds.), *Constructing the self in a mediated world* (pp. 156–175). Thousand Oaks, CA: Sage.

Turkle, Sherry. (1999). Cyberspace and identity. *Contemporary Sociology*, 28(6), 643–648.

Turkle, Sherry. (2012). *Alone together: Why we expect more from technology and less from each other*. New York: Basic Books.

Turkle, Sherry. (2015, September 26). Stop Googling. Let's talk. *New York Times*. www.nytimes.com

Turner, Victor. (1967). *The forest of symbols: Aspects of Ndembu ritual*. Ithaca, NY: Cornell University Press.

Twitter. (n.d.). Search result FAQs. https://help.twitter.com

United States Census Bureau. (n.d.). Quick facts. www.census.gov

Uriu, Daisuke, Ju-Chun Ko, Bing-Yu Chen, Atsushi Hiyama, & Masahiko Inami. (2019). Digital memorialization in death-ridden societies: How HCI could contribute to death rituals in Taiwan and Japan. In J. Zhou & G. Salvendy (Eds.), *Human aspects of IT for the aged population. Design for the elderly and technology acceptance. HCII 2019. Lecture Notes in Computer Science*, vol. 11592. Cham, Switzerland: Springer Nature.

Uscinski, Joseph E., Adam M. Enders, Casey Klofstad, Michelle Seelig, John Funchion, Caleb Everett, Stefan Wuchty, Kamal Premaratne, & Manohar N. Murthi. (2020). Why do people believe COVID-19 conspiracy theories? *Harvard Kennedy School (HKS) Misinformation Review*. https://misinforeview.hks.harvard.edu

Utriainen, Terhi, & Marjaliisa Honkasalo. (1996). Women writing their death and dying: Semiotic perspectives on women's suicide notes. *Semiotica*, 109(3/4), 195–220.

Van Calster, Geert, Alejandro Gonzalez Arreaza, & Elsemiek Apers. (2018, May 15). Not just one, but many "rights to be forgotten." *Internet Policy Review*, 7(2). https://policyreview.info

Van Cleaf, Kara M. (2020). The pleasure of connectivity: Media, motherhood, and the digital maternal gaze. *Communication, Culture & Critique*, 13, 36–53.

van Dijck, José. (2012). Facebook and the engineering of connectivity: A multi-layered approach to social media platforms. *Convergence: The International Journal of Research into New Media Technologies*, 19(2), 141–155.

van Dijck, José. (2013). "You have one identity": Performing the self on Facebook and LinkedIn. *Media, Culture & Society*, 35(2), 199–215.

van Dijk, Teun A. (1995). Aims of critical discourse analysis. *Japanese Discourse*, 1, 17–27.

Veix, Joe. (2018, May 25). Exploring the digital ruins of Second Life. *Digg*. https://digg.com

Vita-More, Natasha. (2019). History of transhumanism. In N. Lee (Ed.), *The transhumanism handbook* (pp. 49–61). Cham, Switzerland: Springer.

Vlahos, James. (2017, July 18). A son's race to give his dying father artificial immortality. *Wired.* www.wired.com

Walker, Rob. (2011, January 9). Things to do in cyberspace when you're dead. *New York Times.*

Walter, Tony. (1991). Modern death: Taboo or not taboo? *Sociology,* 25(2), 293–310.

Walter, Tony. (1993). Death in the New Age. *Religion,* 23(2), 127–145.

Walter, Tony. (2017). How the dead survive: Ancestors, immortality, memory. In Michael H. Jacobsen (Ed.), *Postmortal society: Towards a sociology of immortality* (pp. 19–40). New York: Routledge.

Walter, Tony. (2020). *Death in the modern world.* Thousand Oaks, CA: Sage.

Wambach, Julie Ann. (1986). The grief process as a social construct. *OMEGA: Journal of Death and Dying,* 16(3), 201–211.

Warraich, Haider. (2017). *Modern death: How medicine changed the end of life.* New York: St. Martin's Press.

Watts, Ian. (2009). Red ochre, body painting, and language: Interpreting the Blombos ochre. In Rudolph Botha & Chris Knight (Eds.), *The cradle of language* (pp. 62–92). New York: Oxford University Press.

Weaver, John C., & Doug Munro. (2010). The historical contingency of suicide: A case-based comparison of suicides in New Zealand in the 1930s and 1980s. *New Zealand Sociology,* 25(1), 100–130.

Webb, Lynn M., & Brittney S. Lee. (2011). Mommy blogs: The centrality of community in the performance of online maternity. In Michelle Moravec (Ed.), *Motherhood online: How online communities shape modern motherhood* (pp. 244–257). Newcastle upon Tyne: Cambridge Scholars.

Weber, Max. (1958). Science as vocation. *Daedalus,* 87(1), 111–134.

Weber, Max. (1978). *Economy and society.* Edited by Guenther Roth & Claus Wittich. Berkeley: University of California Press.

Weber, Max. (2011). *The Protestant ethic and the spirit of capitalism* (rev. 1920 ed.). Oxford, UK: Oxford University Press.

Wertheim, Margaret. (1999). *The pearly gates of cyberspace: A history of space from Dante to the Internet.* New York: Norton.

Westerlund, Michael. (2012). The production of pro-suicide content on the Internet: A counter-discourse activity. *New Media & Society,* 14(5), 764–780.

Wexler, Victor. (1976). Made for man's delight: Rousseau as antifeminist. *American Historical Review,* 81(2), 266–291.

White, Michelle. (2009). Review: Networked bodies and extended corporealities: Theorizing the relationship between bodies, embodiment, and contemporary new media. *Feminist Studies,* 35(3), 603–624.

Whiting, Rebecca, & Katrina Pritchard. (2018). Digital ethics. In A. Cunliffe, C. Cassell, & G. Grandy (Eds.), *SAGE handbook of qualitative business and management research methods,* volume 1: *History and Traditions* (pp. 562–579). London, UK: Sage.

Whyte, William H. (1956). *The organization man.* New York: Simon and Schuster.

Wiley, Norbert. (2016). *Inner speech and the dialogic self*. Philadelphia, PA: Temple University Press.

Willim, Robert. (2014). Floating points of reference: Trust, enchantment, and the shifting visibilities of digital infrastructures. Paper presented at *Beyond the frame: The future of the visual in an age of digital diversity*. Nordic Network for Digital Visuality, Stockholm, Sweden.

Winkelman, Michael, & John R. Baker. (2016). *Supernatural as natural: A biocultural approach to religion*. New York: Routledge.

Wolfe, Rebecca, Kristen Harknett, & Daniel Schneider. (2021, June 4). Inequalities at work and the toll of COVID-19. *Health Affairs*. www.healthaffairs.org

Wray, Matt, Cynthia Colen, & Bernice Pescosolido. (2011). The sociology of suicide. *Annual Review of Sociology*, 37, 505–528.

Wreschner, Ernest E. (1980). Red ochre and human evolution: A case for discussion. *Current Anthropology*, 21(5), 631–633.

Wright, Nicola (2014). Death and the Internet: The implications of the digital afterlife. *First Monday*, 19(6).

Yang, Bijou, & David Lester. (2011). The presentation of self: An hypothesis about suicide notes. *Suicidology Online*, 2, 75–79.

Yong, Ed. (2019, July 22). The human brain project hasn't lived up to its promise. *Atlantic*. www.theatlantic.com

Zayas, Luis H., & Allyson M. Pilat. (2008). Suicidal behavior in Latinas: Explanatory cultural factors and implications for intervention. *Suicide and Life-Threatening Behavior*, 38(3), 334–342.

Zelizer, Barbie. (2010). *About to die: How news images move the public*. New York: Oxford University Press.

Zhang, Jie, & David Lester. (2008). Psychological tensions found in suicide notes: A test for the strain theory of suicide. *Archives of Suicide Research*, 12, 67–73.

Zimmerman, Beth. (2007, March 12). Virtual memorial: Family, friends use fallen troops' MySpace pages for mourning. *Navy Times*.

Zuboff, Shoshana. (2019). *The age of surveillance capitalism: The fight for a human future at the new frontier of power*. New York: Public Affairs.

Zussman, Robert. (2012). Narrative freedom. *Sociological Forum*, 27(4), 807–824.

INDEX

Page numbers in *italics* indicate Tables

fear of death, grief contrasted with, 201–2
Fields, Karen, 59
Firstenberg, Suzanne Brennan, 196, 197
"The Forever Social" (fake website), 158
Foucault, Michel, 103, 105
4 Your Eyez Only (film), 132
freedom, mnemonic. *See* mnemonic
    freedom
freedom, narrative. *See* narrative freedom

Gaden, Georgia, 103
Gamble, Clive, 59
Garner, Eric, 133, 228n41
Georges, Thomas, 21–22
Gergen, Kenneth, 65
Gibson, James J., 53, 186
Giddens, Anthony, 39, 61, 112
Gilbey Keller, Emma, 6
Goffman, Erving, 41–42
Goldstein, Alex, 196
Gone Not Gone (company), 162
Google (company), 221n21
Gorer, Geoffrey, 71
Gorski, Philip, 74
Goudsmit, Tamar, 161, 162, 164
Graeber, David, 60
Grant, Ann, 33–34
Graves, Lucas, 70
@GregariousAli (Twitter handle), 138
grief, 25; digital death followed by, 26–27;
    fear of death contrasted with, 201–2;
    online, 31–32; pathologizing of, 37;
    photographs enabling, 66; World War
    I influencing, 74–75
Gross, Nora, 138–39, 143

Haldane, J. B. L., 166
Haraway, Donna, 104
Harvey, David, 66
hashtags, 7, 227nn34–35; against anti-
    Black violence, 139–48, 143, *144*, *147*;
    on Black Twitter, 135; collective mem-
    ory expressed with, 149, 150; as legacy,

153–54; mnemonic freedom demanded
    by, 151; police violence highlighted by,
    134, 139–40, 144–45, 151–52. *See also*
    #IfIDieInPoliceCustody; #IfThey-
    GunnedMeDown
health, mental, 120
Heisman, Mitchell, 109, 110
Hendricks, Michael, 171
r/HermanCainAward (subreddit), 194
Herring, Susan C., 16
Hertz, Robert, 58–59
Hewson, Tim, 162, 164–65
Hick, John, 105–6
Holy Crap I Have Cancer!!! (blog), 80–82,
    101, 108
hospitals, death in, 74–76, 88, 106–7, 191,
    193
Howe, Irving, 39
hunter-gatherer tribes, death in, 58–59
Huxley, Julian, 166

identity, 105, 186–87; the Internet liberat-
    ing, 8–9, 135; social networking sites
    solidifying, 42; writing refashioning,
    150
#IfIDieInPoliceCustody, 7, 134, 150, 153;
    advanced directive compared with,
    147–48; death confronted by, 139–40;
    @GregariousAli beginning, 138; loved
    ones instructed through, 148; suicide
    rejected by, 146; themes of, *147*
#IfTheyGunnedMeDown, 134, 139–40,
    148, 150, 153; photographs compared
    by, 136–37, *143*; racism emphasized by,
    144–45; "socially acceptable" con-
    trasted with "socially problematic"
    photographs for, 137–38; themes of, *144*
immortality, 76; collective, 151–52; digital
    suicide notes achieving, 130–31; mne-
    monic freedom and, 149–52; postmor-
    tem messaging services contrasted
    with, 164; social networking sites
    attempting, 20–21; virtual, 36–37, 173

ABOUT THE AUTHOR

TIMOTHY RECUBER is Associate Professor in the Department of Sociology at Smith College. He is the author of *Consuming Catastrophe: Mass Culture in America's Decade of Disaster*, winner of the Outstanding Recent Contribution Award from the American Sociological Association's Sociology of Emotions section. He has written numerous articles and essays about mass media, digital culture, and emotions.

www.ingramcontent.com/pod-product-compliance
Lightning Source LLC
Chambersburg PA
CBHW020534030426
42337CB00013B/843